Managerial labour markets in small and medium-sized enterprises

Any successful business depends on the quality of its management team. But for a very small firm the relationship between management and economic performance is often much more visible. Understanding the workings of this relationship can be difficult, particularly when studying small firms which have become highly successful in a short space of time, so developing more complex management structures.

This study offers the first systematic analysis of this important labour market. It draws on themes of organizational behaviour, strategy and leadership and addresses the public policy issue – 'the people gap'. By exploring aspects of ownership, motivation, promotion, incentives and training, this study discusses how these issues have very different implications when related to the context of small firms rather than to that of large firms. A central question posed is how far economic performance is likely to be affected by these different patterns of ownership, organizational and management structures.

Routledge small business series
Edited by David Storey

Managerial labour markets in small and medium–sized enterprises

Pooran Wynarczyk, Robert Watson,
David Storey, Helen Short, Kevin Keasey

London and New York

First published in 1993
by Routledge
11 New Fetter Lane, London EC4P 4EE

Simultaneously published in the USA and Canada
by Routledge
29 West 35th Street, New York, NY 10001

© 1993 Pooran Wynarczyk, Robert Watson, David Storey, Helen Short, Kevin Keasey

Typeset in Times by LaserScript Limited, Mitcham, Surrey
Printed and bound in Great Britain by
Biddles Ltd, Guildford and King's Lynn

British Library Cataloguing in Publication Data

A catalogue record for this book is available from the British Library.

ISBN 0–415–10022–4

*Library of Congress Cataloging in Publication Data
has been applied for.*

Contents

Figures and tables

FIGURES

TABLES

Authors

Pooran Wynarczyk is a Senior Research Associate at the Centre for Urban and Regional Development Studies (CURDS), University of Newcastle upon Tyne.

Robert Watson is a Lecturer in Accounting and Finance, School of Management, University of Manchester Institute of Science and Technology (UMIST).

David Storey is Professor of Small and Medium Enterprises, Warwick Business School, University of Warwick.

Helen Short is a Lecturer in Accounting and Finance, School of Business and Economic Studies, University of Leeds.

Kevin Keasey is Professor of Finance and Accounting, School of Business and Economic Studies, University of Leeds.

Preface

In many respects the current volume can be considered as the sequel to our 1987 work *The Performance of Small Firms*. We have added one new author to the team (Helen Short) and arbitrarily shuffled the names around but the present volume may be considered to continue to address broadly similar questions to those in which we were interested in 1987.

The key changes relate to the comments and criticisms which we received on that volume. In particular we can now see that little emphasis was placed in that work on the relatively few small firms which grew rapidly. This volume is about that group of firms.

The second criticism of the 1987 volume was that, while it examined a large number of small manufacturing firms, it did so using only published records. In this volume we have had a closer involvement with the firms themselves, using face-to-face interview techniques as well as consulting publicly available records.

The third major change has come from our own observation of highly successful firms, and what the owners of those firms have told us. In almost all cases owners emphasized the importance of teamworking – as one put it 'ensuring that round managerial pegs fitted in round, and not square, managerial holes'. We realized that the managers referred to in this context were not owners of the businesses, and that here was an almost unre-searched area. The assumption has been, until now, that smaller businesses are owned and managed by the same individuals. Yet the apparent key to success in growing a small business was the ability to assemble a managerial team, frequently comprising individuals who were not owners of the business.

We were therefore fortunate that the Economic and Social Research Council in 1987 had identified managerial labour markets as an important topic in influencing the competitiveness of British industry. The Competitiveness Initiative of ESRC, co-ordinated by Arthur Francis, was the key source of funding for this research. Supplementary funding was also provided by the University of Leeds and we thank both organizations for their contributions.

Over the 5-year period in which this book was written we received considerable help from a large number of individuals. Arthur Francis, as co-ordinator of the initiative, provided us with opportunities for presenting our work. Many of the interviews and some of the preliminary analysis was conducted by Helen Stoddart and Sue Marlow who acted as research fellows on the project. Anne Rees also conducted a significant number of interviews and we thank all of them for their efforts.

Versions of the text have been inflicted on many audiences throughout the world and the feedback which we have received has, hopefully, enabled us to improve the quality of our writing and the sharpness of the arguments. We thank audiences at the 1990 Entrepreneurship Research Conference at Babson College in the United States, at the Helsinki School of Economics and Business in 1989, and at the University of Jönköping in 1991 in Sweden. Closer to home we have made presentations at Manchester, Aston and London Business Schools, at Heriot-Watt University and the Barbican Centre.

Finally we all extend our thanks to Glenda Hall who has typed and re-typed numerous versions of this text with great efficiency and good grace.

1 Background and scope of the text

INTRODUCTION

The main objective of this study is to identify and analyse the managerial factors most closely associated with successful, fast-growth small firms. Within the small-firm sector, any relationships between firm performance and the quality of the managerial inputs are likely to be clearer than for larger firms. At the risk of over-simplifying, large firms with their greater resource base, market power, ability to buy in additional managerial inputs or be bought out via takeovers or mergers, are less dependent upon the quality of their existing management teams than are small firms. The relationship between performance and management is, therefore, likely to be more nebulous and less direct in large firms. Nevertheless, though the performance of small firms will be more closely linked to the quality of its management, the relationship should not be presumed to be obvious and unproblematic. As we shall see, a number of complexities and difficulties emerge, particularly in relation to fast-growth firms, regarding the strength, direction and attribution of causality of these relationships.

In addressing these issues we shall be investigating the nature of the demand of small firms for individuals to act in a managerial capacity and the factors affecting the willingness of such individuals to supply themselves for work as managers. These constitute the basis of the economist's view of the managerial labour market, and it is our intention to combine elements of industrial and labour economics within our analysis. We do not, however, view the economic paradigm as the only valid perspective by which to examine these issues. In this text, we have adopted a catholic, rather than a single disciplinary approach to managerial labour markets in the small-firm sector and have incorporated, where appropriate, insights from the organizational behaviour, strategy and leadership literatures.

To our knowledge, there has been no systematic and comprehensive research on this very important labour market. Indeed there are surprisingly few empirical studies of the motivations, remuneration and incentive packages or performance of small-firm managers. Almost all such studies relate instead to managers in larger firms (Yarrow 1972, Cosh 1975, Baker *et al.* 1988, Cannings and Montmarquette 1991). This is possibly because the vast majority of small firms appear to have neither the need nor the inclination to employ specialized professional managers. Most small-firm owners do not seek growth, and hence their businesses remain small owner-managed affairs from birth to eventual demise. The lack of a growth objective and an inadequate management team are characteristic of the majority of small firms as is the high incidence of failure, around 10 per cent per annum (Daly 1991).

Despite their high failure rates, and the very modest growth achieved by the majority of small firms, there is evidence that in some locations the small-firm sector has contributed significantly to exports, innovation, employment and to economic growth. The classic illustrations include North East Central Italy – the third Italy – (Brusco 1986) or Palo Alto, California in the United States (Oakey *et al.* 1988). For the UK, however, the small-firm sector has made an increasing, yet essentially modest, contribution to economic growth over the last two decades.

Nevertheless, a small minority of small firms do achieve rapid growth and eventually become large enough to become internationally competitive players. These firms may be located in new and dynamic sectors of the economy and can be a significant source of new wealth creation and employment. In other instances these fast growing small firms operate in quite familiar sectors, but bring a particular quality or characteristic to the marketplace (Storey *et al.* 1989). Even though they constitute only a small minority of the total stock of firms in existence, successful fast-growth firms are likely to have an economic impact out of all proportion to their numbers.

A greater understanding of the processes and conditions which produce and sustain these highly unusual firms is of great interest to several groups. In this book, our prime target audience is our academic colleagues with an interest in the managerial factors influencing the growth of the firm. Our intention here is to make original theoretical and empirical contributions to understanding the links between the managerial labour market and firm performance in smaller businesses.

We also hope, however, that our findings will be of interest to those whose task is to improve the performance of smaller firms. This will include financiers, accountants, as well as small-firm owners themselves. Fast-growth small firms are of increasing interest to public and quasi-public policy-makers – such as Enterprise Agencies, Training and Enterprise Councils, etc. For too long (Macmillan 1931, Bolton 1971, Wilson 1979) the limited policy discussion on the performance of smaller firms focused upon a real or imagined finance gap, defined as an unwillingness of financial institutions to provide suitable finance to small firms, even if the firms were prepared to pay the appropriate charge. Our views on this topic are set out elsewhere (Storey *et al.* 1987).

In this volume we address a public policy issue which has been the subject of more recent comment – 'the people gap'. This phrase, attributed to Mr Tim Eggar, a former Small Firms Minister at the Department of Employment, focused on the limitations of the small-firm sector imposed by their human, rather than their financial capital.

We have argued elsewhere that the success of public policy initiatives to encourage the creation and success of fast growth enterprises will be crucially dependent upon the ability to distinguish the potential 'winners' from the majority of small firms at an early stage in the life of the business. Our previous study (Storey *et al.* 1987) was of manufacturing businesses in Northern England established before 1981. It suggested that, ex post, fast-growth small firms could be identified and that they generally had a different management structure from other firms from early in the life of the business. The major differences were that fast-growth firms were more likely to start up with a team of professionally skilled directors (owners) who also had a number of directorships of (ownership interest in) other small enterprises. In contrast, the more typical small firm was owned and controlled by a 'one-man-band'[1] whose previous occupation was of a 'technical' or skilled manual nature and whose management team was often limited to his immediate family. Moreover, this type of firm was more likely to fail than firms with a more extensive management team.

Existing research based upon the management practices of large firms is unlikely to be of much relevance to the small-firm sector. As will become apparent in later chapters, the small firm cannot be viewed merely as a scaled-down version of a large firm. The ownership and managerial structures, recruitment patterns and remuneration packages considered to be appropriate for large firms will often not be suitable for any type of small firm. The rapidly growing small firm has to confront and overcome a number of unique managerial problems over and above those of the typical small firm. For instance, its management structure will need to change constantly in anticipation of, and in response to, the growth, scale and scope of its operations. The managerial problems which the growing small firm must overcome, such as the transition to a formal management structure involving the recruitment and integration of specialist personnel and the development of corresponding control, incentive and communication procedures, is unique to these fast-growth firms.

In this text we shall be focusing upon the following four key managerial issues:

1 In what respects, if any, do the managerial backgrounds, aspirations and motivations of the *founders* of fast-growth small firms differ from those of non-fast-growth small firms?
2 Among fast growth small firms how is the process of growth managed? Where does the firm recruit its managerial talent? How does it promote managerial development? What incentives, remuneration packages and communication systems are instituted?
3 How do these characteristics and experiences differ in fast-growth small firms from both the traditional small firm and the large-firm sector?
4 To what extent is it possible to explain the relative economic performance of small firms in terms of differences in their ownership, organizational and management structures.

A CONCEPTUAL FRAMEWORK

As we have already noted, the majority of small firms have a relatively 'simple' and unchanging management structure, often being owned and managed by the founder and possibly a few close associates. Indeed one of the three components of the Bolton Committee (Bolton 1971) definition of a small firm was that it was owned and managed by the same individual or group of individuals.

It may be the influence of the Bolton Committee which has served to hide the presence within small firms of a group of individuals who exercise managerial functions, yet are not significant owners of the business. Only in firms with perhaps less than ten workers are such individuals totally absent, and yet the vast bulk of research on smaller firms implicitly or explicitly assumes that all managerial functions are conducted by the owner manager. For example the authoritative review by Curran (1986) on research over the period 1971–86, on smaller firms, discussed the internal management of smaller firms only in terms of owner-managers. The non-owner-manager, despite his or her often crucial role within the firm, has been virtually ignored by researchers. The Curran review correctly reflects this void.[2]

It might be presumed that the relationship between the 'quality' of the managerial inputs and firm performance is relatively straightforward and direct. Firms owned and controlled by 'high-quality' managers will generally perform better than firms in the hands of 'low-quality' managers. However, both performance and quality are highly abstract and multi-dimensional concepts. They cannot be unambiguously defined in an empirical context unless their scope is reduced to some small subset of dimensions. Any such reduction, however, necessarily involves choices and value judgements regarding the relative importance of individual dimensions. The criteria for making such choices are generally based upon a (more or less explicit) theory which argues that certain aspects of performance and managerial quality are particularly important, relevant and valued. The theory should also suggest the form and direction that any relationships should take.

Performance and the quality of management are also relative concepts in the sense that both need to be considered in the context of what is humanly possible, given the initial conditions and circumstances within which the firm or the individual operates. Moreover, the actions of managers and firms will need to be judged with reference to their particular objectives. For instance, profit maximization or growth may be a highly inappropriate measure for judging the performance of a small family firm which operates in a specialized niche market and whose owner-managers have no desire for the firm to grow beyond a certain size. Such a firm may deliberately aim to achieve low growth and plan to be only modestly profitable but, from the owner's point of view, it may be deemed highly successful. The strategy may be 'optimal' in providing the owners with a satisfactory standard of living (and leisure time), ensuring that ownership stays within the family group, and may be consistent with other desirable aims such as the maintenance of good working relationships with employees, business associates and the local community. Of course, environmental conditions and objectives can change significantly over a period of time and are greatly influenced by previous management decisions and strategic choices. Hence, the relationships between the performance of firms, the objectives pursued by their owners and skills, qualities and activities of their managers may be highly complex, multidirectional, contingent and far from obvious or unproblematic.

Figure 1.1 provides a diagrammatic representation of how we view these issues.

The figure indicates four boxes which we have labelled environmental setting, organization structure, strategic leadership and organizational performance. These boxes refer to the various classes of 'real-world' phenomena (events, outcomes, processes, behaviours, etc.) that an individual recognizes as belonging to these categories. We have listed some of the possible elements which might be included in each box. The list is meant to be indicative rather than exhaustive because the actual detailed content of these boxes, what is included and (just as importantly) excluded, will vary between individuals. The content is likely to depend upon an individual's particular philosophical and theoretical concerns, the reasons for the individuals immediate interest in the issues, previous experiences and the whole cultural and economic environment within which the individual is situated.

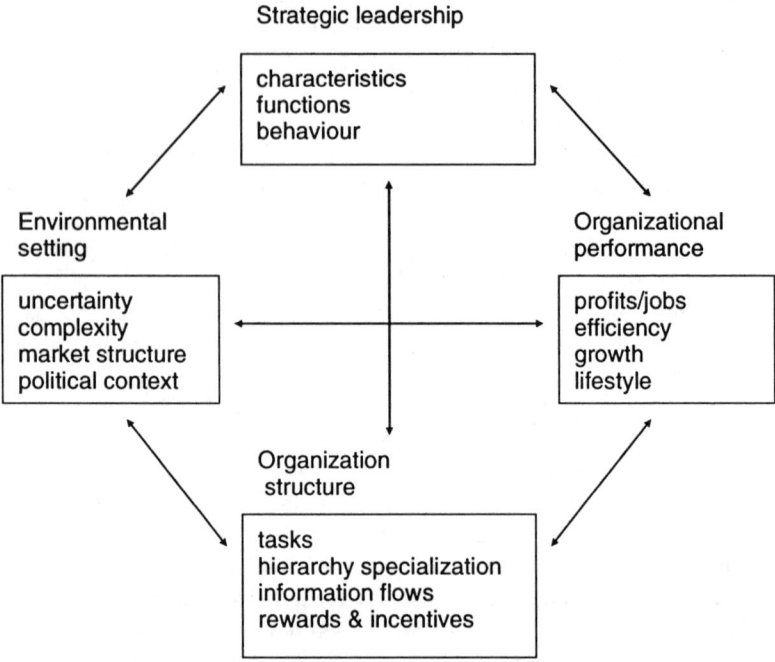

Figure 1.1 Strategy, performance and organization

Despite the necessarily arbitrary nature of this classification scheme, there is some measure of agreement on the content of the boxes. Indeed, the indicative lists in the figure are derived directly from the economic, socio-logical and organizational theory literatures. For instance, the degree of uncertainty, existing market structures and the general socio-economic and legal circumstances within which firms operate, are taken in most theories as part of the environment. Likewise, when viewed as desired outcomes, the achievement of a suitable lifestyle, sales growth, profits or efficiency, are usually seen to be valid performance measures. Hence, the listings of the main sub-elements of our conceptual framework are likely to be reasonably uncontentious and, moreover, we believe that, at this level of abstration, it would make little difference to our argument if one were to shuffle around some of these box contents. Chapters 2 and 3 enlarge upon these themes by reviewing some relevant findings of the economic and sociological literatures respectively, and assessing its implications for smaller firms.

Within, and even more so between, these literatures, however, there is considerably less agreement regarding the relative importance of each sub-element, the choice of empirical surrogates for operationalizing them, or the measurement methods used. Moreover, the nature and direction of any causal relationships is also often in dispute, not merely between each of the four major elements but even between some of the sub-elements. To highlight this absence of consensus over key relationships, Figure 1.1 uses double-headed arrows, illustrating all possible relationships between the four broad concepts. Similar double-headed arrows could, if space permitted, also be shown between the sub-elements.

At this juncture, we are not placing any explicit restrictions on the possible flows of causality (or even inferring whether it is reasonable to speak in terms of causality) between the real phenomena these boxes are meant to represent. For example, the figure does not exclude the possibility that performance could induce changes in strategic choice, which could in turn cause a change in the environment – either directly or via changes in organizational structure. This form of relationship is the form most favoured by those in the strategic management field – see for instance Covin and Slevin (1989).

Figure 1.1 also does not exclude the possibility that the causal flow proceeds in the opposite direction – environment either directly determining performance or indirectly doing so via changes in strategy and/or organizational structure. This latter view has become popular in both the economics (i.e. the so-called structure–conduct–performance paradigm) and organization theory (contingency theory) literatures. (See Reid 1987 for a review of the SCP literature and Ezzamel 1987a, 1987b for a review of the contingency theory literature). Indeed, the political bargaining models of organization of Cyert and March (1963) and especially Cohen *et al.* (1972), seem to suggest that all of these factors interact in such a complex and simultaneous manner that any attribution of causality, or even separation of the various elements, is likely to be misplaced.

It should be clear then that the different approaches place differing emphases upon, and in some cases totally ignore, some of the elements and possible relationships shown in Figure 1.1. For instance, economic theories of organizations (the firm) usually attempt to explain the prevalence and longevity of certain forms of organization in terms of their economic rationality (efficiency). For any given environment, usually conceived of as the existing structure of economic exchange relationships (markets), technology and consumer tastes, firms that are able to respond 'appropriately' so as to exploit market opportunities, as and when they arise, will have a comparative advantage over others. In this sense economic explanations tend to contain an evolutionary mechanism whereby the (economically) strong species of firm survive and prosper, while firms that either will not or cannot respond appropriately to their environment will die. Hence, in empirical tests of economic theories, the emphasis is upon performance measures, such as a firm's sales growth, market share, profitability, growth in employment, the successful launch of new products, etc., that are necessary for survival in various competitive environments.

Until quite recently, few economists explicitly addressed the issues of organizational design, strategy and management choice. This was mainly because the neoclassical framework within which most economists worked, contained strong assumptions regarding the 'rationality' of economic actors, their knowledge set, the speed of market adjustments and the absence of barriers to new entrants. These assumptions implied there was a deterministic (and unidirectional) relationship between market conditions and organizational responses (performance). This effectively made organizational design choices, managerial inputs and strategy issues irrelevant since the firm was merely a theoretical link between factor and product markets (Machlup 1967).

Recently, however, industrial economists have relaxed some of the neoclassical assumptions and recognized the existence of 'bounded rationality', information asymmetries, highly imperfect markets and barriers to entry. This has led to much greater attention being given to issues of strategy and organizational design. Contemporary economic explanations of firm performance now tend to be less deterministic in that it is recognized that market imperfections can produce several 'efficient' responses by individual actors and firms. The roles played by strategic and organizational design choices have, at the very least, become viewed as 'contingent variables'. Nevertheless, most economic theories are still characterized by their 'efficiency' claims and the belief that one or another aspect of firm performance is the dependent (that is the determined) variable. Other theories outside of the economics tradition, such as some forms of contingency theory, also conceive of organizational performance in similar (evolutionary) terms. Here, however, the focus is upon different contingent variables to those in economics, such as choice of technology, the organization of production, control systems, leadership styles, etc. Furthermore a much less well-developed (prescriptive) criterion than that of economic efficiency is employed by which to judge actual firm performance.

It should be clear, therefore, that there are a number of complexities, problems and choices associated with studying the determinants of organizational performance. The choice of any particular theory will highlight certain factors and possibly, either explicitly or implicitly, ignore other relationships and influences. It is fair to say that no existing theory has managed to command universal support on these matters. As we shall see from the reviews in the following two chapters, this should not be too surprising. Such a comprehensive theory is in all probability, impossible. The limited conceptual apparatus of human beings (bounded rationality), their (often) conflicting interests and changing objectives, coupled with the fundamental uncertainties of life and the costs of gathering, analysing and evaluating information seem to be inevitable aspects of the 'human condition', and apply, just as strongly, to social theorists!

PLAN OF THE BOOK

With the foregoing considerations in mind, the remainder of the text is organized as follows. The theoretical and contextual scene is set in Chapters 2–4. Empirical analyses are contained in Chapters 5 to 9, and some concluding remarks in Chapter 10. Chapter 2 reviews a number of economic theories of organizations, their creation, growth, internal management and strategic choices. The chapter also contains a review of the small-firm literature dealing with these topics and some of the general limitations of the economic framework. Chapter 3 examines a number of non-economic theories drawn from the sociological, organizational behaviour and strategy literatures. The main issues reviewed concern the relationships between environments, organizational structure and performance, the formation of organizational goals, the scope for strategic action, and the characteristics and influence of management teams and leadership. As with Chapter 2, the research findings relating to small firms are also reviewed. Chapter 4 then takes the material covered in the previous two chapters and presents a number of empirically testable hypotheses relating to the performance, creation, internal organization and management of small firms.

The second half of the book provides empirical tests of some the hypotheses identified in Chapter 4. This begins with Chapter 5 which provides a detailed description of the data collection procedure. It describes how a group of fast-growing small firms, defined as those which reach the Unlisted Securities Market (USM) within 10 years of starting up, differ from a comparable sample of match firms. The match firms are so defined because they were each chosen on the basis of being identical to one of the USM firms in the sense that they operated in the same sector, were the same age, were located in the same geographical region and were independently owned at start up. The difference between the two groups is that the USM firms are significantly larger and are therefore assumed to have grown faster since start up. Chapters 6 and 7 examine the managerial labour market in USM and match firms from two separate perspectives. Chapter 6 provides an empirical analysis of the labour market for small-firm managers. It uses data collected from managers in small firms themselves to determine the quality of managerial labour recruited, their salaries, and their current satisfaction levels and how these differ between fast growth and match firms. Chapter 7 examines this managerial labour market from the perspective of the owner. The central theme is that a key component in the labour market for owners and managers is the performance of firms. Chapter 8 then undertakes an empirical analysis of the relationship between profitability and a number of ownership, organizational and management factors. All three of these chapters use broadly quantitative approaches to the examination of managerial labour markets in smaller firms.

As a counter-weight to this, Chapter 9 provides a broadly qualitative review of responses of owners to the creation of managerial teams. In particular the chapter is interested in the question of how teams are assembled and provided with sufficient information to enable them to operate efficiently.

Finally Chapter 10 provides a synthesis of the key conclusions.

NOTES

1   The term 'one-man-band' is appropriate in this context since the vast majority were owned and managed by men. Where the wife played a role it appeared to be on a part-time basis as bookkeeper/administrator/confidant. It should be noted, however, that there have been major changes in the 1980s with a much higher proportion of businesses being owned and managed by women (Carter and Cannon 1989).
2   It should be emphasized that our research is about the development of managerial teams which contain not just business owners (major shareholders) but also salaried managers. There is a modest quantity of literature on the creation of new ventures by teams of owners – as opposed to the single founder. For a helpful review of this literature see Kamm *et al.* (1990).

2 The economics of small-firm performance, growth and internal organization

INTRODUCTION

There are two broad strands of the economics literature which relate to how entrepreneurial actions and management organization impact upon small-firm performance, although there has been relatively little work which has been directly addressed to smaller firms. The literature may be broadly defined as either industrial or labour economics and it is our task here both to review and apply those aspects which are of most relevance to the small-firm sector.

The industrial economics literature is replete with models that consider the various dimensions of firm performance, such as the determinants of market value, growth, profits, employment, market share, etc. Generally, these models attempt to measure the impact of one or more input factors upon firm performance. Market structure, the 'quality' of management, labour policies, technological improvement, to name but a few, have all been considered as potentially influencing performance.

Consideration also has to be given to the issues raised by the labour economics literature. In the neoclassical model workers move freely from one firm to another in response to differences in wage rates. The labour market for managers has been argued to be a special case for two main reasons. The first is that the movement of managers between firms appears to be very much less than neoclassical theory would lead us to expect. This is often attributed to the existence of barriers constructed by the firm to minimize managerial movement – thus creating an 'internal' labour market. The second is that the manager is likely to be in a particularly strong position to move out of the managerial labour market by creating a new firm and so becoming an owner.

Our main interest in the industrial and labour economics literatures is to evaluate their contribution to an increased understanding of the economic determinants of the entrepreneur's personal aspirations and organizational design choices, competitive strategies, choice of markets and innovation. Within the firm, their insights into the design of 'efficient' ownership, reward, risk-sharing, managerial recruitment and monitoring structures that improve the firm's prospects will also be central to our concerns. Many of these issues are best addressed from the perspective adopted by the so-called 'property rights' and agency theory literatures (see Milgrom and Roberts 1992). These conceptual frameworks, which view the firm as a nexus of contracts, attempt to specify the ownership, employment and remuneration contracts that are most efficient (suitable) in controlling and motivating managers and other employees to act in the interests of residual claimants (owners). A closely related literature, concerned with exploring the 'efficiency' implications of different organizational forms, centres around the idea that the chief motivation underlying organizational choice decisions is the minimization of 'transactions costs' associated with economic activities. In recent years, this theory has been most closely associated with the work of Williamson (1979, 1981), although the basic ideas are certainly not new to economics (see O'Brien 1984 for a review).

Given the themes outlined above the chapter is organized as follows. The following section provides a brief review of the neoclassical theory of the operation of markets and the role of the entrepreneur, the firm and its internal organization. The neoclassical model which we describe is something of a 'straw man' since it is highly unlikely that any contemporary economist would actually subscribe to all its assumptions. Nevertheless, it allows us to highlight a number of the limitations of the neoclassical framework which have motivated other writers to amend the model to make it more descriptively relevant to actual existing firms and market structures.

The third section presents a brief overview of what has become known as the 'new institutional economics'.[1] This branch of economics provides a much richer view of the relationships between performance and entre-preneurial activities, including the creation, ownership, growth and internal organization of the firm, than was the case in the recent past. Writers in this tradition have recognized that, because of uncertainty, information asymmetries and heterogeneous beliefs, barriers to entry, bounded rationality and/or incomplete markets, there are frequently non-trivial costs associated with organizing economic transactions and in monitoring the actions of self-interested agents. It is only when the neoclassical assumptions are relaxed that the crucial roles of information, managerial choice (strategy) and the internal organization of firms become important theoretical issues, because this opens up the possibility that one form of contracting/organizing may be less costly than another. While these models are a great improvement on the earlier neoclassical models, they can still be criticized on a number of grounds. For instance, the conceptualization of uncertainty is highly constrained in these models and this has allowed economists to posit the existence of Pareto optimal solutions even though such a notion is problematic in a world characterized by, what 'post-Keynesian' economists call, fundamental uncertainty (see Findley and Williams 1985). Moreover, by equating 'efficiency' largely in terms of the maximization of the owner's payoffs, they give insufficient attention to alternative explanations of outcomes such as the exploitation of market power or simply luck. These issues form the basis of the fourth section.

The following three subsections apply the insights gleaned from the economic frameworks to assess the (largely atheoretical) empirical evidence relating to the small-firm sector. We first discuss the nature of uncertainties confronting small firms. The character and extent of entrepreneurship and innovation within small firms is then discussed and the following subsection examines the issues relating to the growth of the firm, managerial recruitment, motivation and firm performance. The final section summarizes the main points discussed in the chapter.

THE NEOCLASSICAL FRAMEWORK

The central concern of neoclassical microeconomics is the determination of relative prices. This is achieved by specifying abstract and descriptively unrealistic assumptions about agents' behaviour and the operation of markets.[2] Agents in the neoclassical model are assumed to be motivated by a desire to maximize their own exogenously determined subjective preferences (utility).[3] Equilibrium market prices in the goods market are determined by equating the supply and demand of goods/services by individuals seeking to maximize their own utility.

To produce a theory of the determination of relative prices, however, the nature of the product market needs to be specified. Perfectly competitive markets are generally assumed, with other forms such as monopolistic competition being viewed as a special case when significant barriers to entry exist. In the perfect competition model, each market is for a homogeneous commodity whose price is uniform, both with respect to all units purchased or sold by an individual, and also across all buyers and sellers. Moreover, because it is usually assumed that there are many homogeneous market participants, each with an insignificant share of the total market, the price is parametric, a datum which cannot be influenced by the actions of any individual agent. Hence, there is no price discrimination and rationing is solely by price rather than quantity. Trading is costless and, because all participants possess the same information set with regard to price, no riskless arbitrage opportunities exist. Buying and selling prices are the same because market participants react instantaneously to any changes in supply or demand conditions.[4]

The requirement that all arbitrage opportunities will be instantly competed away renders it extremely difficult to envisage how any entrepreneur or firm could ever gain from introducing new products or processes since imitation is an option instantly and costlessly open to everyone. Hence, the neoclassical model's assumptions limit its usefulness as a description of the operation of many product markets. For example, the assumption of perfect certainty and equal access to information is totally uncharacteristic of the everyday business world. Furthermore, the model has no plausible explanation regarding the process of adjustment to (exogenously induced) changes. It is assumed that whenever a market is subjected to a random shock all markets adjust completely before any trade takes place. This is clearly untenable – as is most evident in the Walrasian version of the model where resort has to be made to notions of omnipotent auctioneers (see Casson 1982).

The equal access to information assumption of the model implies that market transactions are unproblematic. Entrepreneurial activities are excluded by definition since no obstacles to trade exist because the market-making activities performed by the entrepreneur are not required. All the practical problems associated with business transactions are thereby assumed away: from initially making contact with potential buyers and sellers through to obtaining restitution should one party default on an agreement. The costs incurred by agents in resolving these problems, from search activities through to the enforcement of the contract terms, are also assumed not to exist.

Moreover, the assumption that all units of a good are homogeneous with respect to quality and that all transactors are (essentially) identical, severely limits the understanding of the origin of the firm, its internal organization and its growth. The firm is viewed as a unitary profit-maximizing entity defined by a technologically-determined production function and is, in consequence, little more than 'an interface between factor markets and product markets' (Stephen 1984, p. 4). This is because perfect frictionless markets ensure that each homogeneous firm (market participant) can only earn a 'normal profit', the minimum amount (the opportunity cost) required to keep it in its current market. The firm instantly responds to any changes in market conditions by hiring each homogeneous input, capital, labour, materials, etc., to the point where its (perfectly observed) marginal revenue product is equal to its marginal factor cost. In effect, the firm is a 'black box', and its sole role is:

> to explain and predict changes in observed prices (quoted, paid, received) as effects of particular changes in conditions (wage rates, interest rates, import duties, excise taxes, technology, etc.). In this causal

connection the firm is only a theoretical link, a mental construct helping to explain how one gets from the cause to the effect. This is altogether different from explaining the behaviour of a firm.

(Machlup 1967, p. 9)

Hence, the economic roles and behaviours of individual entrepreneurs, and the vast differences between small firms and large public corporations are essentially equivalent in this framework. Likewise, the management function within firms cannot be adequately addressed since all factor inputs, including the suppliers of specialized management skills, are assumed to perform exactly as specified in the exchange agreement. The assumptions of perfect information and costless monitoring ensure that all transactions, including employment relations, are really 'contingent contracts' that can be costlessly negotiated and perfectly enforced. Problems relating to non-performance or shirking cannot arise because:

firms are able to hire not workers, but units of labour productivity on terms fully contingent on future states of the world. Workers accept not jobs but fully contingent contracts for the exchange of specified levels of productivity for perfectly defined packages of wages and other benefits.

(Yarbrough and Yarbrough 1988)

Firms in the neoclassical framework are, therefore, just another part of the instantaneous market-clearing process. The search for new markets, the development of products and marketing initiatives, the internal organization and management of the firm and all the other complexities of everyday business life have no place in this model of market behaviour.

The neoclassical model of the labour market has many of the same characteristics. There are many firms competing to recruit many workers in a market in which neither the firms nor the workers – or their organizations – have power in the sense of being able to influence market price by their own actions. Workers are able to move freely from one firm to another in response to the opportunity to earn higher wages. By implication firms and workers make few investments in the job so that there are no costs to the worker in leaving the firm and no costs to the firm when the worker leaves.

The observed reality is markedly different for several reasons. Some occupational labour markets are highly segmented in the sense that wage rates appear to be unaffected by the general trend of wages in the economy. Secondly, the level of firm-to-firm movement among certain groups of workers is less than suggested by the neoclassical model. Thirdly the presence of trade unions and nationally agreed wage bargains negates a key assumption of the neoclassical model. Fourthly, both employees and employers make considerable firm specific human capital investments in some

groups of workers, so that quit costs may be high for employer and employee, in the event of the worker choosing to switch firms.

THE NEW INSTITUTIONAL ECONOMICS

Background

It is not our intention to suggest that the neoclassical framework is sterile or
without intellectual merit. Rather, we have pointed out that it does not
realistically address key elements in the processes of firm creation, growth,
internal organization or other managerial issues. The theoretical focus upon
aggregate market outcomes and the lack of empirical applicability to the
actual economic behaviour of firms has in recent years led to the emergence
of several alternative conceptions.

Probably the most influential of these alternative frameworks, at least
within the industrial economics field, is the so-called 'structure–conduct–
performance' (SCP) paradigm stemming from the work of Mason (1949),
Bain (1959), Clark (1961) and Caves (1972). Generally, this approach is
based on the assumption that certain basic exogenous supply and demand
conditions determine market structure, i.e. the degree of concentration,
scale economies, barriers to entry, etc. It is then assumed that there is a
unidirectional causal flow from these market structures, through firm
conduct (i.e. price-setting behaviour, output levels, quality, etc.) to firm
performance (usually evaluated in terms of some 'ideal' Paretian welfare
norm). To date, much of the work in the SCP paradigm has been concerned
with establishing relatively simple empirical relationships. Despite its wide
influence, this work has a somewhat mechanical flavour due to its
theoretical under-development (see Reid 1987 for a review).

Of rather more relevance to our present concerns are the theoretical
developments under the broad title of 'new institutional economics'. Under
this heading we include the so-called 'property rights' (see Alchian and
Demsetz 1972 and Putterman 1989), agency theory (see Thompson 1988
for a review) and internal labour market (see Creedy and Whitfield 1988
and Wachter and Wright 1990) literatures.

Building on the work of Knight (1921), Commons (1934) and Coase
(1937), these otherwise diverse literatures share an emphasis upon the
highly imperfect nature of markets and the importance of market-making
activities of entrepreneurs and firms in creating economic change. Broadly,
the primary focus of this work concerns the 'transactions costs' (or more
generally, 'transactions difficulties') associated with organizing economic
activities, particularly with respect to the introduction of new economic

ideas; that is, innovation and the exploitation of existing market imperfections and information asymmetries.

Basically, transactions costs have to be incurred in order for trade to take place because it cannot be simply assumed that a market, let alone a 'perfect market', actually exists. Thus, in market settings characterized by uncertainty and information asymmetries, an adequate explanation of the behaviour of economic agents and the ownership, internal organization and management of firms has to take into account the relative costs associated with different strategies and ways of organizing transactions.

This perspective also highlights the role of management direction because the existence of incomplete contracts creates the possibility of non-performance (shirking). Hence, there is a need for the monitoring of factors since it is recognized that agents do not give up their own self-interests just because they have entered into an economic relationship.

Initially, this theme was taken up by so-called 'managerial' theorists who posited that managers might maximize objectives other than profits; for example, sales revenue (Baumol 1959), firm growth (Marris 1964) or multi-element utility functions (Williamson 1975). In more recent years this emphasis upon transactions costs and the problems of drawing-up, monitoring and enforcing contracts both within and between economic organizations has formed the basis of explanations regarding ownership structures (Jensen and Meckling 1976, Fama and Jensen 1983a, 1983b), entrepreneurship and innovation (Casson 1982, Silver 1984), the organization of labour (Williamson 1979, 1981, 1984),[5] management information systems (Spicer and Ballew 1983, Waterhouse and Tiessen 1983) and internal transfer price mechanisms (Spicer 1988). The key elements of these explanations in so far as they impinge upon our topic will be discussed below.

The entrepreneur

There appears to be widespread agreement that entrepreneurial activities both induce and result in innovation, or more generally, economic change.[6] Though, as Penrose (1959, p. 33) observes, entrepreneurship is:

> a slippery concept . . . not easy to work into formal analysis because it is so closely associated with the temperament or personal qualities of individuals.

None the less, there have been many theories of entrepreneurship from the seventeenth century onwards (see Casson 1990, Binks and Vale 1990, for in depth summaries of the history of the theoretical development of entrepreneurship). The various theories have stressed different aspects of entrepreneurship, i.e. a special factor of production, a taker of risks, an innovator, etc. From a macroeconomic perspective, entrepreneurship can be seen as a process that both induces economic change (which Schumpeter 1934, p. 64, described as the mainspring of economic development) and as a response to market opportunities that result from economic change. Hence, entrepreneurs can both create market disequilibrium and market equilibrium.

In the first role the entrepreneur is seen as one who 'disturbs the economy's circular flow equilibrium' (Schumpeter 1934) and who 'initiates change and generates new opportunities'. Hence, 'until imitators force prices and costs into conformity, the innovator is able to reap profits and disturb equilibrium' (O'Farrell 1986). In a similar vein, Knight (1921) viewed the entrepreneur as the primary cause of uncertainty. According to Knight individuals face a choice of offering themselves in the labour market for a fixed and certain wage, or becoming entrepreneurs who buy inputs at a fixed price and sell outputs at an uncertain price in the expectation of obtaining an adequate margin. However, the entrepreneur can also be seen as a market facilitator by virtue of being either better informed or having greater insight than other agents in the economy. For this reason Casson (1982) defines an entrepreneur as an individual who specializes in making judgemental decisions about the co-ordination of scarce resources. Table 2.1 encapsulates Casson's market-making view of entrepreneurship

Table 2.1 Entrepreneurship as market making

Obstacles to trade	Market-making activity
No contact between buyer and seller	Contact making via search or advertisement
No knowledge of reciprocal wants	Specification of the trade and communication of the details to each party
No agreement over price	Negotiation
Need to exchange custody of goods and pay any taxes or tariffs due on the transaction	Transport and administration
No confidence that goods correspond to specification	Monitoring, that is, screening of quality, metering of quantity, timing of instalments, observation of contingent events
No confidence that restitution will be made for default	Enforcement

Source: Casson 1982

and provides an indication of the types of judgemental decisions typically required of entrepreneurs. It lists some of the major obstacles associated with the introduction of any form of innovation and the corresponding market-making activities required to overcome them.

Many of these activities require the acquisition and processing of large amounts of highly specialized information, access to financial and other resources and social contacts and adequate technical/negotiating skills. In other words, it is unlikely to be the case that these skills and economic resources are randomly distributed throughout the population. Rather an individual's prior education and experience, particularly knowledge of a closely related market, is likely to be of crucial importance. Also, since access to capital funds will be necessary in order for individuals to act upon their insights, entrepreneurial activities will be concentrated among individuals that have credibility in the eyes of the financial markets and/or have access to personal/family wealth (see Casson 1982, pp. 90–3). Thus the entrepreneur is an individual who is both willing and able to respond to or create market opportunities.

The origin and nature of the firm

The discussion of entrepreneurship emphasized the exploitation of market imperfections. This does not necessarily require the ownership of resources, let alone a requirement for owning and managing an organization (firm). Nevertheless, in practice, many entrepreneurs appear to find that, in order to fully exploit market imperfections, owning and managing a firm is preferable to contracting exclusively with other market participants. This section reviews some of the explanations as to why this should be so.

While there are number of explanations for the existence of firms this chapter concentrates on the perspectives deriving from Coase's (1937) work. Starting from the assumption that significant transactions costs are incurred in organizing economic activities, Coase argued that because the transactions costs associated with using markets were often high, the firm could act as the least-cost co-ordinator of factor inputs.[7] By co-ordinating inputs rather than contracting with external market participants, the firm reduced the transactions costs associated with extensive search efforts and allowed factors to be hired on incomplete contracts. This is particularly important when uncertainly regarding future requirements is high since an incomplete contract allows the subsequent direction of resources to their most profitable uses as circumstances change.

Williamson (1979, 1981, 1985) extended this line of reasoning to produce a theory which explained the relative efficiency of different organizational arrangements (governance structures) in terms of the nature and costs associated with organizing transactions.[8] Williamson's model is based upon two main postulates regarding human nature: bounded rationality and opportunism. Following Simon (1957), Williamson assumes that human decision-makers have limited information-processing abilities. This implies that, at the time of the transaction, economic agents are unable to draw-up complete state-contingent contracts; that is contracts which specify in detail the obligations of each party in any situation which could effect the interests of the parties to the transaction.

Williamson describes opportunism as 'self-seeking with guile'. It refers to the likelihood that, at least some people, some of the time, will attempt to deceive other parties to a transaction so as to further their own interests. When a contract is being negotiated, agents may attempt to misrepresent their intentions or the quality of the goods or skills on offer. This is termed 'ex ante opportunism'. If, after a contract has been agreed, monitoring of performance is either impossible or costly then agents may act opportunistically by, for instance, strategically revealing or distorting information. This is termed 'ex post opportunism'.[9] Hence, the major problem is not that most agents are opportunistic but rather, it is difficult to know who is opportunistic and who is not (McGuinness 1987).

Williamson suggests that certain types of transactions offer greater scope for opportunism than others. The scope of opportunism, and the most appropriate organizational form for controlling it, are related to the following three attributes of transactions:

1 asset specificity;
2 uncertainty; and
3 frequency.

Highly specific assets cannot normally be switched to alternative uses or be sold without a considerable reduction in their current value. This is usually because no alternative use or effective demand for the asset exists outside the present contract. Human capital assets, such as investment in specialized training or detailed knowledge of a particular firm's administrative system, as well as physical assets are relevant here. The main point regarding asset specificity is that both parties to a transaction involving the use of highly specific assets will be 'locked-in' to some extent since potentially both have much to lose if the contractual arrangement were unilaterally ended. For instance, the owners of such quasi-rent-receiving assets would have to take a capital loss if the transaction were terminated. Likewise, because of the lack of availability of comparable assets, the ending of the present contract would hurt the users of the asset's services. Hence, once an investment in highly specific assets has been made, subsequent bargaining when contracts are due for renewal leads to a small numbers bargaining situation, particularly when the winner of the original contract acquires additional first-mover or other learning-by-doing advantages. This situation allows great scope for opportunistic behaviour and, according to Williamson, it renders market contracting all but impossible. High asset specificity requires the entrepreneur to 'internalize' and manage assets within an organization designed to minimize opportunism.

Similar arguments apply with respect to uncertainty. Bounded rationality, when coupled with a high degree of environmental uncertainty relating to the transaction, also increases the scope for opportunistic behaviour. This is because the inability to make detailed plans, particularly when there are many possible states-of-the-world to consider, means that detailed, fully contingent, contracts cannot be drawn-up, monitored or enforced effectively. In conditions characterized by uncertainty, therefore, incomplete contracts and an organization which is both flexible and able to control opportunism are required. The final attribute of transactions that Williamson suggests has important implications in respect of opportunism and organizational design concerns their frequency. The greater the frequency of a transaction, the more it makes sense to invest in sophisticated monitoring and control systems which will significantly reduce bargaining costs on each subsequent occasion the transaction takes place.

Williamson claims that, given the assumption that economic actors (entrepreneurs and firms) desire to minimize the sum of their production and transactions costs for the tasks required, his theory can be used to explain the relative efficiencies of different organizational forms. He developed a typology of the most 'efficient governance structures' associated with different combinations of the frequency of transactions and investment characteristics. This typology is reproduced in Figure 2.1.

Fama and Jensen (1983a, 1983b) have used similar ideas to explain the 'survival value' of different ownership rights, incentive schemes and organizational forms. Here the central concern is with minimization of agency costs, that is the costs associated with writing, monitoring and enforcing contracts between opportunistic agents in an environment characterized by uncertainty and information asymmetries. Within this framework, an organization is viewed as a nexus of (written and unwritten) contracts between factor owners (i.e. the suppliers of risk capital, specialized labour services, etc.) and customers. The central contracts of an organization specify which agents have rights to any residual income and which agents are responsible for particular stages of the decision process. The primary decision processes are seen to consist of decision management (the initiation and implementation of decisions) and decision control (the ratification and monitoring of decisions). Fama and Jensen (1983a) suggest that organizations differ in their degree of complexity, that is the extent to

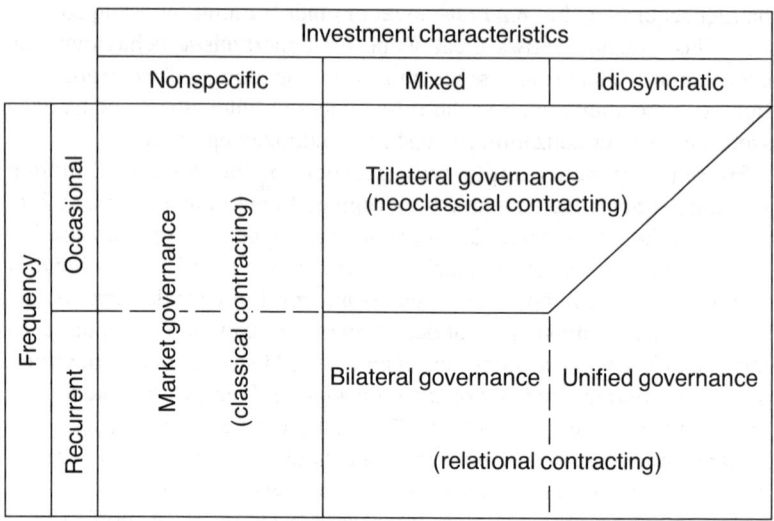

Figure 2.1 Efficient governance

Source: Williamson (1979), reprinted in O.E. Williamson (1985) *The Economic Institutions of Capitalism*. New York: The Free Press.

which costly transfers of information necessary for decision making is required because it is not concentrated in one or a few agents. They develop the following two hypotheses in relation to this issue:

1. Separation of residual risk bearing from decision management leads to decision systems that separate decision control from decision management.

2. Combination of decision management and decision control in a few agents leads to residual claims that are largely restricted to these agents.
(Fama and Jensen 1983a, p. 304)

Basically, their argument is that in non-complex organizations, such as small firms where information is concentrated in one or a few agents, it is efficient in terms of the minimization of agency costs to combine decision management and control and to limit residual claims (ownership) to the decision makers. In contrast, in complex organizations where information is diffuse and where risk-bearing residual claimants (shareholders) are not involved in the initiation and implementation of decisions, it is more efficient to separate decision control from decision management.

Fama and Jensen suggest, therefore, that the traditional owner-managed small firm and the large public company (characterized by a separation of ownership from control), are both 'rational' and efficient organizational forms. Given the diverse information requirements of their respective business operations and ownership structures, both types of organization minimize the agency costs associated with the drawing-up, monitoring and enforcing of contracts between agents.

The labour market for managers

The neoclassical model of labour markets assumes that workers move from one firm to another in response to the opportunity to earn higher wages. The firm, which is perfectly competitive in the product market, cannot pay the worker more than their marginal product. Payments in excess of marginal product are not sustainable since this would raise the firm's costs above those of rivals and, thereby make them uncompetitive and placing in jeopardy the continued existence of the firm. The worker, on the other hand will not stay with a firm when he knows there is an opportunity to earn high wages elsewhere. It is this movement which serves to bring about a state of equilibrium in the market.

However, this stylized view of the labour market is at variance with casual observation. For example, certain groups of workers such as managers, while they move jobs quite frequently, appear to move employers very infrequently, if at all throughout their career. There also appears to be only the most modest of links between the marginal product of the worker and the wage paid. Instead wages are more strongly linked to seniority which, in turn, is often linked to age. Finally it is not clear that an employee's current wage is the sole, or even the most important, factor influencing the choice of employer.

In the same way that the neoclassical theory of the firm is modified by the new institutional economics to provide supposedly greater 'realism', so there is also an adjustment of the theory of the labour market along broadly similar lines. Williamson (1984), for example, applied his transactions cost framework to human assets and to the organization of labour contracts. He argued that where an individual's productivity is easy to monitor and does not involve firm-specific skills then market contracting will be most efficient. However for many management posts, where productivity cannot be easily measured and skills are highly firm specific, a governance structure based on 'relational teams' will be required. Williamson's relational team seems to correspond with, what Ouchi (1980) refers to as a 'clan' form of organization where the firm:

> will engage in considerable social conditioning, to help [ensure] that

employees understand and are dedicated to the purposes of the firm, and employees will be provided with considerable job security, which gives them assurance against exploitation. Neither of these objectives can be raised independently of the other.

(Williamson 1984, p. 92)

By combining the notions of 'bounded rationality' on the part of individuals, with a recognition that some workers could be 'opportunistic' in the sense of not disclosing all the information available to them, Williamson laid the basis for the economic view of 'internal labour markets'. These were a set of long-term employment agreements between a firm and its workers, which are in total contrast to the assumed short termism envisaged in the neoclassical model.

Williamson's arguments were developed by Wachter and Wright (1990) who postulated that there were four factors which, when present simultaneously, explained the existence of an internal labour market. These were (a) firm or match-specific training, (b) risk aversion, (c) asymmetric information, and (d) transaction costs.

Match-specific investments occur when the firm invests its resources in making a worker more productive with their current employer – either in their current job or in a future job with that employer, and ideally relatively less productive with an alternative employer. These investments are worthwhile to the employee if they can benefit through higher earnings in the future or greater certainty of future income. They are worthwhile to the employer if it avoids the need to rely upon recruits from the external labour market and perhaps incurring substantial induction costs for new labour.

We noted above that workers not only place a value upon their current wage, but also upon the probability that they will be in receipt of a stream of income over time. If the employer can provide greater certainty through the types of long-term contracts which characterize the internal labour market, then this is clearly of value to a 'risk-averse' employee.

The central contribution of Williamson is, as we noted above, that where information on effort is distributed asymmetrically, there are opportunities for workers to act strategically. It is in the interests of the employer therefore to minimize the effects of this by entering into a set of employment-related contracts, of the types which form the basis of the internal labour market.

ASSESSMENT

The developments in economics, which we have labelled the new institutional economics, are a significant advance on earlier conceptions of the relationships between the market environments, organizational forms and performance of firms. However, a major problem associated with both the transactions cost, agency theory framework and, indeed, most economic explanations, is the apparent belief that market forces necessarily 'weed-out less-efficient' organizations. Thus, dominant business practices and organizational forms are seen to be, *ipso facto*, efficient. This raises a number of important issues. First, this Darwinian view of organizational evolution whereby 'efficiency always wins out in the end', seems to provide a justification of whatever corporate forms and practices are currently prevalent. Moreover, the economic notion of efficiency is not well defined in an economy characterized by uncertainty and a lack of agreement concerning the initial distribution of wealth (agents initial endowments). In an uncertain world expectations are often confounded because all possible future states cannot be enumerated, much less be assigned probabilities. This implies that, ex ante, an agent can never know whether the 'right' decision has been made because the ex post set may contain outcomes preferable to all those outcomes considered when making the decision. Another implication is that:

> as we only observe a very limited portion of the ex ante set (which, in turn, is at least partially a function of the ex ante decisions made), we can never know ex post whether we made the 'best' decision and can only vaguely discern (usually by comparison to the experience of others) whether we even made a 'good' decision.
>
> (Findley and Williams 1981)

Hence, in an uncertain world, we can never know whether other, un-observed, outcomes would be any more or less efficient than existing arrangements. It should also be apparent that the writing, monitoring and enforcement of a perfect, state-contingent, contract will be impossible.

In addition, efficiency, in the more everyday sense of achieving the 'best' means to some given end, seems to imply the existence of some commonly agreed objective. Hence, the very notion of efficiency is problematic in the context of conflicting interests regarding desired outcomes between various factor suppliers and/or customers and other members of society. The possibility of conflicting interests between, say, shareholders and managers or managers and workers, is, of course, central to the conceptual schemes we have been discussing. Generally, the economics literature overcomes this problem only by uncritically equating efficiency with the interests of the firm's owners in minimizing costs. Even if it were generally agreed that the minimization of costs was a generally desired outcome, the notion of efficiency would still be ambiguous. Any conflicts between agents regarding the best means to this goal or the existence of trade-offs between long and short run costs would still need to be resolved. In addition, uncertainty, idiosyncratic exchange, information asymmetries and entry barriers are features of highly imperfect markets, the very conditions which give greatest scope for self-interested agents to exploit whatever sources of economic power they possess. The assumption that these conditions necessarily produce efficient outcomes seems less plausible than several alternative possibilities such as increasing monopoly power or exploiting some new technological process.

Despite the foregoing criticisms, when shorn of their prescriptive efficiency elements, the economic frameworks can provide important insights into the forms of organization and business practices adopted by new and/or successful firms in particular circumstances. It is the case, however, that the frameworks implicitly or explicitly are constructed on the basis of observing or explaining behaviour in large firms.

THE SMALLER FIRM

Our interest is in the management, organization and behaviour of smaller firms. For this reason we now turn to an examination of the literature on small firms relating to uncertainty, innovation and the evolution and management of the firm since these are key dimensions in which small and large firms fundamentally differ. Our purpose is to assess the extent to which the issues addressed in the new institutional economics relate to smaller firms.

As will be seen in the next three subsections, the small-firm literature has tended to be largely 'descriptive' in character and has not generally been well informed by formal economic theories. Nevertheless many of the same themes addressed within these theories have relevance for smaller firms and it is our task to examine these matters

In undertaking this task we have, at the forefront of our minds, that the small firm is not a scaled down version of a large firm. It cannot be assumed that the issues facing the smaller firm and its behavioural response to them are the same as those facing a larger firm, other than in terms of scale.

As Penrose (1959, p. 19) points out:

> the differences in the administrative structure of the very small and the very large firms are so great that in many ways it is hard to see that the two species are of the same genus . . . we cannot define a caterpillar and then use the same definition for a butterfly.

The converse is equally true. Using the Penrose analogy, we cannot assume that a caterpillar is a small butterfly. Instead we need to identify those characteristics of a small firm which most clearly distinguish it from a large firm and then to theorize on their implications for the key dimensions of management. It is the argument of the remainder of this chapter that these three characteristics are uncertainty, innovation and evolution. The implications for the management of smaller firms of each of these is discussed in turn.

Uncertainty and the small firm

Uncertainty is a key feature confronting small firms and can be of a different order of magnitude and importance than is the case for large firms. Uncertainty facing the smaller firm can stem from several factors. First, it may be simply a reflection of the small firm's lack of market power. The large firm is much more likely to be able to influence price because of its market share and more substantial resource base. Even if its share in a particular market is small, the large firm can constitute a much more credible threat to firms in that market than a smaller firm through its ability to enter a market and, once inside, to compete on the grounds of low price, advertising, etc., and achieve low returns for some years. This is the so-called 'deep pocket' argument (Utton 1984). Moreover, Baumol (1967) argues that large capitalized firms have the option of competing with small firms but that small firms cannot easily choose to compete with large.

The absence of market power for smaller firms means they are invariably price takers. Nevertheless, many large firms also face a highly complex and uncertain environment due to trading in a market with other powerful strategic players. In contrast, some small firms experience a relatively stable and non-complex business environment as price takers in product markets characterized by relatively stable demand or low profit rates. Indeed, the feasible strategic decision set of small firms may be so constrained as to be relatively straightforward because of the limited number of acts/options available: either to continue making low profits or to get out of the business altogether.

The argument indicates that the market uncertainty facing small firms is multi-faceted: it is a function of the degree of power the particular firm has in its market, the number of players in the market, the stability of the market and the firm's perception of the available feasible options. These facets are clearly not independent and their intertwining produces the unique configuration of uncertainty faced by an individual firm. For example, in relation to market uncertainty, many small firms operate in a highly competitive environment. How the competition transforms itself into uncertainty depends upon how orderly the competition is and the degree to which present market incumbents are protected by entry barriers. While, it needs to be recognized that small firms will often find it difficult to erect product differentiation barriers, barriers may still exist because of the niche nature of the market, the existence of information asymmetries and the benefits of being an early entrant.

Another source of uncertainty for many small firms is their limited customer and product base, creating what Williamson refers to as 'small numbers bargaining situations'. A number of studies of smaller firms (for a review see Storey 1982) have shown that many smaller firms have no more than a handful of key customers, and a number have only a single customer. For example, Davies and Kelly (1972) show that more than one third of all small manufacturers sell more than 25 per cent of their output to one customer. In that situation, any difficulties which befall the larger company may lead to the demise of the small company supplier. Similarly many small firms produce only a single product or service, so that again the narrow nature of product/service base will, *ceteris paribus*, cause greater uncertainty than where a diversified range is provided.

One extreme form of this dependence is where small firms act as subcontractors to larger firms. Here the small firm is usually unable to exercise any form of price control and it may also have all other elements of the production process and management controls tightly specified. Here the large firm customer not only sets the price and quantities at which the commodity is to be supplied, but also determines the nature of the inputs, the production method used and even the quality control checks which are to be implemented. While this means that some production and marketing uncertainties are reduced for the small-firm subcontractor, it also means that the latter can become totally dependent upon a single customer. Furthermore, subcontractors are likely to achieve generally lower margins because of their weak bargaining position in negotiations where the purchaser is aware of all of the costs. It may therefore be difficult to build up sufficient retained profit to finance either new developments or overcome difficult periods when orders are in short supply. Hence, if the large customer acts opportunistically or decides to look elsewhere for a source of supply, the subcontractor has less resources available from which to diversify its customer base.

A third source of uncertainty which characterizes small firms concerns the diverse objectives and abilities of the owners of such businesses. It has been shown in several studies (reviewed in Curran 1986) that the owners of small businesses are not commonly motivated by a desire to significantly expand their business; indeed, many deliberately set out to avoid growth. For example, some business owners who have worked in large firms have established their own firms in order to rid themselves of the need to satisfy large company objectives such as achieving growth or increasing market share. A major problem which frequently arises, however, is that these owners often do not see the need to implement even the most basic management practices, such as an appropriate financial information system. It is perhaps for these reasons that studies in both the United States by Phillips and Kirchhoff (1988) and in Australia by Williams (1990) have shown that the small firms most likely to cease trading are those which also experience zero or low rates of growth.

The aspirations of small business owners are heavily influenced by the uncertainties of economic life. To understand these aspirations and the strategies adopted to achieve them, it is vital to recognize that a substantial proportion of the small business owner's overall financial and human capital resources are generally tied up in the business. In many cases, the business is the sole source of employment and income, not just for an individual, but often for an extended family network. The small business owner has, therefore, an undiversified portfolio – often consisting of highly specific physical and human assets – and, as such, is subject to greater risk than agents that are able to diversify their holdings.

Nevertheless, various legal and fiscal rules do allow owners some scope for diversifying their holdings. For instance, the owner of a successful company who becomes aware of opportunities for developing in an associated market may, because of the limited liability provisions, be unwilling to jeopardize the existing company, and the income which can be derived from it, by including within it the new development. Instead the entrepreneur may create or acquire a second company which, if it does not succeed, can be liquidated without threatening the existence of the successful company. In the event of success, of course, the two companies may be combined at a later stage or continue to operate separately. Successful entrepreneurs may, therefore, develop a portfolio of companies from which they and their families derive income. Empirical evidence indicating that the owners of successful small businesses often own several firms can be found in Storey *et al.* (1987). Growth may then be reflected, not just in the performance of a single company, but within the portfolio in general.

The derivation of income, the retention of ownership and the reduction of risk are very powerful motivations for small-firm entrepreneurs operating in uncertain environments. In many cases this is reflected in a resolute determination by entrepreneurs to maintain ownership of the portfolio of businesses within the family. It can also mean that the entrepreneur is prepared to forgo growth which could be facilitated by the injection of external equity or additional debt, in order to maintain ownership and control within family hands (Boswell 1973).

In other cases, uncertainty and fiscal considerations combine to inhibit growth by encouraging directors to distribute company profits rather than using them for reinvestment purposes. For instance, Watson (1990, 1991) showed that some 65 per cent of the total trading profits of small and closely held companies was typically taken out of the business in directors fees. He also developed a directors' remuneration model, based upon tax-minimization behaviour in the context of uncertainty, that succeeded in explaining over 70 per cent of the variance in directors remuneration. Moreover, he showed that the pay-out ratio had a significant negative effect upon the employment growth of these companies. Again, this seems to indicate that small-firm corporate profitability and the after-tax incomes of the directors and their families are closely intertwined. To understand the motivations of the entrepreneur and the strategies adopted by small companies, therefore, requires the nature of family circumstances in a highly uncertain environment to be appreciated. This clearly differs from the case of larger companies where dividend policy is assessed to satisfy the requirements of shareholders and management, and where the options are extensively analysed in the publicly traded market for shares.

Innovation and small firms

To examine the innovatory aspects of small firms the five types of innovation specified by Schumpeter (1934) could be used to form a loose organizing structure. The types of innovation identified by Schumpeter are the introduction of a new good (or improvement of an existing one), the introduction of a new process, the opening of a new market (especially exporting), the identification of a new source of supply of raw materials and the creation of a new type of industrial organization.

The reason that these criteria can only form a loose organizing structure is that they are somewhat ambiguous since each criterion has several dimensions. Take for example the notion of a new good. It is unclear how newness should be defined. One possible measure of newness is a perceived absence of close substitutes, though perceived closeness of substitutes is only one facet of the newness of a good (an excellent example being the introduction of the home computer). There is a clear need to develop an awareness of the other factors that provide a good alternative in the marketplace. For instance, if the image of a good is seen as consisting of product, price, promotion, packaging and place of sale, then perceived newness can reflect any one of these facets or any combination. A Rolex watch, copied in every detail by a Hong Kong manufacturer but sold at a fraction of the price of the original, for many customers will be a new good, a good they can now afford, that has additional perceived value because it imitates an existing good. Its newness, its price differential, only has value because of its imitative qualities. The craze for mountain bikes might be seen as a response to a new good coming onto the market. The newness of this good is derived from a combination of attributes. It is essentially similar in its physical design to previous bikes except that it has more gears and knobbly tyres – hardly a radical new product. However, it is this marginal product change, coupled with a promotion that stresses the ability to access the rugged outdoor life, that creates the image of a new good. This is not just a form of transport, but is also an entry into a certain lifestyle. Hence, newness itself is derived not only from the basic attributes or characteristics of a good, but also related to the ability to influence perceptions (marketing). A similar perspective could be adopted for the other Schumpeterian criteria.

Mueller (1988) reviews a number of plausible arguments as to why small firms may be more innovatory than large firms. These arguments stress the flexible organizational structures of small firms, which help mitigate the control loss and information distortion problems (agency costs) characteristic of large firms, and the superior incentives provided to management for risk taking. Nevertheless, apart from the initial setting-up of the firm, relatively few small firms appear to be innovative to any great degree. For instance, many small firms come into existence only because their owners incorrectly observe market signals. It may be that their owners deem there to be a market for a totally new product where one does not exist. More frequently owners incorrectly assume there to be a currently unsatisfied demand, at a given price level, for an existing product or service. New firm founders may also incorrectly assess their own ability to manage and organize an enterprise so that, even if the market exists, the particular firm in question is unable to satisfy it.

It therefore seems doubtful whether the inability either to correctly identify market signals or to be able to manage a business in such a way as to satisfy the market constitutes innovation. Yet, judging from the high failure rates of small firms, this is a role which small businesses play to a much greater extent than large firms. Conversely, a large number of even those small firms which survive provide 'standard' goods and services provided by many other firms. Again it seems difficult to consider this an act of innovatory entrepreneurship on the part of the business owner.

In practice few small firms could be classified as innovative according to the strict interpretation of the Schumpeterian criteria. The role of small firms is generally much less glamorous than that envisaged by Schumpeter. To illustrate, take again the first of the five types of innovation – that of the introduction of a new good. An initial observation of small firms would suggest that few introduce fundamentally new products in the mould of introducing the home computer for the first time. The more familiar role for small firms is to occupy what Penrose (1959) describes as the interstices of the economy. The characteristics of these firms is that they rarely compete directly with large firms, even though from a statistical classification point of view they may be deemed to be in the same industry.

Small firms will occasionally, but very rarely, introduce a fundamentally new product/service. There are instances when this does happen, and these instances are extensively documented. For example, Rothwell (1986) discusses the development of the semiconductor industry in California as a classic new product initially introduced by the small-firms sector, although subsequently developed by the large-firm sector. A contrary view of the role of small firms in new industries is, however, provided by Shearman and Burrell (1988) in their discussion of the medical laser sector.

While the introduction of fundamentally new products is the exception for smaller firms, many will produce a good that can be defined as new because they offer a new mix of the basic attributes. The smaller firm, operating in these interstices, will produce a product which differs from that generally available from larger firms, in some minor but nevertheless observable respect. Hence, they are likely to regard their rivals as being other smaller firms occupying these or adjacent interstices, rather than the large firms which dominate the main market. It may therefore be necessary to make a distinction between the small firms which produce a standard product/service and those small firms which occupy such interstices. The latter may not be innovative in the Schumpeterian sense of producing a new product, yet they may provide a new good/differentiated product, as defined in the opening part of this section, within the marketplace.

This newness/differentiation may take a number of forms. First, it may be that one firm sees its advantage in terms of its ability to move quickly into exploiting a market opportunity, even where it knows that this will always be followed by competitors. In this case the firm's comparative advantage is in terms of its speed of response. A second area where firms may compete is in the area of marketing. Some firms clearly have a much greater awareness of their markets than others. One firm may have superior market intelligence to that available to most firms in the sense of knowing what its competitors are doing, what their strengths and weaknesses are, and how these can best be exploited. It may also have particularly strong links with customers, having a clear understanding of their preferences.

A third area where a small firm may compete is through the provision of something extra, i.e. a personalized service. For instance, a small office and factory cleaning service firm may have a comparative advantage over a large national company because its customers know that, in an emergency such as a flood, fire or burglary, the owner can be contacted at home at any time and the service provided. It should be noted that these arguments relate also to the issue of competitive strategy discussed by Porter (1980). He suggests that, while small firms may generally be less profitable than larger firms, their ability to identify and occupy niches can lead to an elimination of profitability differentials. Empirical support for this in the United States is provided by Bradburd and Ross (1989) who show that in heterogeneous industries large firms no longer have significant profitability advantages over smaller firms.

In the medium term, the smaller firm occupying a highly profitable interstice is likely to experience entry either from another small firm or from a larger firm. The original incumbent may either beat off the competition, identify another niche and move into it, share the market with the entrant or be pushed out completely. Thus, it is important to recognize that interstices, as well as individual small firms, may therefore be temporary.

The management and evolution of the small firm

The managerial dimensions which most clearly characterize the smaller enterprise will now be highlighted. The first dimension of managerial tasks that characterizes smaller firms is that ownership and management are usually concentrated in the hands of very few people, often a single person. The power to initiate, implement and monitor decisions and appropriate any residual profits lies with that individual and it will not normally be frustrated or diluted by the action or inaction of other managers. In this sense, therefore, the owner/manager can be more certain that his decision will result in a change in the direction of the business. Within the company therefore the small-firm owner/manager is subject to fewer checks and balances than his or her large firm counterpart. Conversely the external effects of any given managerial decision, in terms of its effects on the market place might, as we have noted earlier, be much more uncertain.

The second dimension along which those characteristics of management unique to smaller firms can be examined is that of evolution. As noted previously, the nature, style and functions of management are likely to change considerably as a small company grows and its ownership and management structure evolves. Within the managerial literature there have been a number of attempts to model stages of firm growth, of which the best known are those by Greiner (1972) and Churchill and Lewis (1983). In these models the firm is generally portrayed as moving through a number of stages, although Churchill and Lewis note that it is not necessary for the firm which arrives at the final stage to have passed through every intermediate stage. In the models of both Greiner and of Churchill and Lewis the firm, once it grows out of the early stages is no longer small. Hence, if the discussion is to be limited to small firms, it is more appropriate to examine the stage models proposed by Scott and Bruce (1987) which refer only to small firms.

Scott and Bruce see the firm moving through five stages from inception to maturity with the movement at each stage being triggered by a crisis. The staged development which they propose emphasizes the point that failure to deal with the crises which separate each of the stages can be the cause of the demise of the firm. Conversely, successfully managing the crisis enables the firm to move into the next stage of growth. The model proposes that the early stages of company growth see internal managerial procedures and systems become more formalized, with a movement away from informal methods of communication (the model is, therefore, similar in its emphasis to those proposed by Williamson and Fama and Jensen). From the perspective of this chapter, however, interest is directed to how, and under what circumstances, the firm moves from being flexible and informal, even entrepreneurial, to one in which there is greater formality and clearer systems of responsibility.

This formality of system is most clearly reflected in the way in which the management role and style change as the organization develops. Scott and Bruce characterize the role and style of management in the five stages as shown in Table 2.2. The table also reproduces their characterization of organization structures. It shows that the small business covers a wide spectrum of management styles and organizational structures. These range from very simple at the inception phase of the business to almost the full range of complexity found in a multi-product, multi-divisioned large company at the maturity phase. As the business develops new managerial skills are required, together with new levels of sophistication in existing skills.

These can be achieved in three main ways. First, the owners themselves can develop new skills or implement new procedures. Thus the business founder who, prior to the start-up of the firm may have had a background in marketing, continues to have full responsibility for developing this

Table 2.2 Management role and style in the five stages of small business growth

Stage	Top management role	Management style	Organization structure
1 Inception	Direct supervision	Entrepreneurial individualistic	Unstructured
2 Survival	Supervised supervision	Entrepreneurial administrative	Simple
3 Growth	Delegation/ co-ordination	Entrepreneurial co-ordinate	Functional centralized
4 Expansion	Decentralization	Professional administrative	Functional decentralized
5 Maturity	Decentralization	Watchdog	Decentralized functional/product

function. Or the individual may find that, since the creation of the business, he has developed new areas of interest which he wishes to exploit such as finance or research – these are called 'diversified owner managers'.

Second, new individuals with proven managerial skills may be recruited from outside. Normally these will be professional managers who do not have an ownership interest in the firm, but in some cases the requirement for very specific managerial talent is such that there is a requirement to share the equity. These are considered to be 'external' managers. Third, there may be individuals, who are not currently exercising a managerial function, but who could be promoted into managerial posts. These are often individuals who have worked in the business for some time and whose functions and responsibilities have grown in parallel with the business. They may be considered 'organic' management.

All three methods may be used by the same firm, or it may rely exclusively upon a single procedure. Nevertheless it is the development of skills within the managerial team that both facilitates and stimulates further growth. The factors which influence the chosen combination of insiders/outsiders will vary from one firm to another, and are likely to be heavily influenced by the personal aspirations of the owner. They may also vary from one managerial function to another and reflect the different 'styles' which pervade the business. In this sense they may also vary according to the stage to which the business has developed according to Table 2.2.

The role of the management team in the development of a smaller business is, therefore, both complicated and dynamic. It is one that is not immediately suitable to empirical analysis since the development of the management team will facilitate the growth of the business, and yet the growth of the business will induce changes in the team. To Penrose (1959, p. 46),

> the capabilities of the existing managerial personnel of the firm necessarily set a limit to the expansion of that firm in any given period of time, for it is self evident that such management cannot be hired in the market place.

She argues that not only does the existing team limit the size of the new management team that can be hired, but also that previous plans determine the rate at which new personnel can be absorbed into the firm. Indeed she appears to suggest that, given an existing managerial structure, there is an optimum rate at which new management can be added – too fast and there will be administrative chaos, too slow and market opportunities will be lost.

Casson (1982) analyses this matter with respect to what he defines as the 'internal' and 'external' labour market. He begins with the assumption that labour is of variable quality as regards both integrity and ability, and that the problem of quality control (adverse selection) is of greater significance in the recruitment of delegate decision makers – managers – than in the recruitment of other forms of labour.

For the entrepreneur these uncertainties, together with those discussed earlier, may lead some to a preference for promoting family members to decision-making posts. This only serves to underline further the difficulties of disassociating family from corporate income in smaller firms. Some firms may only enter the external market for lower quality or non-managerial labour to undertake routine and/or closely monitored tasks. Such strategies to reduce the potential adverse selection and moral hazard problems associated with hiring labour can be effective in the early days of a firm's development. Casson points out, however, that this pool of 'internal' labour is unlikely to provide the full range of skills required for the firm to expand significantly, and so the entrepreneur must eventually develop his own skills in the recruitment of labour. Hence, a new firm may move from the internal to the external labour market as it grows. In the early days the firm/entrepreneur is likely to favour the internal market which, in its most extreme form, will be family only management. When that pool of resources is fully exploited, and that may be immediately, the firm will favour the next two most 'internal' sources, notably individuals with whom the entrepreneur has worked previously, and individuals with whom he/she is currently working, but where that individual is not a manager.

Matters are further complicated by the fact that for growing businesses the particular configuration of managerial abilities is rarely optimal at any point in time. In many cases, while the managerial team may have been appropriate for a point in time in the past, it is then unlikely to be relevant to current and future conditions. The stage models assume that the firm is continually reaching managerial crisis points as it develops, and it is the ability to solve these crises that enables the firm to move through the successive stages of development.

While the stage models are helpful in highlighting that managerial styles and roles vary widely, and are constantly evolving, there are several key problems in utilizing them for the present purposes. First, there seems to be a presumption that, while perhaps not all firms follow the pattern of staged growth identified by the models, this is a fairly familiar developmental pattern. For example, Scott and Bruce say 'Not all businesses which survive grow to be large businesses' while Churchill and Lewis point out that previous researchers 'assume that a company must grow and pass through all stages of development or die in the attempt'. To overcome this problem Churchill and Lewis have a third stage (success) which gives the firm the choice to use as a platform for further growth, or as a basis for good lifestyles for owners and managers (the success disengagement stage). In these senses there is a recognition by the authors that there is not an inevitable move from stage 1 to stage 5 through all intermediate stages.

Despite this recognition, the vast majority of the discussion is devoted to factors influencing the movements between stages. The present concern with stage models, however, goes beyond a recognition that some firms may reach a given stage and then 'stick' or even disappear. Instead, as should be clear from the previous discussions of uncertainty and innovation, relatively few firms are likely to move from one stage to another. The crisis points discussed by Greiner and by Scott and Bruce are much more likely to lead to the demise of the firm than to its movement to the next stage, as reflected in the fact that about 10 per cent of the stock of small firms in the UK cease to trade each year (Ganguly 1985, Daly 1991). Thus, it may be more plausible to assume that firms which are currently at or beyond stage 3 in the Scott and Bruce typology either never experienced the earlier stages or existed in those stages for such a short period of time that it could not properly be described as a stage. Another possibility is that some firms will have reached their current size through acquisition rather than organic growth.

Examination of the managerial and organizational dimensions shown in Table 2.2 illustrate this point. The types of businesses which have reached stage 4 may well, at start up, have a managerial and organizational structure more akin to stage 3 than stage 1. In essence the trajectory of development which the fast-growth small firm experiences may be fundamentally different to that of the more typical small business. Furthermore the only firms which are likely to achieve stage 4 and 5 are those which effectively began life in stage 3. Those which started in stages 1 and 2 will have never achieved, or even sought to achieve, the acceleration necessary to generate the need for the later stages.

In terms of Table 2.2 the fast-growth firm, which is the only one likely ever to achieve stages 4 and 5, may well begin with a managerial team of owners and professional managers. The top management role may then be classified as delegation and co-ordination. Even at start-up it would be difficult to imagine the organization structure to be anything other than centralized, but strong elements of functionalism are quite likely. It is also likely that the management of a start-up small firm which is gearing up for rapid growth will have a highly entrepreneurial style, and yet be concerned to co-ordinate the activities of the existing team.[10]

It seems unlikely, therefore, that there is any consistent or single pathway to development. Almost no firms will have passed through each of the five stages of business growth. Indeed it may even be the case that the vast majority of businesses have never moved from one phase to another and that the single most frequent response to the crises which are supposed to induce movement from one stage to another is the collapse of the business.

Despite their limitations the stage models nevertheless do serve to highlight the fact that the managerial role within a small firm varies widely. In a minority of firms the managerial role may be subject to considerable change over short periods of time, as the firm expands rapidly and does, perhaps, pass between stages. In other cases firms may experience the types of managerial turmoil which ultimately results in failure. Probably in most cases, however, there is no movement between stages, but equally no disastrous collapse.

CONCLUSIONS

This chapter has examined the creation, ownership, management and growth of the small firm within the context of the contemporary developments in institutional economics. The economics literature emphasizes the transactional difficulties associated with organizing economic activities between opportunistic agents in imperfect market environments, i.e. markets characterized by uncertainty, information asymmetries, investments in specific physical and human assets, etc. These market imperfections create an important market-making role for the entrepreneur and provide an explanation of economic change and innovation. They also suggest that certain business practices and organizational forms that are able to minimize these transaction and agency costs will tend to survive and prosper at the expense of others. We do not, however, believe that there are any grounds for supposing that this necessarily results in 'efficient' outcomes. In a fundamentally uncertain world populated by self-interested individuals with differing tastes and initial endowments, luck and power are also likely to be important determinants of outcomes. Nevertheless, the economics literature provides a number of interesting insights regarding the origin and growth of firms and the strategies adopted by entrepreneurs in organizing economic activities.

The issues of uncertainty and innovation have been taken as central to understanding the origin, management and evolution of small firms. Probably the key concept is that of uncertainty which largely conditions the financial, production, marketing and motivational options available to smaller businesses. The perceived risk of failure, and the implications for the entrepreneur and his/her dependents is an ever present factor influencing management decisions.

Innovation is the key factor that distinguishes the relatively few growing firms from the majority of small firms that have neither the resources nor desire to expand significantly. Even so, innovation in the context of the small firm, is not usually the grand concept of a totally new product as discussed by Schumpeter, but rather it more properly refers to the ability to offer a product or service which is perceived to be in some way distinguished from that supplied by rivals. The ability and willingness to innovate is only a necessary and not a sufficient condition for growth. Growth induces crises which impose pressure on existing management and create the need for additional managerial resources. Only if additional, suitably qualified and motivated managerial talent becomes available, either through internal and/or external sources, will these crises be satisfactorily negotiated and further growth facilitated.

These issues were discussed in the stage models of firm growth but these tend to suggest that most firms have gone through several stages of growth. This chapter has proposed an alternative view that relatively few small firms may actually make any form of significant transition and that those which achieve a significant size probably had management systems characteristic of 'later' stages even in their early days – the majority of small firms either remain small or fail.

NOTES

1 The term 'new' is used to distinguish recent institutional approaches to economics from the American institutionalist school of the 1930s associated with the writings of Veblen and Commons (see Putterman 1984).

2 Friedman (1953) argues that the use of descriptively false assumptions is justified when the objective is to predict aggregate market behaviour. Provided adequate predictions are possible from the model, the degree of 'realism' of its assumptions will be irrelevant. Hence, from this perspective, attempts to 'realistically' model the behaviour of individual agents and firms are (conveniently) often deemed to be of minor importance.

3 Other important exogenous variables, factors about which the model has nothing to say, include agents' initial endowments, firms' production functions, and the introduction of new economic developments (innovation).

4 Given additional assumptions regarding the full employment and allocation of all factor inputs to activities which provide a return equivalent to their contribution to production, where there is simultaneous equilibrium in all markets a unique equilibrium set of relative prices (and quantities) for all commodities will exist. In this situation, the economy is in general equilibrium and Pareto optimality obtains, in that no one could be made better off without making someone else worse off.

5 See Davies (1987) for a review of the work relating to vertical integration and Casson (1987) for an application to multinational enterprises.

6 The term innovation refers to all kinds of new developments in the economy, not just new methods of production and products (technical innovation) but also to the creation of new enterprises, markets and financial instruments.

7 Commons (1934) was the first to emphasize the importance of the transaction as the basic unit of analysis and Knight (1921) first suggested that firms were better able to handle uncertainty than individuals.

8 Williamson's 'efficiency' explanation of various organizational forms has been extensively criticized because it ignores the effect that differential market power has upon outcomes. He assumes, in Malcomson's (1984) phrase, 'that

efficiency always wins out in the end'. Thus, Williamson's work can quickly become an apology for existing organizational arrangements. These and other criticisms, which also apply to the agency theory explanations, are examined more fully in a later section.

9 In the agency theory literature ex ante and ex post opportunism are known respectively as 'adverse selection' and 'moral hazard'.

10 In making these statements we assume that growth is organic, rather than arising through the acquisition of, or merger with, other companies.

3 Non-economic explanations of firm structure, management and performance

INTRODUCTION

Chapter 2 reviewed a number of economic explanations of the relationships between the internal organization of firms, their market environments and their performance. These explanations emphasized the importance of various forms of 'cost minimizing' imperatives by self-interested agents in the context of either perfect or imperfect markets. Perfect markets are characterized by many buyers and sellers of a homogeneous product, none of whom by their own actions are able to influence price. Information is freely available in the market and there are no restrictions on entry or exit. Entry takes place in response to market opportunities, defined as a situation where price persistently exceeds long run average cost.

On the other hand, in imperfect markets there is uncertainty, barriers to entry, specific (quasi-rent receiving) asset investments and information asymmetries. Such market features create transactional difficulties for market participants. However, they are also the source of new profit opportunities, and of innovation and change in the economy as a whole.

Specific market environments are seen to determine the particular type(s) of internal organization that minimize the (costly) problems associated with the drawing-up of complete, state-contingent, contracts between opportunistic agents. Contemporary economic explanations suggest, therefore, that for any particular configuration of market imperfections, there will also be a cost-minimizing internal contracting and monitoring system. But, assuming incentive and monitoring problems can be overcome, successful firms will tend to adopt forms of ownership rights and internal organization that enhance the firm's value and its probability of survival.

From the above it is clear that even the new institutional economics literature infers that the characteristics of the market (structure) determine the ways in which the firms organize themselves (conduct), which in turn determines their success (performance). The structure–conduct–performance paradigm in which the individual firm passively accepts the dictates of the market remains at the heart of most economic approaches.

Temporary situations of market disequilibrium, as assumed in perfect markets, or long-term disequilibrium as occur in imperfect markets, create opportunities for profits and economic change. The primary role of the entrepreneur in economic theory is therefore to seek out, create and exploit for personal gain market imperfections (Baumol 1968). The key point is that the entrepreneur is still initially seen to be responding to a set of prices, rather than initiating a change. Within the economics framework, therefore, the success or performance of the firm can be seen as being dependent upon the choices made by the firm's strategic decision-makers (the entrepreneur) in response to markets. This involves choices over products, internal organization, financing and production decisions. Ultimately, what is important then, are the characteristics and skills of the firm's management, their ability to organize the firm's physical, financial and human resources efficiently in the pursuit of 'realistic' goals given the existing and potential market conditions.

The presumed ability of the firm to attract, train, retain and motivate suitable agents at all levels of the organization, to devise, implement or monitor the tasks required to attain economic objectives is, therefore, an important (but frequently unstated) assumption of most economic models. Other than the most general (and largely empirically empty) behavioural assumptions, such as the role of self-interests and attitudes to risk, economic models have little else to say regarding agents' behaviour.

Williamson's (1984) notion regarding the efficiency of 'relational teams', or 'clans' (see Ouchi 1980), seems to be a recognition that long-term employment relationships, particularly in respect of specialist managerial staff, need to be based upon something more than unmitigated self-interests. Even so, the development of the economics of the internal labour market, is squarely based on the assumption of self-interest on the part of both firm and employee.

The economics literature largely ignores the social and political processes within the firm whereby goals and decisions are determined, implemented and controlled. It also does not address questions over the attributes of the individuals concerned and the specific strategies adopted in different circumstances to manage conflicts of interest. In particular the view that the structure of industry is a dependent, rather than an independent variable, is heresy.

In this chapter we examine some of the evidence which is argued to provide support for such heretical views. Such perspectives are provided by those from the traditions of sociology and organizational behaviour. We also examine the theoretical and empirical contributions of those interested in business strategy. These explanations of organizations, their management and performance, provide a more detailed picture of the human aspects of economic activities.

One of the two main strands of the organizational behaviour literature emphasizes the importance of different organizational 'structures' upon performance. Here, the behavioural consequences of specific task attributes, management monitoring and control strategies and environmental uncertainties and/or complexities are the focus of attention.

Within the terms of the structure–conduct–performance paradigm, the emphasis is upon the relationship between conduct and performance, but without the economists' emphasis upon structure. The other main strand of the organizational behaviour literature is more 'process' orientated. It stresses the importance of group dynamics (politics) and organizational culture upon decision making and the management of conflicts, the personal motivations, backgrounds, characteristics, forms of interaction and leadership styles of managers and other employees in understanding what goes on in organizations.

The contribution of the business strategy literature is to challenge the view that the firm, ultimately, is responding to the pressures in the marketplace. At least in some respects, it is recognized that some firms are capable of shaping the marketplace. The strategy literature places much less emphasis upon price competition, and more upon other dimensions of competition such as quality, novelty, delivery, service, etc. The firm is assumed to be able to alter the product provided to satisfy client demand, thus moving away from the economists' homogeneous products sold at a single price, towards the view of numerous differentiated markets, in which the firms do indeed have some power.

In developing these views the chapter is organized as follows. We first examine various theories of organization. A brief review of the bureaucratic, scientific management, human relations and contingency theory schools of thought is the main focus of this section. The next section examines the nature and formation of organizational goals. This section emphasizes the essentially political and shifting nature of an organization's objectives. The fourth section looks at strategic management and leadership. The characteristics of leaders, what they do and how they manage to persuade others, both internal and external to the firm, to supply the required quantity and quality of capital and labour inputs are examined in this section. The following section examines where these issues have been addressed in the small-firm literature. The final section presents our concluding remarks.

THEORIES OF ORGANIZATIONS

Apart from the very smallest, most business enterprises currently operating are characterized by two important features. First, relatively few of the internal participants in business enterprises are either part owners of the firm or have any formal (legal) control over its strategic or day-to-day decision-making apparatus. Second, in the 'long-run', such privately owned firms are normally required to make a profit in order to continue in existence. These features of business organizations often result in a third characteristic, namely the existence of hierarchical authority (power) relations between members to ensure that members performance of assigned tasks is (in some sense) 'satisfactory'.

Hierarchical relationships are, of course, not peculiar to privately-owned enterprises. Many public organizations such as government departments, schools, and the armed forces also share this characteristic. However, for present purposes, we are primarily interested in the explanations put forward to account for the existence of different degrees of hierarchy within privately-owned business enterprises.

While the extent of hierarchy differs greatly between firms, the planning and assignment of tasks and control of member's task performance are almost always the function of a relatively small subset of the organization's members, the management, who may or may not also be major owners of the enterprise. The important features of an organization's internal management, its planning and control systems, how tasks are defined, assigned, organized and monitored, normally supply the important elements of the definition of the 'structure' of the organization. Organizational structure variables will usually include such dimensions as:

Specialization   (the extent to which the organization contains specific functions such as finance, production, personnel, etc.);

Standardization   (the extent of variation in and codification of specific tasks);

Formalization   (the extent to which rules, procedures, etc., are written down and adhered to);

Centralization   (the locus of decision-making powers).

There are, of course, wide differences between firms in terms of their internal organization and the question naturally arises as to whether any particular configuration of structural characteristics is 'better' than any other. There have been several attempts to answer this question over the years and the early explanations tended to stress the 'rationality' or 'efficiency' associated with a strict, formal hierarchical organization.

For instance, in the early part of this century Max Weber suggested that the growth of bureaucratic-type organizations formed part of the wider trend towards secular 'rationality' in modern industrial society (see Bendix 1966 for a review). He believed that bureaucratic organizations, based upon legal-rational authority and characterized by formal hierarchy, speciali-zation, the impersonal application of rules by paid officials appointed on the basis of seniority and achievement, were superior to, what he termed 'traditional', organizational forms based largely upon kinship, social status and convention.

Frederick Taylor, an American engineer also writing in the early part of this century, produced a remarkably similar set of ideas, but in relation to specific shopfloor tasks, which he called his 'scientific approach to manage-ment' (see Locke 1982 for a review). Taylor viewed workers as analogous to machines and his objective was to increase their 'efficiency' by introducing systems of hierarchical discipline, the standardization of job performance, the dividing-up of tasks and the specification of the 'one best (scientific) way of doing a task'. By tightly specifying tasks and introducing performance targets and piece-rate wages, he believed that workers would have no discretion regarding workplace practices and managers could be assured that their policies would be implemented in the most efficient manner. Subsequent developments in the classical bureaucratic and/or scientific management framework introduced such familiar management concepts as the optimal span-of-control, job descriptions and the separation of line and staff functions (see Kast and Rosenzweig 1985 for a review).

These ideas have been very influential in shaping many business organiz-ations and still appear to be the guiding lights of many managers. This school of thought puts managers firmly in charge and appears to offer a handy package of principles and checklists that can be applied in any and all organizations. However, even if a narrow, managerial perspective is taken, these 'universalistic' claims regarding 'the one best way' of organizing tasks have been found to be invalid. While there has been a widespread application of these principles among those undertaking 'routine' tasks, attempts to introduce bureaucratic and scientific management practices in some of the more creative types of organizations have been unsuccessful. Often, the introduction of such practices has resulted in lower rather than greater productivity and has in-creased costs, labour turnover and conflict. Examples include where tasks are either relatively unstructured and/or uncertain and where a large element of discretion regarding how the job is to be undertaken is required of the employee, i.e. because the employee possesses 'expert' skills/knowledge or because of the inability of supervisors to easily monitor subordinate's task performance.

A further problem associated with the implementation of classic bureaucratic and scientific management practices is that workers are not machines nor, in many contexts, can the tasks they undertake be seen as analogous to machine operations. Given that many of the tasks they have to undertake may have little intrinsic value to them and may also involve substantial effort, it is unrealistic to expect workers to perform, as programmed, like machines – even if constant, close supervision were possible, cost-effective or desirable. Moreover, many of the tasks which organization members are expected to undertake are not routine or performed under identical conditions on each occasion. Human judgement is required because, as any industrial dispute conducted by means of a 'work-to-rule' illustrates, tasks are often ambiguous, unstructured and incapable of being fully specified by any set of bureaucratic rules. Many work tasks require human initiative and motivation for their successful execution because of the impossibility of constructing a comprehensive bureaucratic set of enforceable rules to cope with every possible contingency. This emphasizes the point made in the previous chapter, namely that it is impossible to write and enforce any fully state-contingent contract in an uncertain world.

What should also be evident is that, by relying exclusively upon monetary incentives, scientific management practices neglect the subjective, personal and interpersonal aspects of work and performance, i.e. achievement, job satisfaction, social/work group recognition, etc. Considerations such as these, beginning with the work of Elton Mayo's famous 'Hawthorne Studies' in the 1930s, led to the development of the so-called 'human relations school'. The Human Relations school was also universalistic in that it assumed that the key to organizational design was a clear understanding of the capacities and abilities of individual workers (Argyris 1972). Managers could improve both productivity and morale if they treated subordinates as unique individuals with their own special needs and abilities. Since it was also usually assumed that workers shared the objectives of the organization, all that the organizational designer had to do was to remove any features of the organizational structure, termed 'obstructions' or 'frustrations', that prevented workers from giving their full commitment to the organization (see Luthans 1985 for a review).

This framework has led to many important insights into the subjective and social aspects of work and has obvious benefits in terms of more satisfied and more highly motivated workers. However, particularly in the context of privately-owned and controlled business enterprises, the key assumption that workers share the same goals as the organization, and will always seek to achieve them given the right conditions, is somewhat fanciful. The idea that there may be fundamental underlying conflicts of interests between different groups of employees and between employees and owners is not seriously considered. In consequence, the major policy recommendation, a universal design based upon the assumption that by attending to workers subjective needs optimal organizational performance would result, has also proved to be unrealistic. This is because it ignores the often divergent interests of organization members, the specifics of the tasks undertaken by different members and the prevailing environmental circumstances within which the organization operates.

In contrast, researchers working within the so-called 'contingency theory' framework suggest that the 'best' method of organizing work 'all depends' upon whether a particular structural configuration achieves:

> some acceptable degree of fit between the tasks, people and the environment. This fit will depend on (will be contingent upon) the prevailing circumstances.
>
> (Buchanan and Huczynski 1985, p. 356)

Hence, contingency theory suggests that there is no one best way of organizing. This contrasts strongly with the universalistic approaches characteristic of earlier theories of organization. As one writer has put it:

> Contingency theory refers to attempts to understand the multivariate relationships between components of organisations and to designing structures piece-by-piece, as best fits the components . . . each situation must be analysed separately . . . . Moreover, choosing a design for the whole is seen by contingency theorists to be restrictive: units of structure may be adopted from all along a design continuum, depending on the situation. Contingency implies that within the same organisation there may be units of bureaucracy, units operating in a matrix structure, and units which are divisionalised. Single design types, neatness, symmetry and permanence are not indicative of 'good' design. The only criteria for good design are task performance and individual/group satisfaction.
>
> (Hunt 1979, p. 189)

Thus, researchers within the contingency theory framework try to identify the important 'situational contingencies' and the particular organizational structure that provides the 'best fit' because this will make the organization 'effective'.

Much of the work within the contingency theory framework is highly deterministic in nature in the sense that it is assumed that one or more variables such as technology, environment or firm size are the direct cause of various aspects of organizational structures. The search for important contingent variables and their definition for empirical testing has been largely atheoretical. Since this work generally contents itself in uncovering low-level empirical associations, the results from different studies are often inconsistent and conflicting. Hence, over the years several contingent variables have been suggested as determining organizational structure.

Early work tended to concentrate upon the influence of the technologies used by the firm, the most important features being the degree of technical complexity (Woodward 1965), and technical predictability (Perrow 1967). The Woodward study asserted that 'there was a particular form of organisation most appropriate to each technical situation' (Woodward 1965, p. 72) and she found a positive statistical association between firms' performance (profits) and their organizational structures. In this sense Woodward's work is very similar to the structure–conduct–performance paradigm in economics since she views performance as being determined by a unidirectional causal flow from an exogenously-given technolgy, working through organizational structures to firm performance.

Environmental determinism has also been very influential within the contingency theory framework, e.g. Burns and Stalker (1961), Emery and Trist (1963), Lawrence and Lorsch (1967). The organization is seen as being in constant interaction with its environment, which would normally include such things as the general economic situation, market structures, the degree of competition in the product and labour markets, the degree of uncertainty and/or complexity, etc. Since the organization is seen as being dependent on its environment, its choices regarding organizational structures will, if it is to be 'effective', be constrained.

Contingency theory considerations have also informed many of the evolutionary stage models of firm growth and development that were also discussed in the previous chapter. All of these stage models assume that, as the firm grows, various crisis points are reached when the existing management structure, which may have been appropriate for the previous stage of development, is no longer able to cope adequately with the new tasks and environment facing the firm. Hence, if the firm is to survive a crisis and continue to grow, then a more appropriate management structure will have to be introduced which 'better fits' the new conditions.

While contingency theory has been very influential and has helped highlight the sort of external constraints on a manager's organizational choices, it has also been extensively criticized (see Ezzamel 1987a for a review). For example, complex dimensions, such as environment, organizational effectiveness and structure, have often been collapsed into a single, and possibly misleading, characteristic. The common tendency has been to dichotomize each of these multidimensional concepts: environments into complex/non-complex; structures into mechanistic/organic; and effectiveness into profitable/non-profitable. Moreover, the deterministic nature of much of this work effectively destroys any notion of strategic choice by management. The notion that the relationships between an organization's structure and its situational contingencies may be a function of managerial choices based upon their perception of the situation is totally absent.

However, dimensions such as technology, size, or environment do not determine organizational structures, independently of the aims and expectations of those who control the organization. As we shall argue later, the crucial factor with new firms is not technology, size, or environment, but rather the managerial choices regarding how technolgy is to be used, what size of firm to create/maintain and what environment to operate in. As Child (1972, p. 2) has noted, the design of organizational structures is essentially a

political process in which constraints and opportunities are functions of the power exercised by decision makers in the light of ideological values.

We now turn to a discussion of the nature of the political processes that lead to the formation and implementation of organizational goals.

The formation of organizational goals

Organizations exist because they are often the most efficient, or indeed the sole, means of bringing about some desired outcome that requires frequent co-operation and contact between several individuals, i.e. the production of particular kinds of goods and/or services. They are then social arrangements ostensibily set up to achieve some specific purpose. The constitution of a chess club, the charter of a university and the memorandum of association of a limited company all contain statements regarding the objectives and activities that the organization has been set up to attempt to achieve.

Nevertheless, it is important to recognize that the stated aims of an organization are really only the public expression of the agreed-upon aims of the individual members that were involved in creating the organization. It is possible that the actual goals pursued by these individuals may differ significantly from the formal stated aims of the organization. Organizations typically survive for many years; during this time they may experience significant growth and develop in unpredictable ways in response to environmental changes which create new threats and opportunities. Over this period new members may be admitted who possibly have different interests and goals from the original members. This, in turn, may profoundly influence the nature of the organization's operations and/or its goals.

These considerations highlight the central ambiguity regarding the nature of organizational goals. The whole notion is problematic since only human beings can really be said to have goals, objectives, purposes, etc. Clearly, even in the (extremely rare) limiting case where an organization contains only people that fully subscribe to the stated aims of the organization, the organization cannot itself be a thinking, goal-seeking being. To suggest otherwise would be to see it as a 'super individual entity having an existence and behaviour independent of the behaviour of its members' (Simon 1964).

In the far more usual case, particularly in regard to business enterprises, an organization will contain individuals with widely differing commitments to the stated aims of the organization and the interests of individual members may conflict. To talk in terms of abstract organizational goals in this context is to obfuscate the important issues relating to whose goals (if any) are actually being pursued and whose interests the organization is actually furthering.

Examined in this light, the notion of organizational goals, and hence the criteria by which performance ought to be judged, raises a number of important questions. For instance, 'How are organizational goals formed?' 'Do goals really precede and inform actions?' 'What determines the subset of organizational members that participate in goal formation?' 'Is it possible to overcome conflicts of interests between organizational members?' 'If so, how are such conflicts resolved?'

Within economics, the traditional model of the entrepreneurial firm, i.e. where ownership and control reside in the same individual, views goals as being jointly determined by the entrepreneur and the prevailing, exogenously given, market conditions. In a perfectly competitive market the entrepreneur will not have any discretion regarding goals: he/she will be forced to pursue profit maximization if the business is to survive. However, as noted in Chapter 2, in more realistic market settings the entrepreneur will not normally be so constrained and he/she may be able to pursue other valued objectives such as maximum sales growth, social prestige or a 'satisfactory' balance between profits and leisure time.

Whatever the entrepreneur's personal goals, the model assumes that these are the goals of the organization because the agreement of other agents within the firm can always be secured at a price via contracting and incentive schemes. Hence, within this model, though dependence upon some other members may constrain his/her choices, there are no goal conflicts because the entrepreneur is the major strategic policy-maker within the firm.

Once, we move beyond a firm owned and controlled by a single individual the possibility of goal conflicts and political bargaining processes to resolve them become important. Cyert and March (1963) produced one such bargaining model whereby the firm was viewed as a coalition of internal and external participants and the bargaining processes between the various sub-coalitions influence both the actual and stated goals of the organization. Within this framework, the organization operates with many unresolved conflicts which are kept in check by the use of 'side payments' (bribes) to various individuals and groups to ensure their participation and co-operation. The use of side payments to contain conflict, of course, assumes that a certain amount of organizational 'slack' exists, i.e. the existence of resources in excess of the amounts strictly necessary for the achievement of existing output levels. Organizational slack, which for the economist is indicative of market imperfections, is therefore important within this political bargaining process since it helps to achieve a degree of stability regarding both organizational goals and agent's continued co-operation.

In principle, depending upon how the balance of power between members is conceived, the model can be applied to any organizational form. For instance, not all members of the organization are necessarily assumed to be equally active or influential in these multilateral negotiations over organizational goals and policies. Participation in goal formation at any particular time or context will be largely determined by a group's degree of cohesion, its assessment of its sources of internal and external power and its willingness to exploit opportunities.

The coalition is not therefore conceived of as a static, unchanging entity. As the organization grows and important environmental features alter, existing, or totally new, groups may become more influential in decision making. Indeed, in a highly fluid, changing situation, where an organization has to continually attend to the interests of several powerful groups simultaneously, the whole notion that goals necessarily precede actions may be problematic. In this context, goals will be ambiguous, and organizational decision making may be more adequately described in terms of a collection of largely random choices. The 'garbage can' model of Cohen *et al.* (1972) is one such model that decouples goals and actions. Here, choices are not viewed as being driven by goals since choices are only possible when problems, solutions and participants combine to produce a feasible coalition capable of any sort of successful action.

While the Cyert and March and Cohen *et al.* models highlight the essentially political and shifting nature of organizational goals and decision-making processes, they tend to underrate the possibility that power may semi-permanently reside in the hands of a subgroup of organizational participants, i.e. the owners or some subset of professional, high ranking, managers. The possibility of an elite determining organizational goals forms the major contribution of the so-called dominant coalition model associated with the work of Perrow (1961), Thompson (1967) and Pennings and Goodman (1977). For instance, Perrow (1961) suggested that the nature of the dominant coalition within an organization will follow a more or less typical sequence.

In a young and/or small organization the model is essentially a variant of the entrepreneurial model since the business is dominated by the owner. As growth occurs during the product development phases, the dominant group will consist of various skill groups (i.e. engineers, research and development staff, etc.). This will normally be followed by management domination when the firm matures. Here the emphasis will shift to improvements in market domination, reducing risks, increased product and financial diversification. Hence, negotiation is less continuous or all-embracing than in the Cyert and March model and any apparent consensus regarding the priorities of different sectional interests is viewed as a function of the asymmetric power of the dominant coalition *vis-à-vis* other sub-coalitions. Obviously, the very existence and membership of the dominant coalition and its ability to dominate the organization will be more or less well defined as the organization develops and responds to internal pressures and external environmental forces.

As Ezzamel (1987b) has noted, these three models of goal formation are not necessarily mutually exclusive. Indeed, all three models are probably required in order to form a comprehensive framework for the study of goal formation in dynamic and growing business organizations:

> in many small, as well as some large, stable organisations the goal-formation process is akin to that described by the entrepreneurial model. Also, in organisations with significant dispersion of power, goals may be formed collectively by the active coalition in a manner similar to that described by Cyert and March. As the organisation moves from one stage of transition to another, power over the determination of goals may change hands from one dominant coalition to another. During the period while power is changing hands organisation goals may be blurred, ambiguous and even confused . . . . Indeed, this is likely to be the case whenever there is no clear set of criteria for ordering goals.
>
> (Ezzamel 1987b, p. 53)

STRATEGIC LEADERSHIP

The previous two sections have indicated that an organization's choice of goals, markets, managerial structure and hence the most appropriate measure of its performance will be greatly influenced by its strategic decision makers. However, much of the work on business strategy, in both the economics and organizational theory literatures, has had little to say regarding the specifically 'human' dimensions of strategic decision making, i.e. the socio-economic, financial, occupational, attitudinal and other personal characteristics of strategic leaders, what they do and how they do it.

The academic literatures have, as indicated in both Chapter 2 and in previous sections of this chapter, tended to concentrate upon the techno-economic factors such as product life cycles, industry analyses, portfolio matrices, financial risk management and market share. Nevertheless, the relatively recent public policy concerns in many countries regarding the regeneration and revitalization of their economies has stimulated academic interest and the study of human resource management within organizations. Moreover, the main focus of this recent work has been on the study of strategic decision makers, within both small firms (entrepreneurship) and large organizations (the manager of managers), rather than on middle or first line managers and workers. One writer has suggested that this focus on top managers is 'inevitable' because ultimately,

> they account for what happens to the organisation. In the face of the complex, multitudinous, and ambiguous information that typifies the top management task, no two strategists will identify the same array of options for the firm; they will rarely prefer the same options; if, by some remote chance, they were to pick the same options, they almost certainly would not implement them identically. Biases, blunders, egos, aptitudes, experiences, fatigue, and other human factors in the executive ranks greatly affect what happens to companies . . . if we want to explain why organisations do the things they do, or, in turn, why they perform the way they do, we must examine the people at the top.
>
> (Hambrick 1989, p. 5)

Clearly, from this perspective, an organization's strategic decision makers are viewed as distinct from the outcomes they produce. The personal characteristics, beliefs and actions of strategic decision makers are not wholly determined by the organization's goals, its performance, structures and/or environments, they have an independent influence upon the shape and direction of all these outcomes. Hence, strategic leadership is viewed as an important 'missing factor' in conventional accounts of organizational performance and evolution.

Whether it is possible to attribute an important independent influence to strategic decision makers upon outcomes (and if so, in what circumstances), will depend upon the answers to three questions. First, 'what are the essential features of the strategic decision making role within organizations?' Second, 'what constraints and other situational contingencies exist to inhibit (or enhance) their ability to achieve the desired outcomes?' Finally, 'are strategic leaders "special people", with rare skills and abilities not present in the majority of the population?'.

Within the labour market economics framework there appears to be a recognition, in principle, that strategic leaders are somehow 'special' and can influence corporate events. First assume that a worker is not paid in excess of his or her marginal product; then if salaries are broadly related to position in the hierarchy, which in turn is related to ability to influence corporate events, then the strategic decision makers must be the most valuable to the organization. The extent to which corporate performance is related to the salaries paid to chief executives however remains unclear (Yarrow 1972, Cosh 1975, Jensen and Murphy 1990).

Within the strategy framework, Hambrick lists four features of the strategic decision making role within firms that distinguishes the roles played by strategic managers from lower level, operational, managers. First, the strategic decision maker has to be concerned with both external and internal spheres. As we have seen, a major conclusion from both the economics and organizational theory frameworks is that if a firm is to have any realistic chance of achieving an objective then its physical and human asset base, external environment and internal organization must be con-figured in such a way to make this feasible. Moreover, given a high degree of uncertainty regarding future outcomes, the firm must also be capable of adapting to any unexpected changes in its specific product, labour and competitor markets and to any wider social and regulatory changes which may have consequences for its long-term viability.

Second, it should be obvious that the tasks of the strategic decision maker are far from routine. Strategy formation, given its innovatory nature, its openess to many competing internal and external influences and their complex interconnections and the often vague and competing performance criteria, seems to be a task beset with uncertainty, ambiguity, complexity and information overload. Third, since a major aspect of any successful strategy is the ability to integrate the various parts of the organization to carry it to fruition, then it should be equally obvious that the task is multifunctional in nature. Strategy formation thus cuts across the usual functional activities since it involves aspects of operations, finance, marketing and personnel. A corollary of this is that it is likely that in a firm of any great size, the strategic decision maker will possess relatively less expertise in these specialist areas than his/her subordinate functional man-agers. This information asymmetry will, in turn, have important implica-tions regarding the exchange of information, the incentive, reward, control and (possibly) ownership systems within the firm and the composition of the strategic decision-making team.

Finally, Hambrick suggests that the ability to 'manage through managers' is an inevitable characteristic of the strategic decision maker. Indeed, for anything other than a very small and uncomplex firm, the ability to delegate to other managers the responsibility for managing the daily affairs of the component parts of the business seems to be a corollary of the first three features of strategic decision makers.

Both the economics and organizational theory literatures have indicated that there are many constraints on the choices available for strategic decision making. The neoclassical economics perfect competition model assumes that the market environment leaves no room for any choice other than profit maximization if the firm is to survive. Only the existence of various market imperfections allow for strategic choices, though the ability of firms to engage in non-profit maximizing behaviour is still seen to be highly constrained by economic imperatives such as the need to respond to product, labour and capital market pressures for survival. This has led to explanations that emphasize the necessarily 'rational' economic basis of organizational choice, generally, the minimization of production, trans-actions or agency costs. The theory of the entrepreneur as the primary creator of change and the exploiter of uncertainty comes closest to con-ceding an important independent role to internal decision making, though it is not well integrated with other economic or non-economic theories of organizational choice and performance.

The organizational theory literature emphasizes the necessity for the organizational structure to 'fit appropriately' with its environment, its technology, its size, its human resources, etc. In this work, strategic leadership, if it is discussed at all, is seen as a dependent variable. Hence, questions such as 'why do certain people get to the top of organizations?', or 'why do leaders do the things they do?', are answered in terms of Darwinian or political processes. Generally, the strategic decision maker is viewed as being jointly moulded by previous sociological influences, such as up-bringing (Collins and Moore 1970, Kotter 1982), education, occupation (Walsh 1988), etc. and the organization of which he/she is currently a part.

For instance, Song (1982) explained the mix of functional areas rep-resented in the top management team in terms of the firm's diversification posture. Similarly, the characteristics of senior managers, such as age (Pfeffer 1983) or their role behaviours (Mintzberg 1973), are viewed as being determined by the age of the industry and the firm's size respectively. Moreover, the political bargaining models regarding organizational goal formation emphasize that the power to initiate, implement and control an organization's direction will, from the viewpoint of an individual, be con-strained by the need to form viable dominant coalitions of interested parties. Generally, the relative ability of different organizations to foster the formation of dominant coalitions will itself be contingent upon a number of internal (ownership structure, product life cycle stage, size, existing management structure and backgrounds, etc.) and external (political attitudes, product, labour and capital market conditions, etc.) factors.

If the unit of analysis is the top management team, that is the dominant coalition itself, then the level of cohesion, commonality of interests and the balance of complementary skills between members become crucial variables which may enhance rather than constrain the influence of strategic decision makers. Indeed, the influence of the top management team's collective characteristics upon organizational outcomes can often outweigh that of the founder or chief executive officer (see Hambrick and Mason 1984, Hambrick 1987, Hambrick and Finkelstein 1987, Bantel and Jackson 1989). For instance, research which has examined the 'strategy–manager fit' dimension (Miles and Snow, 1978, Gupta and Govindarajan 1984, Hurst *et al.* 1989) suggests that the mix of cognitive styles on a top management team will influence both the choice of strategy and the ability to implement it. Other work, which focused on the relationship between innovation and the characteristics of the management team (Hage and Dewar 1973, Kimberly and Evanisko 1981, Bantel and Jackson 1989), suggests that the general level of education and the diversity of functional backgrounds are positively related to the degree of innovative behaviour of the firm.

The level of social and professional heterogeneity within the team has also been shown to influence performance. Murray (1989), using a contingency framework, found that homogeneity improved performance in stable competitive environments but that in turbulent environments heterogeneity produced superior outcomes. These findings suggest that the team rather than the individual founder or CEO should be the unit of analysis.

What the foregoing discussion has illustrated is that, while there are often a formidable array of constraints upon strategic decision makers' freedom of action, none of this implies that they are a passive instrument of external environmental forces and the organization structure of which they are a part. The degree to which they are able to exert some independent influence upon the direction and form of the organizations they lead will, of course, vary with the circumstances. For instance, one could reasonably surmise that the influence of strategic leaders will be most evident where there is a high degree of uncertainty, such as in the case of newly created firms, small firms, firms in crisis or in transitional phases, rapidly growing firms or firms under close ownership and control. Moreover, even in more stable conditions, the ability to decisively influence the course of events may still be possible because of the exceptional characteristics and leadership skills of the firm's top management team.

Much has been said already concerning the necessity for strategic decision makers to possess considerable leadership skills. Basically, leadership is a social process whereby an individual is able to influence the behaviour of others without using overt force or coercion. Hence, successful leaders must possess some form of social, economic, skill or knowledge-based power over their followers. The early theories on leadership tended to view leaders as special people with special characteristics (traits). This work was, therefore, primarily concerned with the search for universal traits possessed by leaders.

Prior to the 1950s, the academic literature on leadership traits concentrated upon various physical, psychological and personal characteristics of successful leaders. Perhaps the only consistent finding from these many studies has been that successful leaders tend to be slightly more intelligent on average than their typical follower (see Luthans 1985 for a review).

In more recent years, the trait approach to leadership has tended to emphasize the various job-related skills required of a leader. For instance, Yuki (1981) identified such skills as creativity, organization, persuasiveness, diplomacy and tactfulness, knowledge of the task and the ability to speak well. Recalling that leadership involves a reciprocal social relationship between the leader and his/her followers, several researchers have examined the impact that subordinates' behaviour has upon the leader. Generally, the style and success of leaders in business organizations has been found to be as heavily influenced by the behaviours and abilities of subordinates as by any inherent personal traits of the leader him/herself (see Greene 1975).

More recent studies have adopted a contingency approach to leadership, stemming from Fielder's (1967) 'least preferred co-worker' framework whereby a leader's effectiveness was related to three empirically derived dimensions: the leader–member relationship, the degree of task structure and the leader's (formal) position power. Other models of leadership have explicitly linked effectiveness with the motivation of subordinates, as in the path–goal and expectancy models first developed by House (1971).

All these frameworks, however, tend to be deterministic and unidirectional. Consequently, the empirical results of these studies have often been in conflict. Hence, the dynamic and multidirectional interactions between the leader's characteristics and all the many other situational contingencies discussed in previous sections tend to be ignored. At this stage of research, perhaps the best one can say regarding leadership is that the ability of any particular individual to become a dominant part of a successful ruling coalition within an organization will depend upon the appropriateness of the fit between the source(s) of his/her social power (ownership, expert knowledge, referent power, etc.) and the other situational contingencies.

One further aspect of leadership concerns the key role of management in developing and sustaining, via example and exhortation, an organizational culture that reduces opportunistic behaviour. In the economics literature, unless monitoring, incentive and sanctioning mechanisms are developed, unconstrained self-seeking is assumed to be the norm. Typically, however, organizational participants do not usually engage in self-seeking behaviour at every opportunity. Their behaviour may also be based upon notions of right and wrong, ethical rules, religious or moral precepts. Indeed, in circumstances where monitoring is prohibitively costly, economic transactions would tend to break down if agents really did engage in unconstrained opportunism. Ethical considerations are often of far more importance than economic interests even when the possibility of being caught out is small or non-existent. As Noreen (1988) has noted

> certain kinds of ethical (ie, self-constrained) behaviour lubricate social and economic systems. If parties to a transaction believe that the other parties to the transaction are honest and act in good faith, the transaction may be possible where it would not have been possible and deadweight losses can be avoided. The crux of the problem is that, by definition, the probability of being caught in an unethical act is small. Thus, sanctions cannot be generally effective in inducing ethical behaviour.

The sociological literature shows that group norms are powerful motivating devices, particularly when the individual seeks group approval and values his/her membership of the work group. Indeed, Bolnick (1975) cites evidence from the experimental literature which demonstrates that group norms and ethical codes are often more powerful motivating devices than economic incentives and that leaders are highly influential in setting these norms.

This work is, therefore, consistent with the literature cited earlier concerning the composition and cohesion of the management team (or, in Ouchi's terms 'clans') and the importance of leaders. If the management team is seen to be trustworthy and their actions and values are consistent and seem to be worthy of emulation, then their scope for successfully implementing new strategies will be greatly enhanced.

The unifying theme of what we have referred to in this section as strategic leadership is that, from an economist's perspective, the discussion takes place in a context which is insulated from the product marketplace in which the firm operates. In terms of the structure–conduct–performance paradigm the emphasis is only upon the conduct–performance component. To view the discussion in these terms, however, fails to do justice to the strategy literature for two important reasons.

The first is that, within the strategy literature, the key decision variables facing the decision maker are much more wide ranging than in the economics literature. In the latter case product price is presumed to be the key variable. In a perfect market the firm is unable, by its own actions, to influence that price. In imperfect markets the firm may be able to influence price, either through actual or threatened output changes or through entry restrictions. In both cases, however, price is the key variable, and it is from product price that managerial decisions stem on investment, research, organization, etc.

The strategy literature, on the other hand, emphasizes that a firm has a much wider range of choice than is implied in the economic model. The first choice is the extent to which it wishes to compete with other firms on the basis of price. Instead the firm may choose to compete on the basis of quality, delivery, design, novelty, innovativeness, etc. If it chooses to compete on one or other of these grounds there may come a point at which the firm is either occupying a 'niche' position, or offering a different product from its competitors. From an economist's perspective these could be measured by the extent to which the cross-price elasticity of demand for the products differed from zero. According to McNamee (1988) this illustrates that the key strategic decision is 'which industry are you in, and how are you proposing to compete in that industry?' Once that decision is made then there follows the more familiar internal organizational decisions to which we have referred above.

The second key difference between the economists and the strategist view of the firm is that the former takes the market environment – structure – as determining how firms behave. It should be obvious from the above that this is directly opposed to the strategist view, where the decisions of the firm determine and define the market. Indeed the strategist will not view it as an SCP relationship, but as a conduct–performance–structure relationship. Here the structure of the industry is seen as the outcome of the strategic decisions made by firms within (and possibly without) the industry.

Despite the fundamental differences in approach between what we have somewhat crudely characterized as the economic and non-economic explanations of firm performance, there have been remarkably few examples of empirical testing of the relative power of these views. Perhaps the nearest to such a test was conducted by Hansen and Wernerfelt (1989) who, for sixty large US companies, attempted to explain performance in terms of profitability, by relating it to a set of 'economic' and a set of 'organizational' variables. The economic variables related to indices of market share, industry profitability, firm size, etc. The organizational variables follow the types outlined earlier – those relating to goal achievement or scientific management, and those relating to the ability of the organization to persuade the employee that it is genuinely concerned with his or her welfare. The study concluded, firstly, that the organizational variables explained a higher proportion of the variance than did the economic variables. Secondly, it showed that the economic explanations are statistically independent of the organizational explanations so when both are incorporated together the explanation of corporate performance is much more powerful than either an economic or an organizational approach.

Though the Hansen and Wernerfelt study utilizes a relatively unsophisticated analytical framework, we feel that this indicates that the performance of firms is likely to be best explained by a combination of the economic and organizational approaches.

SMALL-FIRM RESEARCH

Previous sections of this chapter have reviewed the theory and evidence relating to the organization and management of firms from the perspectives offered by a number of non-economic frameworks. The bulk of both the theory and its empirical testing is derived from observations of large firms, but many of the issues are highly relevant, albeit in a different form, to the management of small and medium-sized firms.

This section reviews some of the relevant strategic and organizational literature which relates directly to the performance of smaller firms. In undertaking this review we continue to remain keenly aware of Penrose's (1959) dictum that a small firm is not a scaled-down version of a large firm, and that the strategic and organizational issues facing the small young firm are fundamentally different from those facing the larger firm.

These differences are reflected partly in the topics covered and the emphasis given in the review. It focuses upon two main issues: first, the personal and socio-economic characteristics of the founders of small firms and their motivations for starting the business; second, and most important, their styles of management, forms of internal organization and relationships with their employees.

The small-firm founder

In her review of corporate strategy and the small firm, Birley (1982) asserts, as we do, that there are major differences between small and large firms, one of which is in terms of goals. She says, echoing the findings of the Bolton Committee (Bolton 1971), that:

> ownership and management of the smaller firm are usually held by the same person or persons, and so the objectives of the firm and the owner become one and the same.

Clearly the statement is true, by definition, for the self-employed worker. It may also be generally true for firms which have less than ten workers, but once beyond that scale there will normally be employees within the firm whose task is to manage the work of others but who are not owners of the business. At that point, which can even occur in the very smallest of firms, ownership and some aspects of management do in fact begin to diverge.

Small-firm researchers, however, appear to have broadly accepted the Birley/Bolton statement. Research on managers within smaller firms and their relationship to firm performance has focused almost without exception upon the founder/owner or group of owners. In the UK the salaried, but non-owning manager in the small firm has, with a few modest exceptions, not been examined.

Strategic, behavioural and organizational literature on the smaller firm, where it is in any way related to firm performance, examines only the owner or owners. Lafuente and Salas (1989) describe a familiar form with their typology set out below:

| experience, origin, personal characteristics of entrepreneurs | $\longrightarrow$ | behaviour of firms (strategy) | $\longrightarrow$ | public and private performance of firms |

In their categorization of entrepreneurs Lafuente and Salas suggest there are three, not necessarily independent, dimensions. The first are personal back- ground characteristics of the individual such as gender, education, age, parental occupation, etc. The second is work experience in terms of whether they worked in a large or small firm, the industry in which they worked and whether or not they had managerial experience. A third dimension is a set of behavioural and motivational characteristics such as their attitudes to risk, whether or not they were unemployed, etc. From these characteristics, a number of typologies of entrepreneurs have been formulated and related to both the probability of an individual becoming an entrepreneur and to their 'success' once in business. There are a number of reviews of this literature such as Storey (1982), Bragard *et al.* (1985), Chell (1985) and Lafuente and Salas (1989).

These studies reach broadly similar conclusions, namely that there are differences in the performance of small firms which are related to the characteristics of the owner. For example several studies show the education level of the founder to be positively correlated with firm performance, except perhaps among those with the highest academic qualifications (Bragard *et al.* 1985). It also appears to be the case that managerial experience, employment within the same industry, and observation of market opportunities are also positively related to 'success' (Monck *et al.* 1988).

Small-firm managers, business strategy, internal organization and firm performance

It is not our purpose here to provide a comprehensive review of work on the role of small-firm founders and firm performance. Instead our interest is to shift the debate away from literature cited above in which the founder(s) or owner(s) *per se* are viewed as the sole managerial resource, and towards the question of how that/those individual(s) manage the process of growth through the employment of non-owner managers. We now examine the strategy and organizational literature on smaller firms where it relates to firm performance, to determine the extent to which the issue is addressed.

Again there are relatively few instances in which these issues are directly addressed. Small-firm strategy is examined by Feeser and Willard (1990) who conclude from their study of high technology firms that the most basic strategic question of 'what market(s) should we enter with what product(s)?' has to be answered correctly to ensure success. As they put it 'the experimental "cut and try, learn as you go" approach does not pay off in the early years'.

Covin and Slevin (1989) argue that organizational structure and strategic posture need to be very different for small firms to operate successfully in hostile, compared with benign environments (markets). In many senses their findings reflect the SCP paradigm favoured by economists since it suggests that in hostile, highly competitive markets, organizational flexibility, with a willingness to undertake risky projects and exercise market leadership, are of clear importance. In a more benign environment, the successful smaller firm places an emphasis upon formality and rules within the organization. In its strategic behaviour in the marketplace the successful firm in the benign environment is more likely to follow than to lead the introduction of new products, preferring to make modest alterations to existing lines.

Even these studies, while they have examined strategy and organization in small fast growing firms, did not address the issue of implementing these strategic decisions, and the impact which this could have on performance. A key element in the implementation of decisions is to be able to assemble managerial expertise for this purpose. In most cases this will consist of a team of non-owning managers. It appears that these issues seem more likely to be addressed by researchers undertaking case study type work, rather than by those using a more aggregate approach.

The study by Grieve Smith and Fleck (1987), using a case study approach to examine business strategies in small high-technology firms in Cambridge, UK, illustrate the point well. Referring to one company they say:

A major factor in Domino's success seems to have been that the founder was conscious from the start of the need to bring in people with business or manufacturing experience to complement the technical expertise on which the company was based.

They continue:

Of concern to many companies was the establishing and keeping of an experienced management team. Many of the newer companies such as I.Q. Bio, Domino and Eicon had recognised a need to complement their founders technical skills and to appoint experienced Managing Directors and management Specialists from large companies. *This awareness, coupled with the willingness of professional managers to join a small company, may be one of the crucial conditions for long term success.*

(our emphasis)

Grieve Smith and Fleck then go on to point out that the small firm can have difficulty recruiting such managerial skills, since it cannot offer as high salaries and cannot provide such a clear career path as the manager could expect in a large company. Their Cambridge cases highlight several important issues which will also be addressed in the empirical sections in this book. For example they refer to the founder at Domino as being conscious, *at the start*, of the need to bring in external managers. They also refer to the need to appoint these individuals *from large companies*, presumably on the grounds that the intention is to grow the company from small to large. Finally, they also refer to the need to bring in managers with different skills to those already in the firm 'to complement the expertise on which the company was based'. This suggests that the founder of the firm has some concept of a balanced managerial team.

Like Grieve Smith and Fleck, we also believe that these are issues central to the success of smaller firms, and we propose to examine them in the empirical sections of this volume.

There are, however, many forms of small firm (young/old, high-tech/low-tech, independent/large firm subsidiary, etc.), each operating in a wide variety of economic environments. There are also many different ways of organizing the operations of any particular small firm and an even wider variety of small firm owners and managers with widely varying motivations and expectations. It would therefore be extremely unwise to generalize on the basis of findings for small high-technology firms alone.

Our previous work (Storey *et al.* 1987) showed that relatively few small firms seek growth. It therefore seems likely that the specialist management or professional employees which small firms recruit will differ from those employed in large companies. In the UK there have been very few studies concerned exclusively with the recruitment, retention or management of these professional employees in the small-firm sector.

A study by Deeks (1972) of managers in the furniture industry found that small-firm managers were likely to be younger than those in larger firms. It also found they were more likely to have moved companies than large-firm managers. Deeks found that almost one-third of non-shareholding managers had worked for more than six companies during their career, compared with studies of larger firms where less than 7 per cent of managers had worked for six firms or more. Thirdly, Deeks found that there were major differences in the levels of educational attainment between large- and small-firm managers. Less than 1 per cent of managers in the (small-firm) furniture industry were graduates, whereas other broadly comparable studies of managers in large firms showed that between 19 per cent and 43 per cent of managers had degrees.

The much more recent findings of Nicholson and West (1988, p. 61) are also supportive of some significant differences between managers in small and large firms. They find:

> Managers in small organisations have made the greatest number of employer changes and upward status moves . . . this finding is easily explained. The larger the organisation the greater the opportunities for internal movement, therefore people in small organisations are more likely to come to their present position from outside.

Nicholson and West (1988, p. 64) also find that:

> twice as many managers moved to smaller sized organisations as moved to larger sized organisations, before finding established career positions in smaller organisations where their talents can find more expressive scope.

There are, however, some doubts about the extent to which the Nicholson and West data on managers in smaller firms refer to owners, and the extent to which they refer to individuals who are managers, but without an ownership stake in the firm. The authors specifically include self-employed small-business owners in their sampling frame, although we have argued that their work histories and backgrounds are likely to differ somewhat from the small-firm manager.

Two other studies (Stanworth and Curran 1973 and Watkins 1983) have examined the attitudes of owners of small businesses to managerial and professional employees. The main findings were that owners were often reluctant to delegate responsibilities to newcomers either because they wished to retain control or because they were fearful that these professional employees would start up in business in competition with them if they were allowed to develop their skills. Also, attempts by newcomers to reorganize work practices frequently led to friction with their employers, who often saw this as a clear criticism of their management skills. Cultural differences between owners and professionals also had the potential to create frictions and endanger growth because:

> functional experts are often cosmopolitans, whose commitment to their professional skills may override their commitment to any particular firm. In the extreme case, their current employer is regarded merely as a stepping stone in their career, to be rejected when further possibilities for career advancement occur elsewhere. Unless the owner-manager can master this new situation by delegating authority to specialists (thus relinquishing an element of personal independence), integrating his longer-standing managers with his new specialists, and coping with the occasional loss of specialists, a quest for growth may be transformed into a battle for survival.
>
> (Stanworth and Curran 1989, p. 166)

CONCLUSIONS

This chapter has reviewed a number of non-economic theories of organizational structures, strategic management, goal formation and management leadership styles. The small-firm research into these topics has also been reviewed.

From Chapter 2, it will be recalled that the economic literature assumes that agents' interests are necessarily incongruent and that, in the absence of explicit monitoring, incentive and sanctioning mechanisms, they will engage in self-seeking, opportunistic behaviour. Organizational outcomes, the performance of the firm, are seen as being the result of the interaction of market forces with the internal organization of economic transactions.

In contrast, the literature reviewed in this chapter has indicated that organizational participants are often motivated by non-economic factors such as loyalty, social and ethical mores and cultural affinities which constrain self-seeking. Thus, though market and other environmental constraints and the possibility of opportunism by individuals may inhibit manager's sphere of freedom, they do not determine outcomes in a mechanistic fashion. The scope for strategic decisions can often be wide, particularly where the management team is able to agree on common objectives and the means of achieving them. Management style, objectives, perceptions and leadership qualities and characteristics may, in many (imperfect market) circumstances, be just as important in determining outcomes as economic factors. However, it should be obvious that both economic and non-economic factors need to be taken into account if we are to understand the dynamics of growth, firm performance and management.

The small-firm literature has tended to concentrate upon the 'typical', low-growth enterprise which makes up the majority of small enterprises. The autocratic management style, limited objectives, lack of resources and suspicion of 'specialist' professional management personnel means that very few of these firms ever need to develop a management team. However, for those few firms which set out to achieve high growth, the recruitment, retention and development of a management structure is essential. Without an adequate solution to the problems this engenders, the firm will either stay small or fail completely. The following chapter will present a number of hypotheses based upon the material presented in Chapters 2 and 3.

4 Small-firm performance and managerial labour markets
A framework for empirical analysis

INTRODUCTION

The previous two chapters of this text have reviewed the theoretical and empirical literatures concerned with the possible relationships between the creation, internal organization and ownership of the firm and its environment, strategic choices and performance. Special emphasis has been given to the distinctive features of, and the empirical findings relating to, the small-firm sector. The purpose of these reviews has been to provide a framework within which to examine the managerial characteristics most closely associated with successful fast-growth smaller enterprises. As we have seen, any attempt to isolate and measure the impact upon firm performance of the management team's inputs is beset by considerable conceptual and empirical problems. Not surprisingly, none of the theoretical frameworks examined provides a comprehensive account of the factors, relationships and processes associated with the successful creation and management of high-growth smaller firms. Although there are a number of common themes running through the various theoretical models, there seems to be little agreement regarding the relative importance or directional influence of different factors.

The discussion has indicated the gap between theoretical concepts and relationships on the one hand and the formulation of empirically testable hypotheses on the other. Theories, by their very nature, are abstractions, and, the more general the theory, the more abstract are the concepts employed and the greater are the difficulties encountered in empirically operationalizing them. Theories, in order to be comprehensible, necessarily focus upon a relatively few key concepts. Human action, however, takes place within a complex, ever changing, and uncertain environment in which other players' behaviour will be influenced by a variety of inadequately understood economic, cultural and personal factors. In this context, notions of causation and relationships between supposedly dependent and independent variables may be inappropriate. For these reasons, empirical scrutiny of these issues is fraught with immense difficulties and it is not, therefore, surprising that there has often been little agreement concerning not only the interpretation of empirical findings, but also their relevance and/or validity.

This chapter provides a discussion of the framework which will be adopted for the empirical analysis of the small-firm managerial labour market. The material reviewed in earlier chapters acts as a basis for framing empirical propositions. Although there are many important dimensions to consider, we have chosen to focus upon three:

1 the labour market(s) for small-firm managers;
2 owner motivations and attributes;
3 organizational structure and management.

Each area will be discussed in a separate section of this chapter, as well as being the subject of an empirical chapter later in the text (Chapters 6 to 8). First, however, we provide a discussion of the framework within which these issues are empirically examined.

A FRAMEWORK FOR EMPIRICAL ANALYSIS

Economic models emphasize the self-interested motivations underlying economic behaviour and the scope for opportunistic actions afforded by various forms of market imperfections. The central aspects of the trans-actions costs and agency theory models are the contracting problems associated with bounded rationality, various sources of uncertainty, the asymmetric distribution of information, the frequency of transactions and investments in highly specific physical and human assets. These models also attempt to identify the most 'efficient' organizational design, man-agerial incentives and monitoring systems for any given configuration of market conditions. Thus, even though it is recognized that markets are generally highly imperfect, such models suggest that competitive pressures drive the more successful firms in an economy to adopt these efficient strategies. Hence, economic models assume that 'optimal' or 'efficient' outcomes are not only possible but are actually dominant.

The notion that 'efficiency always wins out in the end' imputes a strong 'rationality' to economic activities and outcomes. Nevertheless, this distinctive 'Darwinian' emphasis is not necessary to a descriptive theory and fundamentally different conclusions can be drawn from a more descrip-tively realistic set of assumptions. For example, uncertainty, information asymmetries and/or bounded rationality may make it impossible for agents to enumerate (and, therefore, assign probabilities to) all future states of the world. If this is so, the notion of 'optimal' decisions of any sort becomes problematic. Luck or power, rather than economic rationality, are just as likely to determine outcomes. Indeed, for small and/or entrepreneurial firms:

> the whim of the decision maker may be the most important variable determining choice. The entrepreneur who has a 'gut feeling' that his new product or service can be sold may do a little market research and prepare a business plan (particularly if financial backers are involved) but these are typically done to justify the hunches of the entrepreneur. Of course, whim and hunch are difficult to quantify and be scientific about.
>
> (Findlay and Williams 1985)

Moreover, the sociological and organizational theory literatures reviewed in Chapter 3 suggest that, in many contexts, organizational and individual goals may be more accurately described as ex post rationalizations of previous actions. Thus, the 'causal' relationship between goals and actions assumed by economic models is reversed – actions may often determine goals. Consideration of the shifting political nature of goals and actions seems, therefore, to cast doubt upon the notion that it is possible (even ex post) to determine whether or not a 'good' decision has been made, and the notion of an 'optimal' decision is even more problematic. In addition, such theories also emphasize that social and cultural influences, the quality of working relationships, teamwork, the agent's personal characteristics and communication skills, as well as a whole range of non-economic motives, are often of crucial importance in explaining outcomes and behaviour.

We are sceptical of the efficiency claims made on behalf of economic models. Nevertheless, such claims can be decoupled from the more limited and justifiable proposition that self-interested economic agents will design and implement contractual and organizational arrangements which limit the scope and motivation for opportunistic actions. Thus, we believe these economic models provide a number of important insights regarding the important attributes and behaviour of agents and firms engaged in economic activities and the strategies adopted by them to cope with a highly uncertain business world. Moreover, although efficiency claims cannot be sustained, it seems likely that not all strategies will be equally effective and that some matchings of firms and strategies will be more economically successful than others. In this text, we utilize many of these insights to derive descriptive empirical hypotheses relating to management practices, recruitment and remuneration and firm organization and performance. We are, of course, keenly aware of the importance of non-economic factors and motives and attempt to incorporate them into our analysis.

We take as central the strategies adopted by agents to mitigate the contracting and monitoring problems associated with economic activities.

In a highly uncertain and changing environment, transacting with self-interested agents provides ample scope for opportunistic actions and mis-representations. The conceptual limitations (bounded rationality) of agents, the costs of obtaining and processing information and monitoring contracting agents' performance will add to these transactional difficulties. In the extreme, economic transactions between certain parties may cease altogether, perhaps due to information asymmetries between the contracting parties regarding the quality of the goods or services provided. Thus, one or more of the parties to a transaction may have incentives to reveal inside information about themselves in order to facilitate the contracting process. Of course, as we discussed in Chapter 2, such signalling behaviour is only likely to be effective in achieving its purpose if false or misleading information would be either irrational and/or costly for the agent.

In such a context, those agents which manage, either through luck or good judgement, to devise strategies and organizational forms which are able to deal effectively with these contracting problems are likely to be more successful in acquiring and managing economic resources than those agents which do not. The most appropriate strategies, which may be modelled simply on the agent's perceptions of existing successful ventures (imitation) or consist of relatively simple decision rules (heuristics), will, of course, vary with both the objectives of the agents and the particular configuration of contracting difficulties faced. Given that the costs of acquiring and processing information are often considerable, contracting will be conducted, whenever possible, on the basis of observable characteristics. Moreover, we assume that agents are likely to make use of any information concerning the contracting party's 'quality' that is both easily available and objective in the sense of being externally validated by direct experience of the contracting party's capabilities or provided by 'reliable' third-parties and organizations.

THE LABOUR MARKET FOR SMALL-FIRM MANAGERS

The earlier chapters of this text have explored a number of aspects relating to the labour markets for managers. In Chapter 1 we noted that there have been few studies of the labour markets for small-firm managers. This we attribute to the Bolton Committee (Bolton 1971), defining smaller firms to be owner-controlled and so not having non-owning individuals responsible for managing the work of others. For such firms, the only relevant labour market is for owner managers.

None the less, a minority of small firms do achieve notable growth and so need to recruit managerial talent in the form of non-owning managers.

One of the key objectives of this text is to gain an improved understanding of the process by which such managerial talent is acquired and how this process, in turn, affects and is related to the subsequent performance of these firms. However, as noted in Chapter 1, the concepts of firm performance and management 'quality' are complex, multidimensional and not easily amenable to empirical scrutiny.

Chapter 2 reviewed the neoclassical model of labour markets, in which many firms are assumed to compete for labour and no single participant has any significant market power. In such a setting, workers are assumed to freely respond to wage differentials in the market by moving between firms. However, as was noted, barriers to labour movement often exist which make workers less responsive to inter-firm differences in remuneration. The existence of internal labour markets, firm-specific investments by labour and firms, and trade unions were also recognized as factors which may lead to lower levels of labour mobility.

Williamson's (1984) transactions cost framework for analysing the internal labour market for managers suggests that, where individual productivity is easy to monitor and there is also a lack of firm-specific investment by labour, market contracting will be prevalent and the most efficient contractual arrangement. Conversely, in situations where it is difficult to measure the output of labour and where there is considerable firm-specific investment, firms may adopt an internal labour market (ILM) governance structure. Typically, the ILM is characterized by a high level of job security and a formal (rule-based) career structure within the organization in return for a high level of commitment, sustained effort and loyalty to the enterprise.

Finally, Chapter 2 considered the features which characterize the labour market for managers in small firms. While ownership and management are often concentrated in a single individual, it is also apparent that this highly informal management and ownership structure will need to change fundamentally if significant growth is to occur. The problems associated with bounded rationality, the need to monitor increasingly diverse operations, specialist managers and management functions will require the development of a more formal management structure in order to facilitate successful growth.

Since bounded rationality implies that, beyond a certain size or range, no single individual will be able to manage all aspects of the firm adequately, delegation and the recruitment of appropriately skilled managers will be required. Broadly, management skills may be supplied in three main ways: firstly, by existing management developing new areas of expertise; secondly, by the appointment of individuals from outside the firm; and thirdly, by promoting non-managerial labour into managerial positions.

The extent to which these alternatives are used by any particular firm will depend upon its own special circumstances. As suggested in Chapter 2, the process of appointing new managerial talent may exhibit some features of a 'pecking order', whereby the internal labour market, consisting of family members, individuals with whom the entrepreneur has worked, and non-management individuals with whom he/she is currently working, are favoured in the early days of the firm.

This evolutionary view of management development is, however, only one of a number of possible mechanisms by which a management team may be assembled. For example, some firms may be established by highly qualified personnel with a wide range of management skills. Thus, in some circumstances, the necessary management skills may be in place from start-up. It seems possible, therefore, that there is no unique pathway to managerial development for growing small firms.

In contrast to the economic perspective given in Chapter 2, Chapter 3 reviewed the social and political processes which partly determine the behaviour and performance of firms. Nicholson and West (1988) showed that managers in small firms were more likely to move between firms than managers employed by large firms. In addition, there was also more movement by managers from large to small firms than vice versa. However, the sample employed by Nicholson and West combined both small-firm managers and the self-employed owner-manager. These two groups may differ significantly in terms of their work histories, motivations and backgrounds. In particular, it seems likely that the self-employed owner-manager may have previously been employed by a large firm, therefore biasing the results in favour of movement from large to small firms.

With the notable exception of Nicholson and West, the behavioural literature has not developed a model of managerial labour markets amenable to statistical hypothesis testing. We attempt to help remedy this deficiency by examining the following four dimensions of the small-firm labour market for managers:

(a) Managerial attributes and firm characteristics.
(b) The factors which determine managers' remuneration.
(c) The factors influencing managers' job satisfaction.
(d) The factors influencing managerial mobility between jobs and firms.

These four dimensions are considered in turn below.

Managerial attributes and firm characteristics

Individuals holding managerial positions make up only a small proportion of the employed workforce. Generally, the responsibility of directing the work of others is seen to demand a portfolio of interpersonal, motivational and technical skills which only a relatively few individuals are assumed to possess. Typically, the remuneration, social status and satisfaction levels of managerial personnel are higher than for employees generally. Hence, the competition for the relatively few available managerial positions, although often intense, is largely restricted to those individuals that are perceived to possess certain personal, educational, work record and social attributes. In addition, the relevant attributes deemed necessary for the subset of individuals that become managers of fast-growing small firms may differ significantly from those required of small-firm managers generally.

The fast-growth small firm may attract managers with certain identifiable personal characteristics. First, managers with better 'quality' educational qualifications may expect levels of responsibility, pecuniary rewards and career movements that are only possible in a fast-growing firm. Moreover, such managers may also be more likely to possess additional, professionally recognized qualifications. The considerable tasks of successfully managing and financing fast growth suggests such firms will need to recruit professionally qualified personnel (for example, chartered accountants) for both their (presumed) superior technical skills and in order to signal their credibility to outside contracting parties. Second, the career histories of managers of fast-growth firms may differ significantly from other small-firm managers, for example a greater emphasis upon long-term career development motives when changing jobs may be evident.

A third consideration relates to the age of the individual. For a given status (position in a firm's hierarchy), it might be argued that the level of responsibility is likely to be greater in a fast-growing small firm than for small firms generally. Hence, for a given status, a more experienced manager might be required. As experience will be positively correlated with age then, for a given status, managers in fast-growth firms might be expected to be older. Conversely, however, it could be argued that firm growth attracts dynamic youthful managers with new ideas and energy, and that such individuals are attractive to the company because of these qualities. Of course, *a priori*, it is not clear which of these countervailing influences will be the more influential. A further important signal is likely to be an individual's career to date. An employer recruiting through the external labour market can observe the types of firms and previous posts held by the manager and reach a judgement upon whether an individual is likely to possess the requisite skills and experience.

Chapter 2 reported that observers of the process of staged growth in firms pointed to the positive relationship between the specialization of managers and firm size. It could be argued that, as firms grow, managers will be hired for their specific knowledge and skills as well as their general managerial abilities. In addition, it is likely that these skills will become increasingly industry- and perhaps even firm-specific.

Where monitoring is difficult and management skills are highly firm-specific, the creation and use of an internal rather than the external labour market may be preferred. However, the demand for new managers by a fast-growing firm is likely to exceed 'internal' supply. Hence, a fast-growing firm may often have to recruit via the external market to obtain high-quality managers. In such instances, the managers recruited are likely to have held prior management positions and/or have had several years practical managerial experience in a closely related activity. In addition, fast-growing firms may, because they are rapidly becoming large, value highly individuals with experience of the organizational structures and management practices typically found only in large firms. According to the typologies outlined in Chapter 2, the fast-growth firm will need to recruit new types of managers, often to newly created positions to facilitate the next stage of growth. In contrast, firms showing more modest rates of growth may be more likely to replace a departing manager with another of similar type.

It is therefore suggested that managers employed by fast-growth firms may be substantially different, in terms of education, work history, experience and motivations, from managers employed by the considerably less dynamic, but more typical, small firm.

The factors determining managers' remuneration

As noted above, individuals with certain educational, professional and work history characteristics may be attracted to, or be more able to obtain posts with, fast-growth firms. An interesting issue is whether this, largely self-selecting, recruitment behaviour has any consequences for the remuneration of managers with similar attributes but who are employed by different types of firms. For example, are the rewards, in terms of salaries and fringe benefits, to education, experience, training, etc., which accrue to the managers employed by fast-growth firms significantly different from those obtained by their non-fast-growth counterparts?

There are several reasons which suggest that both absolute salary levels and the determinants of remuneration should differ between the two groups. For example, in terms of ability-to-pay and the effort levels required of managers of fast-growth firms, it seems likely that their salary levels will be higher. Moreover, fast-growth firms are likely to compete with large firms for managerial labour to a greater extent than non-fast-growth firms, hence, salary levels in fast-growth firms are likely to be higher. However, as the direct monitoring of effort levels and decisions is likely to be more difficult to accomplish in fast-growth firms, fringe benefits such as share option schemes, profit sharing and performance bonuses, may be used more extensively as a substitute for a fixed salary in order to more closely align the interests of managers with those of the entrepreneur and other major shareholders. Indeed, it seems that there may be a complex trade-off between monetary and non-monetary rewards and other satisfactions and that the relative importance of each factor may differ significantly across the different types of firms and individuals.

The institutional economics and internal labour markets literatures suggest that the basic neoclassical framework of labour markets, by assuming that workers' marginal product is either directly observable or costlessly available, abstracts from the complexities of the situation. Such a framework takes no account of the various market 'imperfections', such as information asymmetries, barriers to entry, teamwork, opportunism, uncertainty, etc., typical of much economic activity within firms. These characteristics create difficulties in measuring productivity and may be responsible for the existence of the various 'rigidities' and the apparent permanent segmentation of labour markets frequently observed in practice. This is particularly obvious in the case of managerial labour markets. Here the service to be supplied is non-standard and uncertain; information asymmetries and agency problems relating to adverse selection and moral hazard are, therefore, likely to be of major significance. In these circumstances, economic agents (firms and workers) will need to make use of observable variables as signals (proxies) of likely productivity and conditions of employment. Given the incentives for opportunistic action, a signal by high-quality agents will only be credible if it is either difficult or costly for low-quality agents to imitate (see Spence 1974). From this perspective, firms (coalitions of shareholders/owners or the 'set of contracts') demand managers for the characteristics they are likely to provide. Thus, the demand for managers depends upon (is a function of) their salary and other financial and non-financial emoluments and their likely productivity, *ceteris paribus*. The latter is signalled by skills, training, previous managerial experience, qualifications, track record, and so on, all of which are assumed to be difficult for low-quality agents to imitate.

Similarly, potential managers are likely to decide to seek employment with any particular firm according to the characteristics of the firm and the emoluments on offer, *ceteris paribus*. In this context, the signals of importance will be observable firm characteristics, such as past and anticipated growth and profits, size, absolute salary and any fringe benefits which attach to the post; all of which influence the likelihood of staying in the post and obtaining higher future wages and future career advancement.

The demand for, and the supply of, managerial labour may be modelled by assuming that there is a range of firms, each with managerial jobs on offer, and a range of potential employees, each with various characteristics. In economic terms, there will be equations which explain the demand for, and the supply of, managers.

Symbolically, let the demand and supply schedules for managerial labour be denoted as follows:

Demand schedule $L^d = L^d(W, D)$ (4.1)

Supply schedule $L^s = L^s(W, S)$ (4.2)

where W = wage, and D and S are vectors of demand and supply relevant characteristics.

If we further assume (somewhat heroically) that the market for managers clears, equilibrium salaries will be established. Therefore, at equilibrium:

$W = W(D, S)$ (4.3)

That is, the level of wages will be explained by the vectors of D and S characteristics.

Any tendency for different types of firm to place differing values on different signals (attributes of workers) will be reflected in their recruitment decisions. Only workers which score highly on certain attributes will become managers in some types of firm, while other signals may be of more importance to a different class of firm. Therefore, it is hypothesized that a relationship exists between firm type and demand relevant characteristics. Assume now that it is possible to partition firms into two groups, namely fast-growth firms (coded 1) and non-fast-growth firms (coded 0). One method of determining whether the signals used by fast-growth firms and other small firms differ in respect of recruitment is to estimate the following logistic function:

firm type (0/1) $= \alpha + \Sigma \beta D$ + Residual   (4.4)

where D = vector of demand relevant characteristics. If the personal characteristics, work histories, etc., of the two groups of managers differ, then one or more of the coefficients in the above equation will be significant. If the managers of both groups are essentially identical, implying no segmentation in terms of recruitment, then the null hypothesis of no relationship between firm type and demand relevant characteristics will not be rejected.

A similar methodology can be applied to determine whether any significant differences between the job/firm attributes of fast-growth and other small-firm managers exists.

Similarly, a wage model can be operationalized empirically by running the following semi-Log form ordinary least square (OLS) regression:

$$\hat{LnW} = \alpha + \Sigma\beta D + \Sigma\beta S + \text{Residual} \tag{4.5}$$

where, $\hat{LnW}$ = log of current wage level, D = the demand vector for managerial labour, and S = the supply vector for managerial labour.

The results from the regression will indicate the firm and manager characteristics that have most influence upon managers' salaries. However, this pooled model assumes that the relative importance of each factor (as measured by the regression coefficients) is identical for both fast-growth and non-fast-growth firms. This restriction can be tested by running separate regressions for the two types of firms and then computing a Chow test F-statistic to determine whether there is any evidence that the relationships differ significantly between fast-growth and non-fast-growth firms. In addition, tests for differences in any of the individual coefficients tests can be conducted.

Given the assumption that the above regression model is an adequate representation of the 'true' model determining managers' salaries, examination of the residuals will show which managers appear to be overpaid, underpaid, etc. If the proportion of unexplained variance is large then it may be concluded that managerial salaries are determined by other external and/or internal labour market factors unobservable to an outsider (or not captured by the present empirical analysis) or, alternatively, that markets take some time to clear (that is, the market is in a state of disequilibrium). For example, managers currently being underpaid (as indicated by a negative residual) may be either (or both) relatively dissatisfied or be expecting to move jobs in the near future, while those currently being overpaid (positive residuals) may be expected to be less likely to be considering changing jobs or perhaps expect to be internally promoted in the near future. Hence, our empirical analysis will also examine the relationship between the wage model residuals, satisfaction levels and actual/anticipated job moves.

While the above analysis has been developed for salaries currently earned, a similar procedure could be adopted for examining changes in wages when the managers last moved jobs. Thus large increases in wages might accrue to those managers with the requisite personal characteristics, employment histories, etc. It would be expected that large increases in wages may accrue to those managers moving to fast-growth firms, as those firms are more likely to have funds with which to pay relatively high wages. In addition, other factors such as promotions, satisfaction levels and fringe benefits might be expected to explain some changes in earnings and job movements.

The factors influencing managers' job satisfaction

The utility function of a manager is likely to be affected by factors other than salary and other financial rewards. Sociological factors might be argued to affect the level of satisfaction which managers derive from their work and will therefore influence their decisions within the labour market. If job satisfaction can be considered as a dependent variable, it may therefore be possible to identify factors which will explain variations in expressed job satisfaction among managers.

A key factor likely to enter the managerial utility function is the achievement of status. However, while status may be an argument in a manager's utility function, it is doubtful whether it acts in a fully independent fashion. For example, a relationship may exist between status and job satisfaction that is contingent on age – for any level of status, the younger the manager, the higher the level of job satisfaction. A similar argument might be applied to gender. As the managerial labour market is largely dominated by males, one could hypothesize that, for any given status, women may achieve higher levels of job satisfaction than males. However, it could be argued that, at lower levels of management, women may feel that their gender is hindering their progression to higher ranks, hence resulting in lower levels of job satisfaction.

A priori, the relationship between educational attainment and job satisfaction is unclear. Managers with high educational qualifications may be more likely to feel their job is insufficiently challenging. Conversely, educational qualifications may ensure an individual is more likely to achieve a high-status job which, in turn, is higher paid and/or provides more job satisfaction. Job satisfaction may also partly depend upon the degree of control over his/her job specification that the manager experiences. For example, the greater the degree of effective control over work responsibilities, the greater may be the satisfaction derived.

The 'boss' typically plays a major role in the working lives of most employees. Given the potential of the boss to affect the level of satisfaction that an individual obtains from a job, it is important to assess this relationship. However, as job satisfaction itself is subjectively perceived by the individual manager, it is that individual's perception of the qualities and abilities of his/her boss, rather than their actual abilities *per se*, that will influence job satisfaction. The level of communication and support in managerial activities from the boss (from the perspective of the manager) are likely to be factors affecting the general level of job satisfaction. In addition to the influence exerted by the boss, the general attitude displayed by the firm towards its staff would be expected to affect job satisfaction. These attitudes towards the welfare of its staff may be reflected in the firm's provision of and general attitude towards training.

The factors influencing managerial mobility between jobs and firms

Under the neoclassical model, equilibrium in the labour market is achieved by labour moving between firms in response to wage differentials. However, as previously noted, in reality equilibrium may never be achieved. First, managers' utility functions may be affected by factors other than wages. Second, labour supply and labour demand may be heterogeneous in quality, hampering labour mobility and resulting in segmentation in the labour market. Finally, there may be markets in managerial labour that are internal to firms. The key areas of investigation in this section concern the extent to which the managerial labour markets in the smaller firm sector can be characterized by managers moving from one firm to another in response to higher wages, following the neoclassical economics model, or the extent to which the market is segmented and, if so, the key dimensions of that segmentation. We will be considering the extent to which individuals move from managerial positions in small firms to managerial positions in large firms (and vice versa), the factors which influence these moves and whether there are any significant differences between owner managers and non-owner managers.

To explain the factors influencing managerial mobility, a distinction is made between those factors which induce a change of job, while the individual remains with the same firm, and those factors which induce a change of employer when the individual changes job. Internal labour markets are more characteristic of larger firms than of smaller firms. The decision by a manager to move from one firm to another is therefore likely to be influenced by the size of the firm, the structure of the hierarchy within the firm and the length of time an individual has been with his/her current employer. For example, the relative lack of internal promotion opportunities within small firms suggests inter-firm job movements will be proportionately greater for small-firm managers than for large-firm managers. However, a fast-growing firm is likely to create several new managerial posts and, if the majority of these vacancies are filled by existing staff, then a possible negative relationship between firm growth and the length of time an individual has been in their current job may exist. This also suggests that firm growth may be positively related to the length of time the individual manager has worked for the firm due to the range of opportunities for promotion and diversification within a fast-growing firm. Furthermore, a growing firm has obvious incentives to retain existing suitable managers.

As noted in the previous section, managers' salaries do not constitute the whole of their remuneration package, because of the provision of fringe benefits in the form of a company car, profit sharing schemes, share options, health insurance, bonus schemes, etc. Therefore, the provision or lack of provision of such fringe benefits is a factor likely to influence the movement of managers between firms and jobs.

The existing empirical evidence on managerial careers broadly suggests that the older the manager, the less likely he/she is to move either jobs or employers (see, for example, Nicholson and West 1988). These results are likely to be particularly relevant in situations where managerial expertise is highly firm-specific and non-transferable. It is also compatible with the predictions of the internal labour market theorists (for example Creedy and Whitfield 1988), who argue that, from a manager's perspective, the key benefit of being part of the ILM is the provision of a relatively certain income over a working lifetime, which implies a continuing status progression with age. Company pension schemes, which, until recently, were not generally transferable, may also have served to reinforce this effect.

One central component of the ILM is the role of firm-specific investments in human capital. This suggests that individuals in receipt of in-house (firm-specific) training may be more likely to stay with the firm. Hence, in-house training would be negatively associated with the likelihood of an individual moving firms since such training makes the individual more valuable to the current employer and (possibly) less marketable externally. This appears, however, to contrast with current UK conventional wisdom which suggests that training is a poor investment and that it is more cost-effective for the individual firm to simply 'poach' trained workers by offering higher wages. The 'conventional wisdom' is likely to be most applicable in respect of general, that is non-firm-specific, training where it would be expected that trained workers would be more mobile after receipt of such training. The *a priori* case for a relationship between training and duration in current job is similar. Interal labour market theory suggests that trained employees will be of more value to the firm and will be more likely to experience rapid promotions.

Gender may also be a factor influencing the length of time a manager remains with a particular firm or in a particular job. The study by Nicholson and West (1988) identified significant differences between the career patterns of male and female managers, although these were less clear among those working in smaller firms. Women were shown to make more frequent job moves than men, and also to make more radical moves.

In explaining the job and firm moves of managers, education might be expected to perform a similar role to that of training, since both constitute supplements to human capital. Thus the higher the level of education of the manager the more likely it is that, if they choose, he or she will become incorporated into an internal labour market. Hence higher levels of education may be associated with more frequent job moves within the firm. In addition, if ILMs and higher levels of education are closely associated, then firm moves will be less frequent and the average duration with an employer will be greater. Alternatively, the attainment of professional qualifications may weaken the ILM effect, as such qualifications add to non-firm-specific human capital, which is more easily transferable.

Therefore, although the neoclassical model of the labour market assumes individuals move firms in response to wage differences, it is unlikely that the remuneration package offered will be the only factor influencing job or firm moves. A whole raft of non-financial factors may also have an influence upon the decision. In addition to the factors considered above, other important influences might include the inherent interest of the job itself, valued personal relationships with colleagues, the risk of being fired, the extent to which the job fits into non-work activities, etc. Hence, any attempt to empirically determine the factors influencing managerial mobility must take into consideration both financial and non-financial factors.

OWNER MOTIVATIONS AND ATTRIBUTES

In small firms, the owner/founder will, initially at least, be the key individual influencing its future operation. Therefore, an owner's business and social skills, educational attainments and motivations are key factors shaping the form of enterprise undertaken and its eventual success or failure. For the purpose of this analysis it will be assumed that the current owners and founder are one and the same person and the terms will be used interchangeably. In a world of uncertainty and highly imperfect information, the founder of an enterprise will need to signal to the suppliers of finance, labour, goods and services that he/she is a suitable person with which to do business. As our discussion of managerial employees indicated, important signals in this respect will be the personal attributes of the owner, his/her educational achievements, business track record and reputation. At the initiation stage, the owner may be the sole managerial resource of the business, hence his/her managerial skills and motivations are likely to be important. In respect of the many small firms that do not experience significant growth, the owner is likely to continue to exercise control over almost all managerial functions within the business. Among the small proportion of small firms that achieve notable growth, the owner will generally continue to be the major influence upon the development of the firm, although he/she may not undertake the full range of managerial tasks. Thus, the motivations for start-up and the attributes of the owner are likely to be particularly important determinants of the organizational form and operation of the enterprise. Many small firms are founded for the attainment of objectives other than purely economic ones and, therefore, evaluating their success in terms of profit maximizing or growth criteria may be highly inappropriate. The purpose of this section is to examine whether the motivations for setting up the firm are related to the founder's personal and business backgrounds. The relationship between motivations, firm performance and structure will be examined in the following section.

Motivations for start-up

There is an extensive literature considering the motivations of individuals establishing new businesses (for a review see Bragard *et al.* 1985). The Bolton Report (Bolton 1971) concluded that the primary motivation of the small business founder was the desire for independence, a finding also emphasized by Curran (1986). Curran further suggests that motivating factors may be categorized as either 'positive' or 'negative' factors. Clearly, a business only comes into existence because the individual takes a positive step into self-employment. However, when considering whether to start a business, many factors will either constrain or favour the alternatives open to the individual. For example, when choosing between the alternatives of starting a business or remaining as an employee, the individual's unfavourable attitude to his/her present employer is likely to act as a constraint on the choice of remaining an employee. With this in mind, a motivation may be considered to be negative where the individual felt pushed into beginning the enterprise because of external pressure. An example of such a negative motivation would be the individual being made redundant, or likely to become redundant, in the foreseeable future. In such cases, the individual would not actively have chosen to begin a new business, and may only have done so because it was considered preferable to unemployment.

In contrast, positive motivations occur when the individual is attracted by the prospect of being in business. This is not to imply that there are no choice constraints but rather, that the founder has, after considering the feasible alternatives available, freely chosen to begin a new enterprise. Some illustrative examples of positive motivations are the perception of a market opportunity, the wish to be one's own boss or the desire to make money.

To examine how these characteristics and business backgrounds relate to the above motivations, we ask why only some people become owners. We consider the background and characteristics which may lead a person to be positively, rather than negatively motivated to start their own business. These include geographical location, general economic conditions, and the gender, age and educational achievements of the entrepreneur. Each are considered in detail below.

Owner motivations may be influenced by geographical location and regional culture. For many decades, the economic success of South-East England, compared with the rest of the UK, was argued to be a product of its above average proportion of small firms and individuals with an entrepreneurial back- ground. Conversely, the long-term economic decline of an area such as North-East England has been popularly attributed to a business environment that is largely barren of entrepreneurial role models. Thus when one part of the local economy downturns there is no self-righting mechanism via entrepreneurship. The presence of entrepreneurial activity as found in the South-East was argued to positively motivate would-be entrepreneurs. Conversely, the relatively high levels of unemployment found in the regions may act to negatively motivate individuals to start up their own firms. Hence, entrepreneurial motivations for starting a business may vary from one geographical region to another.

The general level of economic activity exhibits periodic business cycles of upswings and downswings, reflecting national and international economic and political influences. The different stages of the economic cycle are likely to influence perceptions of economic prospects and opportunities. For example, during the upswing of a cycle, entrepreneurial motivations generally are likely to be more positive than during a downswing. That is, entrepreneurial motivations may be a function of economic conditions which in turn determine the alternative opportunities available.

A study by Carter and Cannon (1989) considering the effect of gender on owner motivations suggested significant differences between males and females in terms of motivations for starting a business. It is possible to argue, from one perspective, that because current cultural stereotypes do not actively encourage women to consider starting up their own businesses, when they opt to set up a business it will be for 'positive' reasons. Alternatively, their 'marginalized' position in the workplace may force them to look for job satisfaction via the route of self-employment. Thus, motivations may be a function of gender, although, *a priori*, the direction of the relationship is unclear.

There has been some discussion in the entrepreneurship literature on the role of age in influencing business start up. For example, Evans and Leighton (1989) suggested that the probability of establishing a business is invariant with age, whereas Storey and Strange (1992) suggest formation rates are highest among individuals in their thirties.

Considerable attention has been given in the literature to the effect of education on business ownership (for example, see Gudgin *et al.* 1979, Dolton and Makepeace 1990). Broadly, it is suggested that education provides access to networks which are necessary for activating entrepreneurial tendencies. However, while higher levels of education should enable the individual to be more effective, once in business, it also means that he or she is also more able to obtain well paid and secure employment in the formal labour market. This might suggest that better educated individuals are more likely to become business owners for 'positive' reasons. However, higher levels of education may lead to boredom and frustration with employment, and hence create negative motivations for starting a business. *A priori*, it is therefore unclear as to which of these hypotheses is likely to dominate.

The start-up decision

The neoclassical economic model of the firm assumes firms come into existence because of the presence of supernormal profits, that is, firms are seen merely as market-clearing devices. However, this model does not indicate who becomes an enterpreneur or the strategies by which individuals exploit these profit opportunities. An examination of the personal characteristics, motivations and cultural values of business owners may help explain why only certain individuals seem willing and/or able to take advantage of economic opportunities that arise. The non-economic literature on entrepreneurs and new firms also suggests the motivations for starting a firm will be an important influence on its eventual performance. Not all founders of new firms will necessarily want to achieve high growth as, for many, the firm is merely a convenient method of self-employment rather than a vehicle to achieve market dominance, high growth or great personal wealth.

The creation of small firms is far from costless, as it entails considerable investments in human and financial resources, product development expenditures, active marketing, the recruitment and installation of formal management systems, etc. Therefore, the personal characteristics and motivations of the business owner will influence the type of firm that is created (founding strategies) and the way in which it is managed (management strategies). The actual establishment of a firm is the first of many strategic decisions that an owner has to undertake and the structure and form of this decision is likely to significantly influence the performance of the enterprise.

We now examine the possible factors influencing the decision to set up a firm. This decision comprises two components – firstly, deciding whether to set up a firm or continue with existing activities (for example, remain in wage employment) and secondly, deciding how, where and when the firm is to be established. The decision depends upon the relative merits of the two states. Moreover, some forms of current activity may lend themselves to enterprise more than others, i.e. employment status, firm size and type, etc. Perceptions of the differences between the alternatives will be a function of personal characteristics (education, risk aversion, marginality) and the experiences gained in business life. The ability to imagine and access new enterprise initiatives may also be a function of personal characteristics and business experience.

The second component of the decision to establish a firm is concerned with the details of how, where and when the firm is to be established. How a firm is established relates to the ways in which the owner produces, manages and sells the product/service. It includes elements such as the structure and form of the initial management team, the degree to which the firm adopts a focused product range and the nature of any initial growth (that is, primarily organic or achieved via acquisition). Where a firm is established may relate to the industry chosen. The industry in which the owner decides to operate will be influenced by current or previous business activities and experience. Finally, the owner has to make the strategic decision on when to enter the industry/market. This decision is partly related to the 'age' and structure of the industry. As the timing of entry into an established market is unlikely to be of crucial importance, we restrict our discussions to new markets. Here the owner has to decide if the gains of being an early entrant (e.g. customer and supplier loyalty) outweigh the potential costs (production and market learning costs).

Motivations, attributes and performance

The above discussion provides background on why the characteristics of owners and their founding strategies may influence the decision on whether or not to establish a firm. We now identify how these factors might be related to firm performance once the firm has been established. We differentiate between those firms achieving fast growth and those that do not.

We have already suggested that fast-growth small firms are more likely to be established by owners with 'positive' motivations. Here we hypothesize that owners establishing firms for positive motivations, such as the perception of market opportunities, are more likely to be interested in growth than those who created a firm primarily to escape from either unemployment or unsatisfactory current working conditions.

A second hypothesis is that owners who set up fast-growth firms will be better educated. Bates (1990), Blanchflower and Oswald (1992) relate business success to educational achievement as education is believed to ease access to business networks and contacts and may lead to other forms of professional and business training. In support of this hypothesis, Storey's (1982, pp. 106–7) survey of the empirical work in this area notes that,

Gudgin *et al.* (1979) showed that firms established by graduates performed significantly better, in terms of turnover, than otherwise similar firms established by non-graduates . . . .

However, Storey notes that the measurement of educational achievement by qualifications may be too crude, and furthermore, his own empirical analysis concludes that:

> no clear relationship exists between the entrepreneur's educational qualifications and the absolute level of turnover of his firm.
>
> (Storey 1982, p. 110)

This lack of clarity in the relationship between owners' education and firm performance may be because the creation of a firm is an act which may be undertaken by any individual, regardless of formal education qualifications. In contrast, access to well paid salaried employment is primarily the province of those who have succeeded in the formal education system. Using the terminology employed by Stanworth and Curran (1973), the small business owner may be a socially marginalized individual who sees the establishment of the firm as a way of escaping from this marginalization and its low income consequences. While some form of basic education is generally necessary to conduct a business activity, it is not immediately obvious that business is an intellectual activity. Nevertheless, because of their higher opportunity costs, fast-growth firms may be more likely to be established by better educated/qualified individuals.

The above suggests that the extent to which the small business owner is able to identify and supply a market gap will influence subsequent firm performance. Successfully identifying and supplying a potential market involves an understanding of one's customers, the means by which they may be accessed, which technology and production methods are appropriate, etc. If these initial decisions result in the firm correctly matching its production, marketing and distribution operations to the perceived market, then economic success becomes possible. Peters and Waterman (1982) suggest that concentration on core activities is associated with successful firms. Hence, fast-growth firms may achieve such success because they have not substantially changed their original product/market focus but have merely enhanced their initial product focus as growth is achieved. However, the success which may accompany concentration on core activities, as opposed to diversification, assumes that the firm can maintain its competitive advantage. An important component of competitive advantage is often the technical/market excellence of the product. Therefore, it may be hypothesized that fast-growth small firms are more likely, at the outset, to invest in R&D type activities to ensure that this competitive edge is maintained. In this context, R&D is defined to include any activity that is believed to produce an improved product or service.

ORGANIZATIONAL STRUCTURE AND MANAGEMENT

The creation of organizational and management structures

While the business owner is a key element (in terms of his/her skills, motivations, aspirations, etc.) in the initial success of a firm, the management of a fast-growth firm cannot fall exclusively upon a single individual owner. The ability to recruit and organize a team of specialist managers is likely to be critical and the skills of the management team assembled will need to supplement those of the entrepreneur. In addition, such managers should also be capable of adding psychological support to the venture.

Deriving testable hypotheses on assembling management teams in a new venture is difficult, as this has not been a focus of interest among theorists. As noted in Chapter 3 there has been some interest in 'teams' of *owners* of businesses (Kamm *et al.* 1990) but little coverage of how owners of small firms develop teams of non-owning managers.

The fast-growing firm will need to ensure it has a well-balanced port-folio of management skills. This will be partly dependent upon the existing skills, interests and objectives of the owner and the strategies actually adopted for the achievement of these objectives. The entrepreneur will have to create an organization capable of successful and sustainable growth which is geared towards the market in which it exists. Therefore, the speed at which new managers are recruited and the quality of those recruited are likely to be related to the objectives of, and the market conditions faced by, the individual firm. The founder of a fast-growth firm will therefore need to invest in managerial talent that will develop and stay with the firm. The search costs associated with hiring managerial talent of a suitable calibre and the consequences of hiring unsuitable individuals are high. As indicated earlier in this text, educational qualifications act as a signal of quality to the managerial labour market, hence lowering agency costs. Therefore, we hypothesize that fast-growth firms are more likely to employ at the outset managers with higher educational qualifications and are more likely to provide higher salaries and fringe benefits as inducements to suitable managers to remain with the firm. In addition, if we assume that the owners of fast-growth firms are themselves well educated and have previous experience of business, it is likely that they make greater use of informal methods for recruiting managers – primarily by approaching those known on a professional basis.

The above discussion reflects the importance to which the fast-growth firm is likely to attach to the extremely risky, yet vital task of selecting key management staff in the early days of the growth of the business. Educational 'signals' may be extensively relied upon and financial sacrifices, in the sense of paying out 'premium' salaries, have to be made to attract the highest quality of staff. Moreover, the risk of a poor appointment (adverse selection) may be reduced if previous knowledge of the individual in question is available (this is analogous to the role played by an internal labour market in a large firm).

Strategic management and performance

Strategic management can be broadly defined as the actions and allocation of resources required for achieving the 'objectives' of the organization. However, while the majority of the strategic literature concentrates on large firms, it is important to realize that strategic management in small firms has to be substantially different. It has already been noted that the objectives of the small business owner need not be primarily concerned with profit maximization. An owner's objectives may reflect family concerns and other personal needs. Competing goals, such as pursuing valued leisure time activities and the cultivation of personal relationships, suggest the objectives of a firm may be more accurately described as profit satisficing, subject to a survival constraint. Such alternative objectives need to be evaluated when considering the strategic posture of the small firm.

A second area in which the small firm may differ from a large firm is in the range of products and services it offers. Large firms are more likely to sell a range of products and services that complement each other in terms of customer perception and in terms of their risk profiles. The adopted portfolio of products/services may be chosen for market penetration reasons or in order to reduce risk; it may choose to combine several product life cycles and to offset the movement of individual markets. In contrast, the small firm is more likely to limit its product/service strategy to ensure its (typically narrow) range of products and services is able to obtain a sufficient number of orders for profitability. This will also apply to the fast-growth firm, which will concentrate in the short term on maintaining a market for its limited product range. When seeking to expand, the small firm is likely to rely on past expertise and select new products close to its existing range and/or find contiguous markets for the existing product range.

Small firms differ from large firms in terms of management skills and resources. The small-firm owner has to create a management culture which is able to function with inputs from a small number of managers. To achieve this, the owner has to learn the skills of recruiting, motivating and 'organizing' managers. This will involve a process of communication, trust and delegation that may be difficult for an individual with 'individualistic' rather than 'corporatist' strengths. Furthermore, the small-firm owner wishing to expand has to judge when it is necessary to make further managerial appointments and the type of appointment required, given the current stage in the development of the firm.

Finally the small firm differs from the large firm in its organizational structure. At start-up, the small-firm owner *is* the organizational structure. Only when the firm begins to grow is there any need to consider more formal structures. Once significant growth occurs, the owner has to consider the limits of his/her own skills and their adequacy in relation to the achievement of valued objectives. The goodness of fit actually achieved between objectives and organizational structure depends upon the nature of the objectives themselves (i.e. are they feasible, clearly articulated and, in the case where several goals are being pursued, are they complementary) and the willingness of the owner to adopt the changes necessary to achieve them. In practice, the organizational structure adopted is likely to be a trade-off between possibly conflicting and changing objectives, past decisions, opportunism and the available resources necessary to achieve them.

The above discussion has highlighted some of the unique characteristics of strategic management within small firms. The remainder of this section examines the factors which may distinguish fast-growth firms from other small firms. It has been suggested that the growing firm would have to be aware of the changing demands in the marketplace. This may entail constant product developments or seeking out new markets and products. Hence, we hypothesize that fast-growth firms may be more likely to recruit personnel for R&D purposes and may have to access the external labour market in a search for suitable managers. Fast-growth small firms are able to offer some of the benefits of working for a large company such as career prospects, competitive salaries, fringe benefits, etc. They are also able to offer some of the benefits of working for a small company, for example, a sense of belonging, greater responsibility, a more informal atmosphere, etc. With these types of benefits on offer, the small fast-growth firm may be able to compete in the external labour market for its managerial talent. In contrast, the more 'typical' small firm has little to offer the manager seeking a progressive management career.

Organizational structure and performance

Few small-firm owners need to create a formal managerial structure requiring the employment of professional functional specialists. The majority of businesses remain small either because the line of business has few growth prospects or because the owner/manager does not seek growth. Nevertheless, many small businesses employ one or more persons to undertake 'managerial' duties without that individual becoming an owner of the business. For the few small firms that seek to achieve growth, the creation of a management team with specialist skills is essential. It is our argument that the composition of the management team in terms of skills, the recruitment process, its organization and motivations will largely determine the success of the growth process.

Small-firm growth may be hampered by the inability or unwillingness of the original owner to relinquish control over the firm's operations. Beyond a certain size and complexity of operations, the reluctance to delegate decisions to management personnel is less likely to result in sustained growth because the owner, no matter how 'gifted', will be limited by his/her specialist knowledge and time constraints.

This suggests that success in firms, beyond those of the very smallest size, is significantly influenced by the ability of the initial entrepreneur to create a management team and to delegate important areas of decision making requiring specialist knowledge to members of that team.

Chapters 2 and 3 indicated that the causes and implications of various firm structures can be complex. As the firm grows, it becomes more 'differentiated' and, from the owners viewpoint, control losses can occur. The more differentiated the firm becomes, the greater are the benefits to be derived from the division of labour and from the employment of functional managers to undertake specialist tasks. However, such managers may not share the same motivations or goals as the owners or other managers. Moreover, due to information asymmetries, the monitoring of specialist functional managers performance may be difficult. Such control losses may be attenuated if the organization has some means of integrating these diverse functions and ensuring the goals and actions of managers are congruent with those of the owner(s).

Unfortunately, models of organizational performance suggest that factors influencing the internal organization of firms are complex, and that it is difficult to empirically separate individual components. Organizational research suggests the behaviour of employees/managers can be influenced by factors such as personalities, skills, control and reward systems, etc. In other words, the performance of the firm will be greatly influenced by the nature, or 'quality', of the psychological, sociological and physical interactions between the individual members of the organizational team.

From an empirical viewpoint, it is difficult to measure notions of quality. One approach, which was developed in the 1960s, has been to relate performance measures to measures of organizational climate. Organizational climate refers to the individual's perceptions of his/her work environment, and can be perceived as the link between the set of factors connected with organization, environment and personalities and subsequent firm performance. Studies have demonstrated how changes in organizational structures, systems and practices have altered climate measures and individual performance (e.g. Pritchard and Karasick 1973 and Lawler *et al.* 1974). These studies have measured climate in slightly different ways but their basic assumptions are fairly consistent. They assume good management is reflected through clearly defined individual, group and organizational objectives and standards of activity. Furthermore, the various needs of the organization are assumed to be effectively communicated to participants. Of particular interest is the assumption that properly motivated and rewarded individuals will perform better. Therefore, it may be hypothesized that fast-growth firms may have to quickly develop an organizational climate which properly motivates and rewards participants. Organizational climate can, of course, be measured by considering several dimensions, including current salary or fringe benefits. A more direct measure of organizational climate, however, might be a direct assessment of job satisfaction, or an individual's perceived assessment of the managerial qualities of the top person in the organization

CONCLUSIONS

This chapter has presented a framework within which we believe testable empirical hypotheses concerning the management, organization and performance of fast-growth firms can be formulated. There have been occasions in which it has been difficult to operationalize theoretical concepts. Nevertheless our purpose has been to present a framework of analysis from which hypotheses can be clearly derived.

5 Research methods and company characteristics

INTRODUCTION

This chapter discusses the various ways in which the issues outlined in Chapter 4, relating small-firm performance to managerial practice, will be subjected to empirical testing. Too frequently, researchers have presented their research results without any justification for either their choice of research method or their sampling criteria.

This chapter begins by arguing that our approach attempts to combine the best features of both quantitative and qualitative research approaches. It critically reviews some existing studies of fast-growth small firms, highlighting appropriate aspects of their methodology. Our chosen approach is to identify a group of fast-growth firms, and then compare them with another group of 'otherwise similar' firms which have not grown so quickly. The main body of this chapter is devoted to the identification of both the fast-growth firms and to the second group of firms, which we refer to as 'match' firms.

The final section of the chapter demonstrates that the chosen firms satisfy our requirements. The fast-growth firms have both grown rapidly in the past and have plans to continue this rapid expansion. While the match firms are similar to the fast-growth firms in terms of their age, location, ownership and trade, they have shown modest, but not spectacular, growth.

THE TESTING OF HYPOTHESES

Our prime interest concerns the extent to which the better *performance* of certain *smaller firms* can be attributed to superior *managerial practices* within these firms. A raft of problems are immediately apparent in researching such a statement, but three key terms in the above sentence require detailed explanation and review.

The first is that of *performance*. Our earlier work on this topic (Storey *et al.* 1987) demonstrated some of the difficulties associated with measuring the performance of smaller firms. Several points emerged, the first of which was that a number of criteria for assessing performance can be utilized. For example, the conventional, financially based, criteria can be employed, such as profitability or asset growth but, in the context of smaller firms, the analysis can be difficult to interpret. We showed there were major differences between firms according to whether the trading or retained profit definition was employed. We also showed that, when profitability was 'normalized' by a measure of firm size, performance varied considerably depending on the measure used. For example the use of net assets or total assets in the denominator could change significantly the relative ranking of firms according to profitability. We also showed that the time period over which profitability was measured was a key determinant of small-firm performance for two reasons. This was partly because of the exceptionally high failure rates of small firms, with perhaps 10 per cent of the existing stock of small firms failing every year (see Ganguly 1985 and Daly 1991). It is also the case that, even for firms which survive, there is considerable year-to-year variation in profitability and/or growth. Hence it is important to recognize that the time period over which performance is examined can lead to significantly different interpretations of relative performance.

Difficulties with obtaining unambiguous measures of small-firm performance also occur when non-financial measures are used. For example one measure of performance among small firms is survival over a period of time (Reid 1991). Here the problem is that no distinction is made between firms which merely survive, and those which grow rapidly and make a major contribution to national employment and output (welfare). A second measure of small-firm performance which is frequently used is that of job creation (Storey and Johnson 1987). While this is a helpful measure, particularly for public policy makers concerned about job generation, it has limitations in respect of the concerns of other interested parties. While employment is often correlated with other performance measures it cannot be simply assumed that firms which grow rapidly in terms of employment are necessarily the same as those which are the most profitable or which grow fastest in terms of assets.

None of these measures of performance are, then, uniformly superior to all others and each have their own advantages and disadvantages. The financially based measures of the performance of small firms generally use information derived from Companies House. This has two major disadvantages; first, while company accounts have been audited, the regulatory regime for smaller firms is such that they are subject to considerably less public scrutiny than is the case for publicly quoted companies. In that sense the reported financial information is both less reliable and less diagnostic than the information supplied by large, particularly publicly quoted, firms. We have also noted that the performance of small companies is extremely volatile in the sense that it is subject to much greater fluctuations over even relatively short periods of time. Hence, even if information were only a few months out of date, a company's trading position could have changed considerably during that time. A second disadvantage of Companies House data is that it tends, in any event, to be out of date. In practice we showed that, while companies are required to submit audited financial accounts to the Registrar of Companies within nine months of their accounting year end, less than half actually did so. Hence, although the data has historic value, it offers only a guide to the current trading position of the firm. Despite our reservations over such data, the analysis in Chapter 8 of this volume does use Companies House data for a sub-sample of firms on the grounds that the widest possible range of performance measures are needed. It was our judgement that the data did have historic, if not current, value and that, since our objective was to track the development of the firms, it did constitute a useful source of information which was worthy of analysis.

The use of employment data as a measure of performance can also have similar disadvantages to that of financial data. In our earlier work (Storey *et al.* 1987), we used Census of Employment data, but this was at least three years out of date. Furthermore this information is subject to severe restrictions in terms of access, and most researchers are excluded from it.

An alternative, and much more frequently employed approach, is to use the results of interviews with owners or managers of firms. In such interviews firms are asked a number of questions about their business performance such as sales turnover, profitability, employment and recent changes in these indices. This has the advantage that the information collected is generally much more recent than that available either from Companies House or through the official statistics.

Even so, this data source also has several disadvantages. The first is that there is no way of checking the validity of the information provided. The second is that a technical term such as 'profitability' is subject to a number of interpretations. If information were being collected on this topic it would be quite surprising if all respondents used the same definition. Thirdly, interviews, by definition, can only take place with firms which are currently in business and therefore exclude that important segment of firms which were recently members of the small business population, but which have currently ceased trading. Also, only firms which agree to be interviewed can be the subject of research. The biases which this imparts is an issue which is rarely addressed. Fourthly, information obtained from interviews is likely to be subject to inconsistencies, reflecting differences in the personal characteristics, motivations and qualities of the interviewers.

The final problem associated with defining the concept of performance is that, within the UK, there is no comprehensive single listing of the population of small firms. The nearest available is the list of firms registered for payment of Value Added Tax (VAT) but even this excludes most of the firms below the minimum threshold point at which tax is payable.[1] It also excludes firms in sectors which are zero rated. Most importantly from a research perspective, however, the data base is not accessible to researchers outside the government sector. The absence of a comprehensive data base therefore means that any sample of firms identified by the researcher and which also agree to be interviewed risk being unrepresentative of the population of smaller firms. It also means that the inferences drawn from the analysis of responses cannot necessarily be generalized to the small-firm population as a whole. Even so, it is possible to be more confident about some sampling procedures than others. (See the debate between Storey and Johnson 1986 and Gallagher and Doyle 1986.)

The second key term highlighted at the start of this section was *smaller firms* and in discussing the question of performance above, reference has been made to some characteristics of small firms. Indeed the focus of the preceding chapters has been to highlight the differences between small and large firms other than those of pure scale.

The third key term of *managerial practices*, includes both the creation of appropriate organizational structures and the motivations of owners as well as the recruitment, remuneration and retention of non-owning managers. In examining the managerial context we may regard managers as workers who supervise and co-ordinate the tasks of others. Handy *et al.* (1988) make it clear in their studies of managers in five countries that small firms in all these countries are both different to larger firms, yet also have some common managerial characteristics.

Clearly Handy *et al.* recognize that managerial issues in smaller firms differ fundamentally from those in larger firms. The essence of these differences are that, in small firms, individuals undertaking managerial tasks need to be less specialized and more 'general' and flexible than managers in large firms. The task itself may also differ in several respects. Owners are likely to have not only a greater variety of decisions to take but their short time horizon referred to earlier means that decisions often have to be taken more quickly, and perhaps on the basis of less information. For managers in smaller firms decision making is also likely to be required to be quicker than in large firms, and will mainly involve consultation with the owner alone.

Discussion of the managerial practices in small firms also has to recognize the dynamics of change. In particular, for those fast-growing small firms which although constituting only a very small proportion of the population, but which make a disproportionately large contribution to economic activity, the management team will be constantly developing. The range of skills within the team is subject to change over time both in response to, and as a cause of corporate development. A key ingredient to success is therefore likely to be the ability of a small company to recruit, develop, retain and motivate key managerial personnel.

STUDIES OF FAST-GROWTH FIRMS

Setting aside problems relating to deriving a suitable sample, there are two main ways in which small-firm researchers have investigated differences in firm performance. The first is to collate a sample of small firms and then distinguish, on the basis of performance measures stated by the firms, between high performing and low performing firms. Illustrations of this include Storey (1982), which subdivided a group of new firms according to their employment size, their sales and their profitability to test for factors affecting these performance differences. A similar strategy was adopted by Lafuente and Salas (1989) who, in their study of new Spanish firms, asked founders to agree or disagree with the statement that their firm was very or considerably profitable. The authors emphasize that 'profitability should be interpreted more in terms of the entrepreneur's satisfaction with the activities of the firm, rather than in terms of economic profits'.

Turok and Richardson (1989) interviewed a group of small firms and then attempted to identify the characteristics of those defined as 'growth' firms. For their purposes they defined 'growth' as a firm which, either increased its employment by more than three workers in the previous twelve months, or which currently employs more than ten workers and has shown an appreciable growth over the last two–five years.

A similar approach is adopted by Solem (1989) in a study both of Norwegian and Wisconsin (USA) small firms. Again a sample of small firms is selected and the characteristics of the above-average performers is contrasted with those of the remainder. In this study a successful firm is defined as one having sales growth above the median for the industry.

The disadvantage of these types of studies is that, even where the sample of firms is relatively large, there will be considerable firm-to-firm variation both in actual performance and also in the factors influencing firm performance. In our earlier analysis (Storey *et al.* 1987) we identified several factors which might be expected to affect the performance of smaller firms – where performance was defined in terms of either profitability or survival. Specifically we argued that the trade in which the firm operated and the age of the firm were potentially very important factors. Since all firms in that study were single-plant independent companies and were located in North-East England, both ownership and location were explicitly held constant. In principle, however, these might also be expected to affect performance.

Our previous analyses provided some support for the hypothesis that the age of the company influenced its probability of survival/failure in the sense that younger firms were more likely to fail. We were, however, unable to show that there were major differences at a broad sectoral level between manufacturing companies. Subsequently Variyam and Kraybill (1992) have shown, for USA data, that both sector and firm age are major determinants of firm employment growth.

For these reasons the firm's age, sector, ownership structure and the region in which it is located are explicitly taken into account in the methodology employed in the current study.

The matching approach

While both case studies and more general surveys have yielded many helpful insights into the factors influencing the performance of smaller firms, they have two key disadvantages for our current purposes. It will be recalled that our focus is upon the management of smaller companies and its impact upon corporate performance. This means that to make an assessment of the impact of management a considerable amount of 'soft' data has to be collected. This can only adequately be assembled through interviews and discussions with the key managerial personnel involved in undertaking, implementing and assessing the effectiveness of management decisions.

Such an insight into managerial practices in smaller firms could be achieved through case studies, with a small number of firms being intensively studied over a period of time. In this way it would be possible to understand the way in which key decisions were made and implemented. Some insight might also be gained about the expected impact of these decisions upon the operations and performance of the firm. It might even be possible to relate decisions to the financial performance of the company.

An illustration of the successful use of the case study approach for smaller firms is the interesting work of Shearman and Burrell (1988) who chronicle the development of small firms in the new industry of medical lasers.

However, for our purposes the case study approach was also not deemed to be appropriate for the following reasons. Firstly, because of the small number of firms in the medical laser industry, Shearman and Burrell were able to study all firms in the industry. They were therefore able both to study the evolution of the firms and the industry simultaneously. Our interests are, however, more diffuse and relate to obtaining quantitative relationships between dimensions of management and small-firm performance more generally. While the case study method will provide many useful insights, it is too resource intensive to enable more than a handful of cases to be analysed. Thus, a move towards quantification and statistical analysis requires a much larger number of firms than can be handled under the case study approach.

We have argued above that both cross-sectional and temporal variations in the performance of individual small firms are substantially greater than for larger firms. Hence, one option open to the small-firm researcher is to increase the sample size, so enabling the factors thought to affect small-firm performance to be explicitly accounted for. In doing so, however, this means either that the costs of the research rise substantially if the same face-to-face discussion mode is to be used, or point towards a switch to a cheaper but less 'rich' mode such as postal questionnaires.

We judged the latter to be unacceptable, partly on the grounds of risking a low response rate and all the biases which follow from this. However, our prime concern was that if we were to fully understand the issues associated with the management of a small company then face-to-face contact between ourselves and the owners and managers was vital. Given that objective, we set out to achieve a sample size which would enable us to undertake some statistical analysis, yet also provide the opportunity for face-to-face interviews.

The research strategy therefore had three key assumptions. The first was that the performance of an individual small firm will be affected by four variables over which management has relatively little direct control once the relevant decisions had been made. These variables are sector/trade, location, age of firm and ownership structure. They are also variables which can be relatively easily held constant by the researchers. The second is that differences in performance between firms in the same sector/trade, in similar locations, of similar age and with similar ownership structure can be attributed primarily to differences in management, however defined. Thirdly, it is these differences in the multifaceted concept of management which it is our task to explore.

Factors needing to be held constant

This section makes the case that it is not possible to isolate the impact of management quality and practice upon firm performance on a cross-section of firms without explicitly controlling for sector, age, location and ownership. Each of the variables we discuss individually.

Sector

Our earlier work (Storey *et al.* 1987) was unable to identify a level of sectoral disaggregation that led to improved predictions of small-firm failure. This was because, although all firms were in the manufacturing sector, disaggregation was only possible at the two-digit classification level.

The factors which influence the performance of an individual small firm, however, are highly trade-specific. Illustrations of this are whether or not a new competitive product is launched on the market, or any changes in the purchasing decisions of a government department or a major retailer, or the entry into the market of a new firm from overseas. In this context the relevant concept of sector is that defined by economists as an industry, i.e. where firms either do compete against one another or could compete with one another.

The problem in practice is that many small firms operate in tightly defined submarkets (Porter 1979, Bradburd and Ross 1989) hence the concept of an industry has to be very tightly drawn. An illustration could be the segments or niches in the construction industry. These will include small firms as diverse as those involved in the construction of one-off individually designed luxury housing, to the case of a small firm specializing in effluent and drainage for industrial wastes. While both may be considered to be part of the construction sector, under almost no circumstances could they ever be considered as competitors. Furthermore the 'external' factors influencing the development of their business are likely to be wholly different.

For these reasons it is essential that the precise nature of the trade in which the firms operate is taken into account in explaining performance. In deriving the firms to be included considerable attention is devoted to ensuring the firms are precisely matched in terms of trade(s).

Age

There is clear evidence that small business performance is strongly related to age. Ganguly (1985) shows, using the VAT registrations data, that the probability of firm failure is inversely correlated with age. Our previous work (Storey *et al.* 1987) also showed that in explaining both growth and profitability in small firms, age had an independently identifiable effect. It suggested that, *ceteris paribus*, younger firms were more profitable and faster growing. Finally it has been shown (Storey 1985) that the median new firm in the manufacturing sector reaches its peak employment in its fourth or fifth year of life. After that it tends to remain at that level or, if anything, it may slightly contract.

The early years of a firm's life therefore tend to be highly unstable. During this period the firm is likely to be particularly vulnerable to decisions made by its bank, or one of its major customers, or by changes in tastes and fashions in the market. In many instances the unexpected loss of a single order or the refusal of the bank to extend credit facilities can lead to the demise of the firm. At the same time the firm is also having to grow quickly in order to achieve a minimum efficient scale, and the owner is also likely to be keen and enthusiastic about developing the business. Conversely, as the firm becomes older, it is more likely to have a more diversified customer base, so that the occasional unanticipated loss of an order is unlikely to prove to be disastrous. The bank is also likely to be more willing to extend credit since the firm will have a longer established trading record and the owners are likely to have more personal assets (e.g. a house) which can be used for collateral. For some owners who have been in business for several years there may be a loss of interest in developing the business and so growth rates may slacken off. Clearly these factors do not operate in all cases, but they can be of significance in the small-firm sector more generally. For all these reasons it is necessary to explicitly take into account the age of small firms when making performance comparisons between them.

Ownership

The Bolton Committee (Bolton 1971) identified three characteristics of a small business: that it had a small share of the market; that it was owned and managed by the same individuals; and that it was legally independent.

It is the concept of legal independence when the firm starts in business which can affect performance and therefore needs to be held constant. This distinguishes between a small independent firm and one which is a subsidiary of a large firm. The subsidiary may be able to enjoy the 'deep pocket' protection of the parent, perhaps even with access to the parents branding. The subsidiary is more likely to enjoy access to finance at the relatively low rates enjoyed by the parent. It is also less likely that the individual who manages the business will be a significant equity owner.

For all these reasons there will be considerable managerial differences between the new independent firm and the new subsidiary. It is only the independent firm which embodies fully the characteristics of the 'Bolton' small firm.

In practice, however, many small firms experience major changes in ownership patterns. The share capital of the firm may be extended, changed in character, sold to other private groups, sold to the public, sold to the management, etc. For our purposes, however, we are concerned to examine only companies which were independent at start-up, even though subsequently they may have undergone significant ownership change.

Region

The region in which a small business is located can be of some importance in determining its performance. Most small businesses sell their output locally and so the buoyancy of the local market is a factor influencing performance. Equally there are factors such as educational attainment, or managerial expertise among business owners, which have been shown to be both positively correlated with small business success and shown to vary between UK regions (for a recent review see Westhead and Moyes 1992).

Both Mason (1991) and Keeble (1990) have shown that successful small firms are more likely to be concentrated in the prosperous south of England, than in other regions of the UK. They also show that the regional distribution of government aid to small business is disproportionately concentrated in firms in the south of England, although not in a wholly predictable manner.

For all these reasons it is appropriate to recognize that location can affect the performance of a small firm. It is therefore not appropriate to compare the performance of a small firm in one part of the UK with that in another. Location needs to be explicitly taken into account when assessing firm and managerial performance.

Firm selection

The issues discussed above lead us to the view that to examine the relationship between the nature of management and its impact upon firm performance in smaller firms any study needs to satisfy the following criteria:

1 Clear and unambiguous measures of 'performance' need to be specified.
2 Face-to-face discussion between researchers and the owners/managers of the small firm have to take place.
3 Sufficient firms are needed to facilitate statistical analysis and so provide generalizable results.

To satisfy these criteria data were collected from a group of 'fast-growth' companies and from 'match' companies. A 'fast-growth' company was defined as one started as an independent business but which had reached the Unlisted Securities Market (Junior Stock Market) within about ten years of commencing business.[2] Each such company was then 'matched' with another firm, in the same trade, located in the same region, of approximately the same age, and which was also independent at start-up.

This research methodology is called 'one-for-one matching' since for every fast-growth company there is one other firm which is matched with it in all four respects. It is assumed that since there is a clear difference in the performance of the two groups of firms, and that since these differences are not attributable to differences in trade, age, ownership or location, that they are likely to primarily reflect differences in the management qualities and motivations between the two groups of firms.

The key advantage of this research method is that it is simple to implement and understand. Since publicly available data on USM companies is plentiful it is relatively easy to identify the fast-growth firms. Furthermore, because all the firms in the sample are relatively young, the person who had been instrumental in building the business from its early days is frequently either the current chief executive or occupies another senior management post. There were, of course, instances where a change of ownership meant that the founder was no longer in a senior position but, since our interest was in how the business developed, in these cases we interviewed the founder rather than a recently appointed chief executive. In a couple of cases in which none of the founders were available for interview we spoke to an individual with a detailed knowledge both of the firm since start-up and of the founder.

While the methodology is relatively simple and straightforward there are several issues which need to be highlighted and discussed. The first is the assumption that the fast-growth companies outperform the match companies, and secondly that reaching the USM is a clear indication of that performance.

Clearly, while any company which reaches the USM within approximately ten years of start-up is one which has grown quickly in comparison with most small firms, not all fast-growth firms aspire to a quotation on the USM. By therefore selecting only young USM entrants to be regarded as being fast growers, other smaller firms which may have grown quickly are excluded. However, while it is true that some firms which have not even considered a USM listing may have grown as quickly as one choosing a USM quotation, the convenience of the USM group as a sampling frame of fast-growth firms more than compensates for these disadvantages. As we show later in this chapter the fast-growth firms selected in this way are, age-for-age, considerably larger than the match firms. Furthermore, since we are primarily interested in the relationship between performance and management, the USM criteria is especially useful because it requires the firm to recruit and implement management systems which are at least sufficient to satisfy the demands and expectations of the external capital market.

In short the methodology ensures that, with minimal effort, a collection of fast-growth firms which have either recently experienced substantial

managerial change or which has such systems from the outset, are identified. It does not imply that this constitutes a population of fast-growing
smaller firms in the UK. Nevertheless there can be no doubt whatsoever
that all USM firms which reached the market within ten years of start-up
are fast-growth firms and that this satisfies our research requirements.[3]

The second inference of the use of one-for-one matching is that each
fast-growth firm outperforms its match on conventional criteria such as
asset and employment size for a given age, profitability growth, etc. It must
be emphasized that, while on a one-for-one basis the fast-growth firms will
always outperform the match firms, it is possible for the performance
distributions of the two groups of firms as a whole to overlap. For example
a fast-growth firm in public relations or advertising may have lower sales
turnover, or fewer employees or lower rates of profit growth than a manufacturer of printed circuit boards which is a match firm. This serves to
emphasize that, while the fast-growth printed circuit board manufacturer or
advertising agency will always outperform its own match, some individual
match firms may outperform some fast-growth firms in other sectors.

This also underlines a point which will be made continuously throughout
the text; the match firms are certainly not to be considered as poor
performing businesses. Indeed they appear to be performing considerably
better than would be expected from a random group of smaller firms in
Britain. The unifying characteristic of the match firms is merely that they
are not growing as rapidly and have not experienced the fierce turbulence
of change, characteristic of their USM/fast-growth counterpart. It is
certainly not appropriate to view them as poor performing small firms.
Indeed a few of the match firm owners we interviewed expressed a keen
interest in seeing the results of this study because they were considering
rapid growth. The fact that other match firms are small, and propose to stay
that way, highlights the heterogeneity of firm performance within the
match group which it was our intention to generate.

A third point about the use of one-for-one matching is that it assumes a
combination of variables need to be held constant to enable adequate
matching to take place. It assumes that it is the combination of the sector in
which the business operates, its age, ownership and location which need to
be matched simultaneously, rather than separately on a univariate basis,
which characterize both the fast-growth and the match firms.

To some extent the matching methodology parallels the pioneering
approach adopted by Hitchens and O'Farrell in a stream of work examining
regional performance differences in smaller firms (O'Farrell and Hitchens
1988, 1989). They use a matched pairs design to compare, for example,
firms in South Wales with those in East Anglia and Avon County (Hitchens
and O'Farrell 1991). In deriving their pairs they identify four key sectors in

the two regions. Firms are then randomly selected, taking broad account of company size, ownership and age with a view to ensuring that the samples of firms in the two regions do not differ significantly according to age, size, ownership and trade.

It should be clear that while their objective in the matching of firms is similar to that of the present study, Hitchens and O'Farrell do not use one-for-one matching. This means that in their studies which compare two regions, while the numbers of firms in each region are broadly similar, significant differences in other dimensions are possible. In the current study, however, we have chosen to ensure exactly the same number of firms appear in each group – i.e. fast-growth and match – except (on those few occasions) where we explicitly attempt to raise the sample size by including those fast-growth companies which we were unable to match. Our development of the O'Farrell and Hitchens approach reflects the fact that in the present study we have judged that differences in the nature of the management of small companies will only be identified when the combination of the four variables are simultaneously held constant at the individual firm level.

Perhaps the methodology which most closely resembles the one used here is that employed by Feeser and Willard (1990). They also identify a group of fast-growing companies – in their case in the computing industry. From the INC Magazine data base they identify thirty-nine independent companies in the same industry which have also grown at a below average rate for the industry. They also endeavour to ensure that the mean ages of the fast growers was not significantly different from the other firms.

While there is an attempt by Feeser and Willard to ensure that firm growth rates are not a reflection of age, sector or ownership, their methodology differs from ours in two major respects. First, while their sampling frame compared thirty-nine firms in both the fast-growth and the low-growth groups, only eighteen low-growth and twenty-four high-growth firms responded. It is upon these unequal numbers of firms that the analysis is undertaken. Secondly, their findings are based on a postal survey, rather than from face-to-face interviews.

Information collected

Given that the objective is to relate the nature of management to the performance of the firm, two types of information were collected both from fast-growth and match firms:[4]

1 data derived from personal interviews with the owners of the companies;
2 data derived from personal interviews with managers within the business.

Fast-growth companies were defined as those which reached the USM within approximately ten years of start-up. At the time the sample was drawn (the end of 1987) there were 181 companies which were known to have qualified on the strict ten-year grounds, and of these 125 were quoted on the market in 1991. The vast majority of the remainder had moved on to a full listing or been acquired.

Each of the eligible companies was then contacted both by phone and letter to explain the purpose of the research and to ask for an opportunity to discuss the development of the company, since start-up, with a founder/ major shareholder, and also with an individual who currently was a senior manager.

This phase of the research proved to be extremely difficult and time consuming. Typically the senior personnel in USM companies proved to be extremely busy; indeed many frequently appeared in the financial press, and a few appeared to have even achieved media cult status. Hence, it proved difficult to get to talk to such individuals, and doubly difficult to persuade them to spare at least three-quarters of an hour of their own time, together with a similar time for their managers, to participate in a research project of this type. At this stage of the fieldwork sometimes ten to twenty calls would have to be made in an effort to arrange interviews.

Despite these problems we felt that, given the nature of the managerial questions we wished to address, it was not appropriate to modify our original methodology by abandoning the use of face-to-face interviews in favour of, for example, postal questionnaires. Although the latter was used in a helpful study on the background of USM chief executives by Slatter *et al.* (1988) the level of detail which they required on the internal management of the company was considerably less than in our study. Furthermore it was thought important for the researchers themselves to visit these companies in order to have a more comprehensive understanding of soft elements such as 'feel' or 'culture', which only direct visits can provide.

Once the interviews with the owner and manager(s) of the fast-growth firms had been conducted, an attempt was then made to identify a match firm. The four characteristics of the fast-growth firm – trade, age, region and ownership – were used for the identification of a match.

Since our focus of interest was in the nature of management, and the development of the management team, two further eligibility conditions for the match firms were applied. The first was that the match firm needed to be of sufficient size to employ individuals who could be considered as managers in the sense of supervising and being responsible for the work of others. This largely explains why all match firms chosen were, relative to the underlying population of small firms, far from being 'slow growth' companies. Secondly, since we were interested in the development of the firm since start up, we focused primarily on those cases where the key founder was still employed within the firm.

In applying these additional eligibility requirements it serves to re-emphasize the point that the match firms cannot be regarded as poor performers. Instead they covered a considerable range of firms, some of which were very similar to the fast-growers. More normally they were well established small firms, of modest significance in their trade, and normally with at least a single tier of (non-owning) management.

There are no suitable lists of firms from which qualifying match companies can be immediately drawn. For those trades where comprehensive directories are produced, it is possible to identify firms of the approximate age and size required and which are located in the appropriate region. But such trades remain the exception in the UK and frequently the researcher is required to cold call on the basis of *Yellow Pages* and to discuss the firms in the industry with a friendly (or possibly unfriendly!) voice at the other end of a line in order to obtain a potentially suitable match firm. We estimate that approximately eight telephone calls were made in order to identify an eligible match company. Once such a firm had been identified, however, it proved very much easier to speak to the owner than was the case for the USM executives. We were also delighted with the fact that once eligible companies were identified there were very few instances of refusals by owners to participate in the research. Instead most owner managers were enthusiastic participants.

Finally it is appropriate to discuss the nature of these interviews with both owners and managers. We had undertaken a prior study using a matching methodology comparing fast-growth firms with match firms (Storey *et al.* 1989) and we were therefore reasonably confident about the issues which we wished to address in this study. Furthermore the bias in our disciplinary backgrounds made us more comfortable in analyses using quantitative methods. Nevertheless we realized that there were a number of dimensions in this study about which it would be unwise to expect tightly defined and quantifiable answers to some questions.

For these reasons we chose to administer two questionnaires, one for managers and one for owners. Both questionnaires contained a minority of 'open-ended' questions, with the majority being of a fixed format type. All interviews were tape recorded and the researcher then undertook a verbatim transcription of the interview.

Coding of the fixed format questions presented no problems, but considerable care had to be exercised over the 'open-ended' questions. To eliminate researcher bias a single researcher undertook to read all the questionnaires in no particular order, and identify key words or phrases which best encapsulated the replies. These were then placed in a coding manual and numbered, and frequency tabulations produced. A second researcher then took the coding manual codes and, without knowing the frequency distributions, collapsed the codes into a set of manageable groups, ranging in some questions to four or five groups, and in others perhaps to twelve groups.

In this way we hoped to combine the benefits of asking open-ended questions with our concern to provide a quantitative assessment of the frequency and importance of issues raised (Gephart and Wolfe 1989).

The firms and their characteristics

In total sixty USM companies were interviewed but in this study most of the analysis will be undertaken of only forty-nine companies. These were companies about which we were able to obtain complete information, and for which we were also able to obtain full information about the match company. Of the eleven remaining USM companies, two were excluded on the grounds of age, two on the grounds of being unable to obtain an owners interview, even though one was conducted with a senior manager, and the remainder because of the problems with obtaining a suitable match according to the criteria specified.

Sectoral composition

In December 1987 there were 605 companies which had been quoted on the USM at some stage since the market opened in 1980. The first two columns of Table 5.1 show the sectoral composition of all companies which, in December 1987, had been quoted on the market at any time since 1980. They are called All. They therefore represent the overall sampling frame for the study.

Using the Hoare Govett USM company classification, rather than the Standard Industrial Classification, the table categorizes those companies on the USM which are known to have been more than ten years old when they reached the market. These are called others – OTHs and are categorized in the second two columns. Included in the third set of two columns are those firms which are known to be less than ten years old when they reached the market, and which existed in December 1987. These are called young fast growers – YFGs. It is this latter group from which the companies to be interviewed were primarily drawn, with interviews ultimately being conducted with sixty out of 125 eligible companies.[5] The final two groups of columns in Table 5.1 show the sectoral composition of the forty-nine USM companies which were both interviewed and for which a suitable match was found. As stated in Note (2), forty out of the forty-nine firms

Table 5.1 Sectoral composition of USM companies

	All		OTHs		YFGs		Interviewed and matched	
	No.	*%*	*No.*	*%*	*No.*	*%*	*No.*	*%*
Electricals	106	18	23	14	28	22	11	22
Paper, advertising and newspapers	50	8	20	12	11	9	9	18
Miscellaneous industrials	140	23	42	26	32	25	12	25
Property, finance investment	60	10	6	4	13	10	4	8
Leisure	36	6	5	3	8	6	2	4
All others	213	35	66	41	33	28	11	23
Total	605	100	162	100	125	100	49	100

reached the market within ten years of start-up, with thirteen years being the longest taken by any firm.

From Table 5.1 it can be seen that there are some sectoral differences between the YFGs and the OTH firms. For example the YFGs are much more heavily concentrated in the electricals sectors and in property, finance and investment, and perhaps slightly more concentrated in leisure. Conversely they are more weakly represented in the all other category.

The two final columns shows that the sectoral composition of the USM companies interviewed in this study closely correspond with the sectoral composition of the YFG group. The only area of difference is that the current study contains a stronger concentration of firms in the paper, and primarily advertising sector, than might have been expected. By defini- tion the sectoral distribution of the match group of firms is identical to that of YFGs interviewed.

The performance of young (YFGs) and long established (OTHs) USM companies

Tables 5.2(a) and 5.2(b) show the rates of profit, expressed as a proportion of turnover, of USM companies. Both tables distinguish between YFG companies – defined as those known to have reached the market within ten years of start-up, and OTHs which are those known to have taken longer than ten years.

Table 5.2 (a) Arithmetic mean profitability[1] of USM companies in years prior to flotation

Year	OTHs	YFGs	t	Interviewed and matched	t
1 Year prior	0.141	0.134	0.48	0.140	−0.35
2 Years prior	0.105	0.102	0.24	0.097	0.29
3 Years prior	0.089	0.090	0.11	0.078	0.71

Source: Hoare-Govett Unlisted Securities Market directory

Table 5.2 (b) Arithmetic mean profitability[1] of USM companies

Year	OTHs	YFGs	t	Interviewed and matched	t
1987	0.124	0.094	1.79[2]	0.060	0.74
1986	0.129	0.081	2.45[3]	0.095	0.26
1985	0.120	0.088	1.93[2]	0.092	−0.13
1984	0.102	0.093	0.50	0.091	−0.56
1983	0.068	0.072	0.23	0.047	1.19

Source: Hoare-Govett Unlisted Securities Market directory
Notes: [1] Defined as profit before interest and tax/sales
[2] Significant at 10 per cent level
[3] Significant at 1 per cent level

The third group are those companies interviewed in this study, 81 per cent of which are YFGs.

Table 5.2(a) shows that in the years prior to flotation there is no evidence of any difference between the OTH and YFG firms in terms of their profitability. There also appear to be no differences between the YFG and the interview companies. The age of the company therefore appears to be unrelated to performance in the years prior to flotation, and certainly the companies which we have included here are not unrepresentative of both all USM companies and of YFGs. Finally it is also interesting to observe for all groups that, as flotation approaches, profitability rates rise quite markedly.

Table 5.2(b) shows that, when a time series set of data is examined, there do appear to be some differences between the three groups. In all three of the most recent years for which data are available, the longer established OTH firms appear to have higher rates of profitability than the YFGs. It also appears that, in 1987, the firms which were interviewed in this study performed less well than YFGs, but these differences are not apparent in earlier years.

Geographical distribution

Table 5.3 presents data on the geographical distribution of both the USM and the match firms. It can be seen that three-quarters of USM companies, and 70 per cent of match firms are in London and the South East, whereas only 34 per cent of all businesses registered for VAT in 1986 were in these areas. This confirms the results of earlier work by Mason (1985) on the geographical distribution of USM companies as a whole which found that 59 per cent of such companies were in London and the South East, with this rising to 72 per cent for companies in the electronics and electricals sector. Subsequent work by Mason *et al.* (1988) and by Martin (1989) have shown that the regional distribution of both Business Expansion Scheme funds and venture capital, respectively, are concentrated in the South East. Martin, for example, finds that 60 per cent of venture capital investment, 1984–7, was in the South-East region.

For these reasons the regional distribution of fast-growth firms, while heavily concentrated in the South East, is only to be expected from the work of others. Nevertheless it is interesting that the sample of USM, and hence match firms, is even more concentrated in South-East England than might have been expected from this earlier work.

In a few instances it was not possible to identify a match firm which was of broadly the same age, operating in the same trade, and in the same region. In these cases we gave priority to the criteria of sector and age, so that in Table 5.3 there are some marginal differences in the regional distribution of USM and match firms, though most differences were more apparent than real, being due to the match firm being located just outside the geographical boundary occupied by the USM firm.

Other characteristics of sampled firms

Table 5.4 provides data on a number of the characteristics of the sampled firms. It shows that both the USM and match firm groups are of a very

Table 5.3 Regional distribution of sampled firms

Region	USM companies		Match companies	
	No.	*%*	*No.*	*%*
London and South East	37	76	34	70
Midlands, West and East Anglia	4	8	6	12
North of England and Wales	8	16	9	18
Total	49	100	49	100

Table 5.4 Other characteristics of surveyed firms

		USM	*Match*
1	Median year of establishment	1976	1976
2	Median current employment	250	24
3	Expected median employment change over next two years	+ 40%	+ 28%
4	Median expected change in turnover next year	+ 30%	+ 22%
5	Mean number of establishments in the UK	10.4	2.2
	N =	49	49

similar age, but that their current sizes, in terms of employment, are very different. The median USM company currently has more than ten times the employment of the median match firm. A second indication of size is shown in the final row of the table which demonstrates that the average (arithmetic mean) number of establishments is 10.4 for the USM companies compared with 2.2 for the match firms.

Given that the USM companies have grown significantly faster than match firms from start-up, it is not surprising that the former also propose to continue growing significantly faster in the future. For example in the next year USM companies were expecting turnover to grow by 30 per cent, compared with 22 per cent for the match firms. Over the next two years median expected employment was expected to grow by about 40 per cent among USM companies and 28 per cent among match firms.

Employment change in firms

While Table 5.4 showed that expected median employment change for USM and match firms was 40 per cent and 28 per cent, respectively, total employment in both groups was expected to rise even more spectacularly. USM companies, as a group, expected to more than double their employment in the next two years.

It is also interesting to see the extent to which the firms in both groupings move between, or stay within their original size bands over the period (Table 5.5). For example, out of the original forty-six match firms with less than 100 employees in 1986–7, forty-one expected to continue to be in this grouping in 1990–1. Of the twenty-two USM firms with less than 100 workers in 1986–7, only five expect to be in that sizeband in 1990–1.

Table 5.5 Employment growth in USM and match firms

	<100 Workers				100–249 workers				> 250 workers				Total			
	Match		USM		Match		USM		Match		USM		Match		USM	
	N	EMP	N	EMP	N	EMP	N	EMP	N	EMP	N	EMP	N	EMP	N	EMP
Empl.1986/7	46	949	22	818	3	610	23	4994	–	–	4	2456	49	1559	49	8358
$\bar{x}$														31.8		170.6
Empl.1988/9	45	1200	9	461	4	1015	24	5714	–	–	15	15540	49	2215	48	21715
$\bar{x}$														45.2		452.4
Expected empl.1990/1	41	1233	5	234	6	970	25	6370	1	500	16	36445	48	2703	47	44249
$\bar{x}$														56.3		941.5

CONCLUSION

This chapter has explained both the reasons for the methodology which we have chosen to employ, and also provided a general picture of the characteristics of the firms generated by the use of the methodology. It has argued that a research study of the relationship between managerial inputs and firm performance in small firms needs to employ both a quantitative and a qualitative mode.

To achieve this we have combined quantitative measures of firm performance with face-to-face interviews with owners and managers. The need for these interviews to be conducted on a face-to-face basis meant that, given our limited resources, it was necessary to carefully select the firms which we interviewed.

Our methodology consists of analysing the results of face-to-face interviews with owners and managers in forty-nine fast-growth companies, defined as those which reached the Unlisted Securities Market within approximately ten years of start-up.

Our previous work has shown four major factors affect small-firm performance: location, trade, ownership and age. We therefore decided that comparable interviews needed to take place with a 'control group' of owners and managers in forty-nine firms that were identical to the fast-growth companies in these four respects. In essence the argument which is put forward is that once location, age, sector and ownership are held constant, then differences in small-firm performance are likely to be strongly influenced by managerial qualities, which it is our task to investigate.

There can be little doubt that the fast-growth companies included in this study have experienced fast growth. Employment in these firms has risen from an average of 170 two years prior to the interview, to 450 at the time of the interview. It was projected to rise to 940 in a further two years.

The second strand of the procedure, identifying the match firms, was very time consuming, but ultimately effective. Thus both groups of firms are generally about twelve years old, heavily concentrated in the computing and business service sectors and are primarily located in the South East of England.

NOTES

1 Currently an annual sales turnover of £36,600.
2 As we show later, while our intention was to take only firms reaching the market within ten years, only 81 per cent of our sample satisfied this condition. Three companies took thirteen years to reach the market, two took twelve years, and four took eleven years. Since the choice of the ten-year ruling was, of itself, somewhat arbitrary we do not feel that the inclusion of companies which took

slightly longer than this to reach the market in any way invalidated our claim that they were fast-growth. Furthermore since the match firms were chosen to reflect the age distribution of the fast-growth firms this does not in any way invalidate our methodology.

3   The fact that in 1993 it was announced that the USM was to be wound up in no way undermines our argument. Our purpose in selecting firms quoted on the USM was that it constituted a useful 'proxy' for growth. We were not interested in them because they were on the USM, but simply because a group of them had grown very quicky, and because the fact that they were on the USM enabled them to be identified. Furthermore, the real focus of our interest was related to their early growth rather than their generally recent market quotation.

4   In addition to the interview data, we also obtained from Companies House the audited financial accounts covering the four-year period from 1985 to 1988 for seventy-two of the firms sampled. This financial performance data was used in the analysis presented in Chapter 8 of this text.

5   It should be noted that in Table 5.1 YFG plus OTH does not add to 'All'. This is because some of the all companies have moved either to a full listing, been acquired, or been suspended or cancelled. In other cases it has not been possible to determine the age of the company and so these have also been excluded.

6 The labour market for managers

INTRODUCTION

This chapter provides an empirical analysis of the labour market for small-firm managers primarily using data obtained from interviews with managers. As has been stressed throughout this volume, there are many types of small enterprise, ranging from family operations producing exclusively for a local market to dynamic, high-growth businesses that are internationally competitive. Our focus here is upon the extent to which the 'quality' of managerial labour recruited, their salary determinants, their current satisfaction levels and their anticipated job moves significantly differ between fast-growth and match firms.

Chapter 5 provided a detailed exposition of the need to distinguish between fast-growth small firms and the remaining bulk of the small-firm sector. It emphasized that we used as the criterion for fast growth that of reaching the Unlisted Securities Market (USM) within approximately ten years of starting to trade. It was pointed out that this was not the only criterion by which fast-growth smaller firms could be identified, but it had the great advantage of convenience. For each USM company we then identified a match firm which was identical to the USM company in the sense of being in the same trade and region, was of a similar age and also began as an independent business.

Since, in terms of size for a given age, the performance of the USM and match firms were very different it would appear that our selection criteria has been successful in identifying a sample of fast-growth firms. Moreover, as this difference in performance could not be attributed to the four factors which we had explicitly held constant between the two groups – age, ownership, sector and geography – it is our contention that this difference in performance is indicative of major 'internal' differences between the firms. The most important of these is likely to be the management of the firm and in this chapter we test for differences between the managers currently employed in USM firms and those currently employed in match firms.

Although using the USM quotation was a convenient method of identifying fast-growth firms, this definition has a number of special characteristics which need to be taken into account when undertaking empirical analyses and interpreting the subsequent findings. The most important feature is that, although the USM was set up explicitly in response to the Wilson (1980) Committee's findings of a 'finance gap' in relation to young rapid-growth firms, a USM listing nevertheless still imposes considerable additional cost burdens upon the firm (see Buckland and Davis 1989). A USM listing also usually requires significant organizational changes and the recruitment of specialist management personnel (Bannock and Doran 1987) – particularly in regard to management accounting and financial reporting functions. For instance, firms seeking a listing (or wishing to raise additional capital once listed) need to maintain outside shareholders' confidence in the firm's management and in its economic potential to ensure that sufficient equity is raised at the lowest possible price.

Young firms without an extensive trading record that seek a USM listing typically have an information asymmetry problem, whereby insiders know more about the true value of the firm than outside investors. One method by which insiders of high value firms can signal this information to outsiders is by appointing managers that are perceived to be of high quality. Hence USM firms may, *vis-à-vis* the recruitment practices of similar unlisted firms, exhibit a preference for appointing managers with externally validated attributes such as the possession of professional or high academic qualifications or those with work histories in well known large organizations.

Often the prospectuses of firms seeking a listing claim to have introduced (or are about to introduce) new remuneration schemes in order to attract, retain and motivate executive personnel. Hence, USM firms appear more willing to signal to outsiders that managers are acting in shareholders best interests by designing remuneration packages which tie at least part of manager's pay to increases in firm value, i.e. executive share option schemes or share-based profit-sharing schemes set up under the Finance Acts. Moreover, managers with attributes highly valued by the external (possibly, large firm) market will only be tempted to move if either high salaries are offered or if the job has other desirable features such as a range of fringe benefits, better working conditions, career progressions, etc. In essence, large firms and USM firms may be competing with one another in the same market for managerial labour to a far greater extent than with small unlisted firms. Hence, it may be that the pay and conditions attaching to jobs within large firms, which are likely to operate highly developed internal labour markets (ILMs), are the relevant benchmark (opportunity cost) for USM managers. If so, then it is to be expected that the 'quality' of individuals recruited and the pay and conditions attaching to USM jobs will be superior to those of non-USM small-firm managers.

This chapter will present empirical analyses in respect of USM and match firms relating to the following four dimensions of the managerial labour market:

1 recruitment decisions;
2 managerial remuneration;
3 levels of managerial satisfaction;
4 anticipated job moves.

The structure of the chapter is organized around these four dimensions. First, we examine the recruitment decisions made in the two types of firm. The personal attributes of the managers, their recent job histories and the attributes of their current jobs will be detailed. The next section examines the remuneration of the two samples of managers. It models remuneration for USM and match managers in terms of human capital attributes, firm/job specific factors and external labour market conditions. Modelling the satisfaction levels of managers is the subject of the fourth section, while the following section examines manager's anticipated job moves. The final section contains a summary of the main findings and presents some concluding remarks.

RECRUITMENT DECISIONS

This section examines the recruitment of managers currently working in USM and match firms. The basic question which our empirical analysis seeks to address is, 'are there significant differences in the personal and job/firm characteristics and career histories of the individuals recruited into the two sectors (USM and match) of the small-firm managerial labour market?'

Job moves

To provide our first insight into these questions Table 6.1 (a) details the most recent job moves of USM and match firm managers. Of the 97 managers included here, one-third were in post following a within-firm (internal) promotion, while the remaining two-thirds were formerly employed by another enterprise and are regarded as external appointments. A slightly higher proportion of the USM managers were internal promotions than were the match managers (36.7 per cent and 29.2 per cent respectively).

Table 6.1 (a) also shows that 64.9 per cent of all managers had held a managerial position prior to their current post. However, only eleven of the forty-nine USM managers (22.4 per cent) had not previously held managerial posts while the corresponding figure for the match managers is significantly higher at 47.9 per cent.

A similar pattern is evident in respect of the size of the managers previous employer. It can be seen that 64.5 per cent of externally recruited USM managers had previously been employed in a firm with more than 500 employees, whereas this was the case for only 38.2 per cent of externally recruited match managers.

The relative importance of experience in the same industrial sector appears to be greater for match firms than for USM firms. Thus only four of the thirty-one external appointments (12.9 per cent) in the USM sample had moved from firms operating in the same industrial sector, compared with seven out of thirty-four (20.6 per cent) of current match managers. As will be seen later, this appears to be true even after controlling for the significantly higher proportion of USM firm external appointees that were professionally qualified accounting/finance specialists where industry-specific experience is likely to be of relatively little relevance to the performance of their duties.

Turning now to Table 6.1 (b) it can be seen that this makes an initial distinction, in row (ii), between match and USM managers. It then distinguishes in row (iii), for each of these, between external and internal appointments. Then in row (iv), for each category, a distinction is made

Table 6.1 (a) Job moves

Total	All	Match	USM
No. of cases	97 (100.0%)	48 (49.5%)	49 (50.5%)
No. of internal promotions	32 (33.0%)	14 (29.2%)	18 (36.7%)
No. of external appointments	65 (67.0%)	34 (70.8%)	31 (63.3%)
No. of previous managers	63 (64.9%)	25 (52.1%)	38 (77.6%)
No. with no previous managerial experience	34 (35.1%)	23 (47.9%)	11 (22.4%)
No. recruited from large firms > 500 employees	33 (50.8%)*	13 (38.2%)*	20 (64.5%)*
No. recruited from same sector	11 (16.9%)*	7 (20.6%)*	4 (12.9%)*

Note: * as a percentage of external appointments

Table 6.1(b) Job moves

Row

(i) All managers (*100%, N = 97*)

(ii) Match = 48 (49.5%)   USM = 49 (50.5%)

(iii) External appointments = 34 (70.8%)   Internal appointments = 14 (29.2%)   External appointments = 31 (63.3%)   Internal appointments = 18 (36.7%)

(iv)

Manager = 19 (55.9%)	Non-manager = 15 (44.1%)	Manager = 6 (42.9%)	Non-manager = 8 (57.1%)	Manager = 23 (74.2%)	Non-manager = 8 (25.8%)	Manager = 15 (83.3%)	Non-manager = 3 (16.7%)

(v) Large-firm recruits = 13 (38.2%)   Large-firm recruits = 20 (64.5%)

Manager	Non-manager	Manager	Non-manager
9 (47.4%)	4 (26.7%)	13 (56.5%)	7 (87.5%)

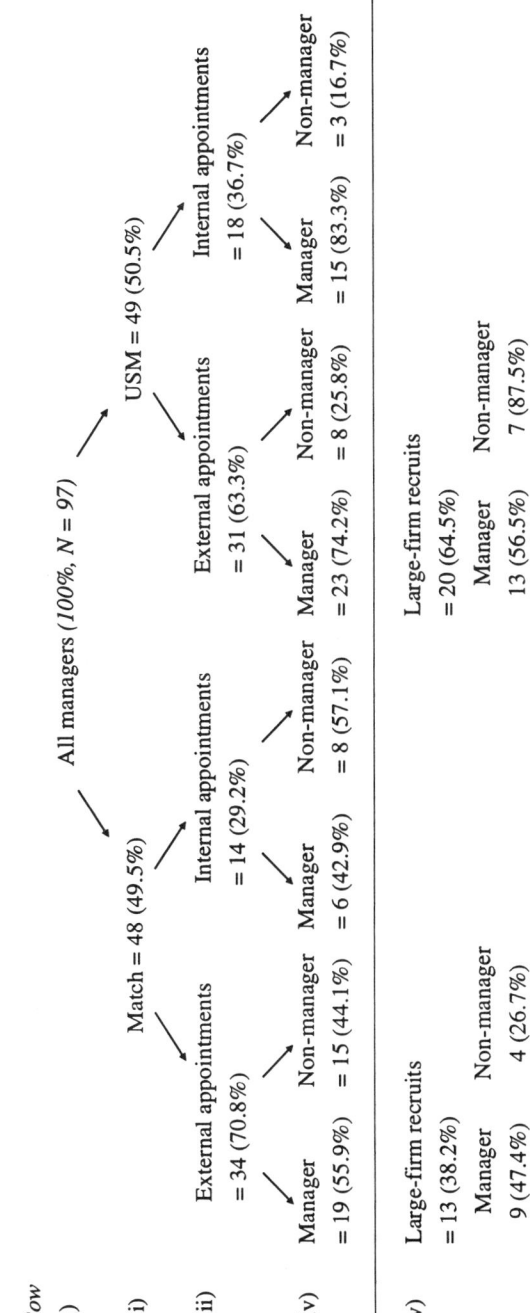

between those individuals who were managers or non-managers in their prior job. Finally in row (v), for external appointments, the proportion coming from a large firm is shown.

The findings of row (i) to row (iii) of Table 6.1 (b) have been discussed in relation to Table 6.1 (a). Row (iv) of Table 6.1(b), however, shows that, relative to the match sample, few of the USM external appointees had been recruited from a non-managerial post (44.1 per cent compared with 25.8 per cent, respectively). Row (iv) of Table 6.1 (b) also shows that USM firms, as might be expected given their greater size, have more than one tier of management since 83.3 per cent of the internal promotions were from one managerial position to another. The comparative figure for the match firms is only 42.9 per cent. Moreover, in row (v) it is shown that of the eight USM external appointees that had not been managers in their prior post, seven (87.5 per cent) had been recruited from large firms. The comparative figures for the match group are that of the fifteen (44.1 per cent) external appointees only four (26.7 per cent) had had large-firm experience. These findings suggests that USM companies are more likely to appoint individuals with large-firm experience and/or previous managerial experience. For match firms neither of these requirements appears to be of such importance.

Table 6.1 (c) presents a Logit model, where the dependent variable is a dichotomous variable coded 1 if the individual is a USM manager and 0 otherwise, which indicates that statistically significant ($p < 0.05$) differences exist between the groups in terms of the four job history attributes discussed above, even after allowing for the (significantly) greater number of financial personnel contained in the USM sample.

In summary the job moves data suggests that the key distinctions between USM and match managers lies in the finding that current USM managers are significantly more likely to have been previously employed

Table 6.1 (c) Logit model for managers' job moves

Variable (All O/1)	Coefficient	t-value
Internal/external	− 0.665	− 2.27
Non-manager/manager	0.642	2.55
Same sector/different sector	− 0.700	− 2.07
Small firm/large firm	0.634	2.16
Non-financial/financial	0.747	2.68
Constant	4.052	14.15
$X^2 = 97.3$ d.f $= 6$ $p = < 0.01$		

in a large firm. It also appears that current USM managers that have changed employer are also much more likely than match managers to have changed sectors.

Job history

Table 6.2 examines job history characteristics of the sample of managers. It examines the percentage change in salary which managers obtained upon moving jobs, their satisfaction levels in their previous jobs, the fringe benefits associated with their previous jobs and whether or not they received training in those jobs. As with the previous table, Table 6.2 distinguishes between USM and match managers, external and internal job moves and according to whether or not the individual was a manager in their previous jobs. Table 6.2 shows the percentage change in salary through a job move is very much greater for USM managers than for match managers (30.8 per cent and 9.4 per cent respectively). From row (iii) it can be seen that the percentage change in salary is greater for both USM and match managers where there is a change of employer (external) than is the case for internal (same employer) job changes. This difference is clearest in USM firms where external appointees obtained an average 40.3 per cent rise compared with only a 14.6 per cent rise for internal job changes. For both groups of managers row (v) demonstrates that external moves appear to generate a salary increase of 24.5 per cent, compared with internal moves which generate a salary increase of only 11.4 per cent.

Row (iv) in Table 6.2 provides some interesting contrasts. It shows that those external managerial appointments to USM firms, who were not managers in their previous firms, obtained an average 36.9 per cent salary rise. On the other hand external appointees to match firms, without previous managerial experience, only received on average a 3.7 per cent rise in salary. Given that those individuals without managerial experience who are appointed to managerial positions in USM companies were much more likely to have previously worked for a large firm this might suggest that working for a large firm was a substitute for prior managerial experience.

The final row (v) in Table 6.2 shows clearly that for all managerial appointments the increase in salary obtained by external moves is more than double that obtained by internal moves. It also shows that for all managerial appointments those with previous managerial experience were able to obtain salary increases with job change which were approximately double those negotiated by those without prior managerial experience.

All managers were asked about the level of job satisfaction which they experienced in the job prior to their current job, (i.e. *not* their current job). They were asked to score that job according to a scale in which zero was

Table 6.2 Job history characteristics

Row	Characteristic	All managers
	Δ Salary (%)	20.6
	Satisfaction	6.5
	Car (%)	62.6
(i)	Profit share (%)	32.0
	BUPA (%)	43.3
	% from large firms	35.1
	% from same sector	44.3
	Training in previous firm (%)	50.0

Row	Characteristic	Match	USM
	Δ Salary	9.4	30.8
	Satisfaction	6.5	6.5
	Car	47.8	77.8
(ii)	Profit share	20.8	42.9
	BUPA	28.3	59.1
	Large firms	29.2	40.8
	Sector	43.7	44.9
	Training	51.2	48.9

Row	Characteristic	External	Internal	External	Internal
	Δ Salary	10.2	7.3	40.3	14.6
	Satisfaction	6.3	7.0	5.5	8.2
	Car	40.6	64.3	79.3	75.0
(iii)	Profit share	23.5	14.3	35.5	55.6
	BUPA	28.1	28.6	57.1	62.5
	Large firms	38.2	0.0	64.5	0.0
	Sector	20.6	100.0	12.9	100.0
	Training	53.3	45.5	53.6	41.2

Row	Characteristic	Manager	Non-man.	Manager	Non-man.	Manager	Non-man.	Manager	Non-man.
	Δ Salary	15.6	3.7	6.1	8.1	41.4	36.9	16.0	7.7
	Satisfaction	7.3	4.8	6.3	7.5	5.5	5.3	8.1	8.7
	Car	63.2	7.7	83.3	50.0	87.0	50.0	76.9	66.7
(iv)	Profit share	36.8	6.7	16.7	12.5	43.5	12.5	46.7	100.0
	BUPA	42.1	7.7	50.0	12.5	63.4	33.3	53.9	100.0
	Large firms	47.4	26.7	0.0	0.0	56.5	87.5	0.0	0.0
	Sector	31.6	6.7	100.0	100.0	13.0	12.5	100.0	100.0
	Training	50.0	58.3	66.7	20.0	40.9	100.0	46.7	0.0

Row	Characteristic	All external	All internal	All with previous managerial experience	All without previous managerial experience
	Δ Salary	24.5	11.4	24.2	12.9
	Satisfaction	5.9	7.7	6.7	5.9
	Car	59.1	70.3	77.0	32.8
(v)	Profit share	29.2	37.5	39.6	17.7
	BUPA	41.9	47.7	53.4	23.0
	Large firm sector	50.7	0.0	34.9	32.3
	Sector	16.9	100.0	47.7	38.2
	Training	53.5	43.1	47.5	54.0

totally dissatisfied and ten indicated totally satisfied. The average satisfaction scores for their prior jobs is shown as the second element for each
of the main rows. The satisfaction levels of current USM and match
managers in their previous jobs are identical at a score of 6.5. Not surprisingly those managers who subsequently moved employers (externals)
scored their previous job much lower than those managers who stayed with
the same employer. Thus row (v) shows that the externals scored their prior
job at 5.9, whereas the internals scored it at 7.7. Row (iii) indicates that this
finding, while it is true for both current USM and match managers, is
clearer for the former than for the latter group.

The following three elements of each of the rows in Table 6.2 indicate
the proportion of managers having the three key fringe benefits of car,
health insurance and membership of a profit sharing scheme. It shows that
current USM managers were much more likely to have had these benefits
in their prior job than current match managers. This is shown in row (ii). It
might have been expected that a difference would have existed between
current USM managers having made internal job moves and those having
made external moves, in the sense that the latter might be moving from an
employer which did not provide these benefits to one which did. Row (iii)
indicates that this is not the case, with there being no clear difference
between external and internal movers. Instead row (v) of Table 6.2 demonstrates that it is the movement into a managerial position for the first time
which is the key factor in explaining access to fringe benefits. Thus
managers with prior managerial experience are more than twice as likely to
have had fringe benefits in their prior jobs than those moving from a
non-managerial position.

The sixth element in each of the rows of Table 6.2 shows that 35 per cent
of managers previously worked in a firm with more than 500 workers. Our
real interest is in the third group of tables which show that, of those moving
into their current firm from outside (externals) 38 per cent of match
managers previously worked for large firms, compared with 64 per cent of
USM managers: confirming the results found in Table 6.1.

The penultimate element in each of the rows of Table 6.2 shows that
44.3 per cent of all managers moved to their current job from a post in a
firm in the same sector. Row (v) shows that this includes, by definition, all
those moving jobs with the same employer, but only 16.9 per cent of those
who changed employer. The third row shows that it was managers in the
match firms who were more likely to have been formerly with another firm
in the same sector (20.6 per cent) compared with only 12.9 per cent of
managers currently in USM firms. Prior managerial experience does not
seem to be related to prior sector.

The final element in each of the rows of Table 6.2 shows the proportion of managers who indicated they received training in the job prior to their current job. From the first and second rows it is clear that while exactly half of all managers indicated that they received training in their previous job, there was virtually no difference between those who subsequently became USM managers and those who subsequently became match managers. Indeed throughout the tabulations the training variable appears to vary very little. This might suggest that formal training is not a powerful determinant of subsequent career patterns.

Managers characteristics

We now move on to an examination of the personal characteristics of the managers in the sample. These data are presented in Table 6.3, which is structured in the same way as the previous table. The personal characteristics examined are age, gender, formal educational qualifications, years of managerial experience and tenure in current post.

The first element of row (ii) of Table 6.3 shows that although there is no difference in the average age of the USM and match firm managers, the final row shows that the average age of those whose previous post was a managerial position (40.1 years) is significantly higher than those whose previous post was not managerial (33.9 years). For both USM and match managers, those that were externally recruited from a managerial post are the sub-sample with the highest average age – the difference being more marked for the match firms than for the USM firms.

Of the ninety-seven individuals in the total sample, element three shows that eighty (82.5 per cent) are male and the proportion of males is slightly higher for the USM group than for the match group (85.7 per cent and 79.2 per cent respectively). It is interesting to note that row (v) indicates that while 90.5 per cent of males had managerial experience in their prior jobs, this was the case for only 67.6 per cent of females.

The fourth element of Table 6.3 provides data on the educational qualifications of the managers. For ease of presentation, we have simply distinguished between those having a degree level and/or post-graduate professional qualification from the remainder. As can be seen from the table the USM managers are, on average, more highly qualified than the match managers since 57.1 per cent of the former have a degree level or above qualification compared with 35.5 per cent of the latter. An examination of row (v) indicates that external and internal appointments have virtually identical qualifications, but those with previous managerial experience are more likely to have higher qualifications (54 per cent compared with 35.3 per cent).

The total number of years of managerial experience of managers in the

Table 6.3 Managers' characteristics

Row	Characteristic	All managers
(i)	Number	97
	Age	37.9
	% male	82.5
	% post-graduate	47.4
	Years managerial experience	9.0
	Years in post	3.3

		Match	USM
(ii)	Number	48	49
	Age	37.9	37.9
	% male	79.2	85.7
	% post graduate	35.5	57.1
	Years experience	8.5	9.5
	Years in post	3.6	3.1

		External appointment	Internal promotion	External appointment	Internal promotion
(iii)	Number	34	14	31	18
	Age	38.4	36.8	38.6	36.6
	% male	79.4	78.6	93.6	72.2
	% post graduate	41.2	28.6	54.8	61.1
	Years experience	9.1	6.9	10.9	7.0
	Years in post	3.5	3.7	3.1	3.1

		Manager	Non-man.	Manager	Non-man.	Manager	Non-man.	Manager	Non-man.
(iv)	Number	19	15	6	8	23	8	15	3
	Age	43.1	32.4	40.2	34.3	39.7	35.6	36.7	36.0
	% male	94.7	60.0	83.3	75.0	95.7	87.5	80.0	33.8
	% post graduate	47.4	33.3	33.3	25.0	60.9	37.5	60.0	66.7
	Years experience	13.1	4.0	10.3	4.4	13.2	4.4	8.1	1.7
	Years in post	3.5	3.6	3.9	3.5	3.3	2.5	3.4	1.7

		All external appointments	All internal appointments	All with previous managerial experience	All with no experience
(v)	Number	65	32.0	63.0	34.0
	Age	38.5	36.7	40.1	33.9
	% male	86.2	75.0	90.5	67.6
	% post graduate	47.7	46.9	54.0	35.3
	Years experience	10.0	7.0	11.7	4.0
	Years in post	3.3	3.4	3.4	3.2

sample are shown as element five of the table. This demonstrates that the USM managers have on average an additional year's experience compared with the match managers. The row (iii) figures show that for both USM and match groups the external appointees are the more experienced. The largest differences, as one would expect, are between those whose previous posts were managerial and those that were not. Since relatively few individuals tend to move from a managerial position to a non-managerial and then back to a managerial post, the number of years of managerial experience for those who did not occupy a managerial position in their prior post closely corresponds with the number of years in their current (managerial) post.

Current job characteristics

The managers' current job characteristics are shown in Table 6.4. Slightly under 30 per cent of managers are currently engaged in predominantly accounting/financial functions and this percentage increases to 42.9 per cent for the USM sample. The row (iii) figures clearly show that both USM and match recruit this financial expertise externally. Thus three times as many match firm finance professionals came to their present post from outside the firm as from inside. For USM companies more than twice as many came from outside as from inside. The final row indicates that finance professionals are also much more likely to have had prior managerial experience than is the case for the sample as a whole.

In terms of managerial status – defined as the number of management levels between the manager's current post and the board of directors – element two of Table 6.4 shows that USM managers are (in absolute terms) slightly further from the top of the management hierarchy than are match managers. However, because the USM managers generally work for significantly larger firms, this does not imply that they occupy less onerous or less responsible positions than their match counterparts. For both groups of firms, those recruited from non-managerial posts (whether internally or externally) generally occupy lower positions in the management hierarchy.

No clear pattern seems to emerge between the USM and match managers in terms of whether or not they have received a significant element of training in their current post. Nevertheless it is interesting to note that the internally promoted group within the USM sample (whether coming from a managerial post or not) appear the most likely to have been in receipt of training. Overall the uniformity of pattern tends to confirm our earlier observation in Table 6.2 that training experience is not a key factor influencing managers careers.

Large differences, however, exist between USM and match firm managers in respect of current salaries. Element four of row (ii) in Table 6.4

Table 6.4 Current job characteristics

Row	Characteristic	All managers
	Financial %	29.9
	Status	1.2
	Training	39.2
(i)	Salary (£000's)	26.4
	Satisfaction	8.2
	Car	78.4
	Profit share	61.9
	BUPA	66.0

Row	Characteristic	Match	USM
	Financial %	16.7	42.9
	Status	1.1	1.3
	Training	37.5	40.8
(ii)	Salary	20.6	32.1
	Satisfaction	7.9	8.5
	Car	68.8	87.8
	Profit share	45.8	77.6
	BUPA	52.1	79.6

Row	Characteristic	External	Internal	External	Internal
	Financial %	20.6	7.1	54.8	22.2
	Status	1.1	1.1	1.3	1.4
	Training	38.2	35.7	29.0	61.1
(iii)	Salary	18.6	25.3	32.0	32.3
	Satisfaction	8.0	7.7	8.5	8.5
	Car	70.6	64.3	90.3	83.3
	Profit share	38.2	64.3	74.2	83.3
	BUPA	50.0	57.1	74.2	88.9

Row	Characteristic	Manager	Non-man.	Manager	Non-man.	Manager	Non-man.	Manager	Non-man.
	Financial %	26.3	13.3	16.7	0.0	56.5	50.0	26.7	0.0
	Status	1.1	1.1	1.0	1.3	1.2	1.5	1.3	2.0
	Training	31.6	46.7	16.7	50.0	30.4	25.0	60.0	66.7
(iv)	Salary	21.4	15.1	25.7	25.0	35.1	23.0	35.7	15.3
	Satisfaction	8.1	7.9	7.5	7.9	8.7	8.1	8.5	8.7
	Car	79.0	60.0	66.7	62.5	100.0	62.5	93.3	33.3
	Profit share	47.4	26.7	66.7	62.5	78.3	62.5	86.7	66.7
	BUPA	47.4	53.3	83.3	37.5	78.3	62.5	93.3	66.7

Row	Characteristic	All external	All internal	All previous managerial experience	All without previous managerial experience
	Financial %	36.9	15.6	36.4	18.0
	Status	1.2	1.3	1.1	1.3
	Training	33.8	50.0	36.5	44.1
(v)	Salary	25.0	29.2	27.8	19.3
	Satisfaction	8.2	8.2	8.4	8.0
	Car	80.0	74.3	88.9	58.8
	Profit share	55.4	74.3	69.9	47.1
	BUPA	61.5	75.0	73.0	44.1

demonstrates that on average, the USM managers receive an additional £11,500 per annum compared with their match counterparts. Within the USM group those coming from managerial positions (either externally or internally) receive the highest salaries (about £35,000), while the three internally promoted non-managers receive on average less than half that amount. Overall the key determinant of current salary would appear to be working for a USM company and prior managerial experience. These matters will, however, be examined in much more detail in the following section.

Data on current job satisfaction levels are shown as element five of Table 6.4. It appears that USM managers are more satisfied than their match counterparts. This contrasts with data in Table 6.2 on job satisfaction in their prior job where there was no difference whatever between the two groups. A second comparison is that the satisfaction scores in their current job are very much higher than in their prior job. Thus current USM managers score their job at 8.5 and current match managers score 7.9. In their prior job both scored them at 6.5.

Currently it appears from row (iv) that externally recruited managers coming from other managerial positions are most satisfied. This is the case for both USM and match managers.

The inclusion of fringe benefits as part of their current jobs is shown in elements six to eight of Table 6.4. It shows that USM managers do considerably better than their match firm counterparts in terms of fringe benefits. In both groups, those coming from previous managerial posts are also more likely to be in receipt of all three fringe benefits in their current post. There appears to be little evidence of any differences in respect of whether or not the manager was internally promoted or was an external appointment.

Recruitment summary

The USM and match firm managers differ from one another in terms of human capital attributes and their job histories. The USM sample, in addition to scoring more highly in terms of human capital, also have higher current salaries and have higher current job satisfaction scores.

There are major differences in manager and job/firm attributes between USM and match managers when stratified by work history factors. However, the USM firms are on average approximately four times as large in terms of employment as the match firms, despite there being no difference in the ages of the firms in the two sectors. These results suggest that, to some extent, these two sectors of the small-firm managerial labour market are segmented in the sense that they each tend to recruit managerial labour with different attributes to undertake what may be fundamentally dissimilar jobs within organizations that differ significantly in terms of size and regulatory constraints.

MANAGERIAL REMUNERATION

This section examines the determinants of managerial salaries in our samples of USM and match managers. The extent to which managerial salaries can be related to firm/job specific and individual manager human capital attributes (or signals) is the main focus of the empirical analysis.

A renumeration model

This section presents a model for empirically examining managers' remuneration in USM and non-USM small firms. It assumes economic agents (firms and workers) make use of observable signals (proxies) of likely productivity and conditions of employment. The signalling literature suggests that, given the possibilities for opportunistic action, a signal by high-quality agents will only be credible if it is either difficult or costly for low-quality agents to imitate (see Spence 1974). From this perspective, firms (coalitions of shareholders/owners or the 'set of contracts') demand managers for the characteristics they are likely to provide. Thus, the demand for managers depends upon their total remuneration (defined as salary and other emoluments) and their likely productivity. The latter is signalled by skills, training, previous managerial experience, qualifications and track record, all of which are assumed to be difficult for low-quality agents to imitate.

Similarly, potential managers decide upon moving to any particular firm according to the characteristics of that firm and the salary plus emoluments (remuneration) on offer. Important signals in this context will be observable characteristics such as past and anticipated firm growth/ profits, size, job security and expected career progression.

Assume now a range of firms, each with managerial jobs on offer, and a range of potential managers, each with a range of human capital characteristics. Equilibrium salaries are set in the familiar manner. Symbolically, demand and supply are:

$$L_d = L_d(W, D) \tag{6.1}$$
$$L_s = L_s(W, S) \tag{6.2}$$

respectively, where W = remuneration, and D and S are vectors of demand and supply relevant characteristics.

At equilibrium:

$$W = W(D, S) \tag{6.3}$$

That is, the level of remuneration will be explained by the vectors of D and S characteristics.

We empirically operationalize the salary model by estimating the following OLS regression for a pooled sample of USM and non-USM firms:

$$\ln(W) = \alpha + \sum_{i=1}^{i} \beta_i D_i + \sum_{j=i+1}^{j} \beta_j S_j + e \tag{6.4}$$

where, $\ln(W)$, the dependent variable = log of current salary, D is the demand vector and S the supply vector for managerial labour.

The results of this model will indicate those firm and manager characteristics that have most influence upon managers' salaries. However, it implicitly assumes the relative importance of each factor (as measured by the regression coefficients) are identical for both USM and match firms. To test for this we run separate regressions for the two groups and then compute a Chow test F-statistic (with Toyoda's 1974 adjustment for heteroscadasticity where necessary) to determine whether either the intercept or any of the coefficients differ significantly.[1]

In summary, since the null hypothesis is that there is no relationship between managerial salaries and the supply and demand relevant characteristics included in the model, we test the following three alternative hypotheses:

H1: The determinants of managers' salaries in USM and match small firms do not differ significantly and that the salary levels of both groups can be explained by the same equation.

H2: Managers' salaries in the two groups of firms differ, but this merely reflects differences in the quality of individuals recruited and/or differences in job or firm characteristics.

H3: Managers' salaries in the two groups of firms differ, and that the main salary determinants also differ (i.e. their respective salary equations differ significantly).

The key distinction between H2 and H3 is that the estimating equation for both groups will be similar if H2 is upheld, and will be significantly different if H3 is upheld.

To test these hypotheses, data on thirty-five variables which, from the discussion above, may be regarded as providing dimensions to the managerial labour market, were analysed. The full list of variables is shown in Appendix 6.1.

Since several of these variables are close proxies for one another, and are highly correlated in our sample, they cannot all be entered into the estimating equation without causing statistical difficulties. Given our specific interest in the USM/match dimensions of the managerial labour market, our preferred model is, therefore, a reduced form model containing a positive constant term and the ten variables and *a priori* expected signs.[2] For the *FB* and *Func* variables no expected sign is specified.

Age(+)   managers' ages in years
Age2(−)   managers' ages squared
FS(+)   log of firm size/status in hierarchy
Qual(+)   possession of first or higher degree, or post-graduate level professional qualification
FB(+/−)   possession of all three fringe benefits (company car, profit sharing and private health insurance)
Func(+/−) accounting/finance position held
Loc(+)   firm located in London and south-east region
Ind(+)   financial services sector firm
Man(+)   previously holding a managerial post
Big(+)   previously employed with a large firm (employees > 500).

With this model, all firms in the sample, irrespective of any specific firm and/or individual human capital attributes, are assumed to pay some minimum total managerial remuneration (salary plus fringe benefits). This is represented by the positive constant. Salary is then augmented according to the firm and individual manager attributes represented by the independent variables. For example, previously being employed in a managerial capacity, previously being employed in a large firm and possessing higher educational qualifications should, given the previous discussion, all be associated with larger salaries and, therefore, are expected to have positive coefficients. Positive signs on the managerial function, location in South-East England and financial service sector firm variables are also expected due to the high external market demand for financial personnel in that region in the post 'big-bang' era. Large-firm employment alternatives, ability to pay, relative workloads and previous empirical studies all suggest that firm size and status within the managerial hierarchy will be positively related to managerial salaries. The impact of fringe benefits on salaries will depend upon whether or not these are complements or substitutes for money wages. The inclusion of the *Age* and *Age2* variables with positive and negative signs respectively assumes that the relationship between managers ages and salaries is of an inverted U nature, i.e. age has a positive effect upon salaries up to a certain age after which greater age has a negative effect.

Remuneration model results

If USM firms are shown to pay higher salaries than match firms, even after controlling for individual manager and firm attributes, then pay, as well as recruitment, can be seen as a dimension of segmentation. The OLS regression results shown in Table 6.5 are designed to indicate the returns (in terms of salary levels) to managers with specific personal and employing firm attributes. A pooled model which has been estimated using data on all ninety-seven managers and separately estimated regression equations for each of the two groups of managers are shown.[3]

Turning first to the pooled model, which is a restricted model since it assumes that the coefficients for both types of managers are the same, it can be seen that the overall relationship is significant at 1 per cent confidence levels and that 69 per cent of the variance (as measured by the adjusted R^2) in the salaries of the ninety-seven managers has been explained. It can also be seen that seven of the ten independent variables are individually significant at least at 5 per cent levels. The significant variables and their signs are as follows:

Age (+)
Age2 (−)
FS (+)
Qual (+)
FB (+)
Man (+)
Loc (+)

This implies that individuals that previously held managerial positions elsewhere, relatively high status managers working for larger firms located in the London and the South-East region, who have either a higher education degree or some form of post-graduate professional qualification, who also obtain all three fringe benefits earn significantly higher salaries than other managers. However, the positive coefficient on the *Ind* variable is significant at 10 per cent levels and, therefore, suggests that financial services sector firm managers obtained higher salaries than managers in other industrial sectors. In addition, the positive coefficient on the *Big* variable is almost significant which implies that previously being employed in a large firm may have some marginally positive impact upon salaries.

There is no evidence from this model that fringe benefits are used as a substitute for salary, or that managers undertaking accounting/financial functions have significantly higher wages. The significance of the location variable probably reflects a combination of the higher living costs associated with South-East England (and hence, a lower real wage for a given

Table 6.5 Wage model results

Variable name	All	USM	Match	Coefficient difference
Qual	0.299	0.194	0.445	− 0.251
	(3.87)	(1.61)	(4.19)	(1.56)
Age	90.256E-3	101.134E-3	39.245E-3	21.889E-3
	(3.73)	(1.51)	(3.03)	(0.32)
Age2	− 1.023E-3	− 1.216E-3	− 0.905E-3	− 0.311E-3
	(3.47)	(1.43)	(2.93)	(0.36)
Big	0.185	0.15	0.012	0.172
	(1.44)	(1.66)	(0.12)	(1.13)
Man	0.170	0.221	0.228	− 0.007
	(2.08)	(1.585)	(1.99)	(0.04)
Ind	0.233	0.177	0.252	− 0.075
	(1.69)	(1.07)	(0.77)	(0.20)
FS	0.062	0.065	0.026	0.039
	(2.49)	(1.85)	(0.60)	(0.69)
FB	0.458	0.354	0.562	− 0.209
	(5.64)	(2.93)	(4.58)	(1.20)
Loc	0.283	0.279	0.284	− 0.005
	(3.67)	(2.02)	(2.84)	(0.03)
Func	− 0.098	− 0.048	− 0.240	0.192
	(1.10)	(0.39)	(1.60)	(0.96)
Constant	0.319	0.248	0.591	− 0.343
	(0.68)	(0.20)	(1.10)	(0.27)
$\overline{R}^2$	69%	52%	70%	
F	22.23	6.29	11.76	0.86
	(10,86)	(10,38)	(10,37)	(11,75)
Age at which wage is maximum	44.1 yrs	41.6yrs	43.8yrs	
Maximum wage (including constant) (excluding FS)	£10,072	£10,494	£10,234	
30-yr-old wage	£8,215	£8,914	£8,618	

Note: Figures in parenthesis are 't' statistics

money wage) as well as the generally tighter labour market conditions characteristic of this region in the study period. The coefficients on the *Age* and *Age2* variables implies that age has a positive impact upon salary levels up to 44.1 years of age after which it has a negative effect upon salaries.

The separately estimated equations for the USM and match firm samples reveal some interesting features. For instance, the USM model is unable to explain as great a percentage of the variance in salaries as the match firm model, 52 per cent and 70 per cent respectively. Moreover, there are only two statistically significant variables common to both models, the fringe benefit (*FB*) dummy variable and location (*Loc*) dummy variable used to capture regional differences in external labour market supply/demand and real/money wage differentials. This seems to suggest that the relative importance of factors may differ between the two groups of firms. The Chow test *F*-statistic of 0.86 is not, however, significant at conventional confidence levels indicating that, overall, the individual equations for determining USM and match firm managers salaries are essentially identical. The results of interaction tests on each of the individual variables and the constant term, shown in the difference column in the table, confirm this. Using the match managers as the reference category, these results indicate that none of the differences in any of the estimated parameters in the two equations are individually statistically significant at 5 per cent confidence levels.

However, as can be seen from the table, even though the separate models are able to explain a large proportion of the variance in managers salaries, relative of the pooled model, fewer of the ten independent variables are individually statistically significant. Correlations between the independent variables appear to be reducing their individual statistical significance in the separately estimated equations where there are much fewer degrees of freedom.

Examination of the intercepts and the two coefficients relating to the managers age in the two models indicates that, *ceteris paribus*, the salary levels of similarly aged managers in both types of firm do not differ significantly within plausible age ranges – though it should be noted that the strength of the statistical relationship between salaries and age is far stronger for the match managers than for the USM managers. For instance, ignoring the increment due to firm size, the estimated salary levels of a 30-year-old working in either a USM or match firm who falls into the joint reference category (i.e. someone who had not previously worked for a large firm, was not a manager in his/her previous job, who does not receive all three fringe benefits, and who currently works for a non-financial services firm that is not located in the South-East) are within £300 of one another (£8,914 and £8,618 respectively for USM and match firms).

Differentiating salary with respect to age reveals that the influence of age is at a maximum at 41.6 years of age in the USM firms and 43.8 years in respect of the match firms. The implied maximum expected salaries (again ignoring firm size) for the reference category at these ages will be £10,494 and £10,234, respectively.

The almost statistically significant negative coefficient on the *Func* variable, which indicates that managers in match firms that are engaged in a financial/accounting capacity earn significantly less than other specialisms, can be explained. It does not imply that professional accountants are less highly valued by match firms since *Qual* has a large significant coefficient – in fact much larger than that for the USM firm model. We interpret the result to reflect the fact that match firm managers engaged in a financial capacity were more likely to be unqualified personnel. They could be more accurately described as 'bookkeepers' or 'accounting clerks'. Match firms' accounting control and financial systems are not normally subject to extensive external scrutiny by capital market analysts and/or are more likely to be under the direct personal control of the owner-manager. The returns to professionally qualified financial managers in match firms are actually higher than for those employed by USM firms. The net effect of being a professionally qualified manager employed in a financial capacity in a match firm is 0.205 (0.445 – 0.240), while for USM firms it is only 0.146 (0.194 – 0.048).

Managerial remuneration: summary

Our attempt to model the determinants of USM and match firm managers salaries has been relatively successful, both in terms of the estimated models' explanatory power and in terms of the plausibility and signs of the significant variables. From the results presented above, it is clear that USM managers are more highly paid than their match firm counterparts and that a number of individual human capital and firm specific attributes provide important signals which influence salary levels.

However, due to collinearity between the independent variables and the relatively small sample sizes, what is less clear is whether the relative importance of the various factors differ between the two groups of firms. For instance, the managers age and qualifications appear to be more important determinants of salaries for those working in match firms than those in USM firms, where firm size and previously being employed in a large firm are of relatively more significance. Hence, although match firm managers are much less likely to possess externally validated qualifications than USM managers, those who are qualified can expect to earn significantly higher salaries than other match managers. Also, should the match firm be of a similar size to a comparable USM firm, the match firm manager can expect to earn a comparable salary.

The pooled model is well defined in terms of the significance levels of the individual variables and there is little evidence to suggest significant differences exist between the salary determinants of the two groups. The

£11,000 average difference in salaries between the two groups appears, therefore, to be largely due to segmentation in terms of recruitment decisions (i.e. USM firms employ higher quality managers) and differences in firm/job characteristics such as size rather than being due to the two groups having significantly different earnings equations.

Our greater success in explaining the relative salary levels of match firm managers than USM managers suggests that there are determinants of USM managers' salaries which have not been captured by our variables. Whether the inclusion of omitted variables relating to employment conditions or market factors, either internal or external to the firm, would materially improve the explanatory power of the models remains an interesting question for future research. For instance, it seems possible that, given the importance of performance related remuneration schemes, etc., inclusion of firm performance variables will be likely to improve the explanatory power of the USM salary model to a far greater extent than for the match firms. It may also be that the USM managerial labour market, being very young and turbulent, is relatively 'inefficient' in the sense that some managers are simply underpaid or overpaid. Alternatively, our cross-sectional analysis may be too static. Labour markets are not frictionless, moving jobs is often a costly process and agents have to invest considerable energies in seeking out information concerning opportunities elsewhere. Markets may simply take some time to clear.

A MODEL OF MANAGERS' SATISFACTION LEVELS

The above section examined managerial salaries and how it is possible to explain why these differ (primarily) according to the type of firm and the human capital of the manager. In this sense it is an explanation derived from the discipline of economics.

We now move away from relying exclusively upon observing how manager's career histories and remuneration can be explained in terms of economic and human capital variables. Instead our focus shifts towards asking questions about reasons underlying managerial behaviour. In so doing we therefore move somewhat away from a 'mainline' economics focus towards one which is more generally associated with the behavioural sciences. Hence we explicitly recognize that there may be subjective variables which influence managers behaviour in the labour market, which are, at least partly, independent of salary/remuneration. Even so our methodology continues to be that favoured by economists.

This section attempts to model the expressed levels of job satisfaction of the managers in USM and match firms. It is clear the salary levels, human capital and job history characteristics and the size and regulatory constraints of the firms they work for, differ between USM and match firm managers. Moreover, as was shown in Table 6.4, the levels of job satisfaction of USM managers was significantly higher than that of match managers. It is our objective to determine the extent to which managers satisfaction levels can be explained by differences in human capital, job history and job/firm specific factors.

Theoretical and statistical considerations

In addition to the level of remuneration being offered, the manager making a choice of whether or not to move jobs will also take account of other factors affecting his/her overall level of job satisfaction. Complex trade-offs between non-pecuniary factors and monetary rewards may have to be undertaken at this stage. Of course, the factors that may influence an individual's anticipated level of satisfaction in a new job are likely to be many and varied. Anticipated satisfaction levels will depend on the individual's personal characteristics, interests, current and alternative employment opportunities, the relative prospects of being promoted and the skill content and other attributes of the job undertaken. Actual satisfaction levels once employed within a firm will, in addition to the above, be influenced by how well prior expectations have been fulfilled, external environmental and internal organizational factors that affect the individuals tasks and the scope within the firm for developing valued working relationships with co-workers – particularly the working relationship the individual experiences with regard to his/her immediate superior in the organization.

In the economics literature, models of employee satisfaction have generally taken the following form:

$$SAT = \alpha + \sum_{i=1}^{i} \beta_i D_i + \sum_{j=i+1}^{j} \beta_j S_j + \beta_{j+1} W + e \tag{6.5}$$

where SAT is an index of job satisfaction, ΣD are the demand relevant human capital, job history and personal characteristics, ΣS are the supply relevant job/firm characteristics and W is the wage rate.

In our analysis, however, the model described by equation (6.5) will be augmented in two respects. First, the job/firm characteristics vector (ΣS_i) will include additional variables which reflect owner's perceptions of their firm's organizational characteristics and the manager's perceptions of their immediate superior (their boss). Given the previous discussion, these, essentially non-economic, variables should have a significant influence upon managers levels of satisfaction even after allowing for the influence of remuneration.

Second, when examining the effect of trade union membership upon employee job satisfaction, an additional dichotomous explanatory variable representing union membership, U, has often been included (see for example, Freeman 1978, Borjas 1979, Kochan 1980 and Freeman and Medoff 1984).

In a similar manner, to examine job satisfaction among USM and match firm managers, an additional dummy (taking a value of unity for a USM and zero for a match firm) could be included in equation (6.5). Coefficients could then be estimated using pooled data to determine whether the satisfaction levels of the two groups of managers differ significantly, i.e.

$$SAT = \alpha + \sum_{i=1}^{i} \beta_i D_i + \sum_{j=i+1}^{j} \beta_j S_j + \beta_{j+1}W + \beta_{j+2}U + e \qquad (6.6)$$

If the estimated coefficient on the additional variable U were significantly positive then it could be concluded that the satisfaction levels of the USM managers were significantly higher than that of the match managers. Such a pooled model is, however, incomplete because it assumes only the intercepts differ and that the other coefficients in the model are the same for both groups of managers. Moreover, as we have seen, since there are systematic differences between USM and match managers in terms of personal and job history characteristics, the model described in equation (6.6) suffers from selection bias. As the USM and match firm managers are not random drawings from the same underlying population of managerial labour, the determinants of USM/match membership will need to be controlled for in some manner.

As levels of job satisfaction, salaries and USM/match group membership are all related, a simultaneous estimation method is needed to allow for selection bias. Job satisfaction in equation (6.6) is a function of salaries while, as we showed in the previous section, salaries differ across the two sectors and are a function of USM/match membership. From the individual manager's viewpoint the decision to obtain employment in either type of firm depends upon expected net benefits and so is also related to expectations of salary and satisfaction levels, personal and human capital attributes and preferences regarding job/firm specific characteristics.

Group membership has therefore to be treated as an endogenous variable by augmenting our separately estimated salary models as follows:

$$W_u = \alpha + \sum_{i=1}^{i} \beta_i D_i + \sum_{j=i+1}^{j} \beta_j S_j + \beta_{j+1}Z_u + e \qquad (6.7)$$

$$W_{\mathrm{m}} = \alpha + \sum_{i=1}^{i} \beta_i D_i + \sum_{j=i+1}^{j} \beta_j S_j + \beta_{j+1} Z_m + e \tag{6.8}$$

Equations (6.7) and (6.8), which allow the coefficients in the two sectors to differ, describe the USM and match firm sector salary models respectively. The Z variables in equations (6.7) and (6.8), following Lee (1978), Schwochau (1987) and Meng (1990), are defined as follows:

$$Z_{\mathrm{u}} = -f(U) / F(U) \tag{6.9}$$
$$Z_{\mathrm{m}} = f(U) / 1 - F(U) \tag{6.10}$$

where $f(U)$ is the density function of the standard normal variable and $F(U)$ is the cumulative distribution function of the standard normal variable. A probit estimate of USM/match firm membership is first used to derive functions (6.9) and (6.10) and then the estimated values of the Zs are inserted into equations (6.7) and (6.8) as correction factors for any selectivity bias.[4]

The predicted values of an individual's wage derived from equations (6.7) and (6.8) can then be viewed as the market wage for that individual given his/her human capital attributes, firm type and other job/firm characteristics. These predicted values (or rather, their antilogs since the Ws are the natural log of managers salaries) can then be subtracted from the individual's actual salary to obtain an estimate of whether the individual is relatively underpaid ($w-\hat{w} < 0$) or overpaid ($w-\hat{w} > 0$) given his/her market wage (or opportunity cost).

It is to be expected that the job satisfaction of relatively underpaid (overpaid) managers will be lower (higher) than that of similar individuals, occupying similar posts in similar firms but who are more (less) highly paid. Hence, this new variable, which measures the deviation from the estimated market wage, $(w-\hat{w})$, is assumed to be positively related to satisfaction levels. It can be inserted into the separately estimated satisfaction equations as follows:

$$SAT_{\mathrm{u}} = \alpha + \sum_{i=1}^{i} \beta_i D_i + \sum_{j=i+1}^{j} \beta_j S_j + \beta_{j+1}(w-\hat{w}) + e \tag{6.11}$$

$$SAT_{\mathrm{m}} = \alpha + \sum_{i=1}^{i} \beta_i D_i + \sum_{j=i+1}^{j} \beta_j S_j + \beta_{j+1}(w-\hat{w}) + e \tag{6.12}$$

Managers' job satisfaction: univariate results

Earlier in Tables 6.2 and 6.4 we reported managers satisfaction levels in their previous and current jobs, respectively. This section relates, via correlation coefficients, satisfaction to organizational factors, boss ratings, personal characteristics, job history, and the other job/firm factors discussed earlier. The analysis contained in Tables 6.6 to 6.8 is a preliminary univariate analysis to set the scene for our multivariate model to be discussed in the following subsection.

The data on the characteristics of the organization are derived from questions to owners of both USM and match firms who were given eight, one-sentence, descriptions of their organization. For each description there were five optional responses ranging from 'very much like this' to 'not at all like this'. These responses were then given a score ranging from unity for 'very much like this' to five for 'not at all like this'. High scores therefore indicate disagreement with the statement.

The one-sentence descriptions of the organization are shown as single-word descriptions in Table 6.6. This shows the arithmetic mean scores, with standard deviations in parenthesis for USM, match and all firms. It can be

Table 6.6 Organizational characteristics mean scores and standard deviations

Variable	All	Match	USM
Market orientated	1.86	1.94	1.78
	(1.24)	(1.39)	(1.09)
Crisis orientated	3.52	3.25*	3.78
	(1.28)	(1.36)	(1.16)
Cost orientated	1.88	1.88	1.88
	(1.19)	(1.27)	(1.13)
People orientated	1.89	1.96	1.82
	(0.97)	(0.92)	(1.01)
Innovation orientated	2.27	2.33	2.20
	(1.37)	(1.45)	(1.29)
Security orientated	2.27	2.29	2.24
	(1.29)	(1.30)	(1.28)
Rules orientated	3.64	3.48	3.80
	(1.33)	(1.40)	(1.26)
Leader orientated	2.18	1.94**	2.41
	(1.23)	(1.06)	(1.35)

Notes: * Significant at 10% 2-tail
** Significant at 5%

seen from the *All* column that owners, in general, were most likely to agree that their firms were *market* orientated, *cost* orientated and *people* orientated. Not surprisingly they were least likely to agree that their firm was *crisis* orientated or *rules* orientated.

Clearly a different perception of organizational characteristics would have been obtained by asking identical questions of managers as well as owners, but this was not done. The scores in Table 6.6 are therefore the only data on the characteristics of the USM and match firms as organizations. It shows that for two of the eight organizational characteristics there are significant differences between USM and match firms. USM firm owners are less likely to agree that their firm is either *crisis* orientated or *leader* orientated than match owners. For all other descriptions there appears to be no significant difference between the responses of the two groups of owners.

All managers were asked about their relationship with their boss, on the grounds that this could be a key, non-salary related item influencing current job satisfaction. A total of twenty-one dimensions for assessing this relationship were provided. Each manager was then asked to rate their boss on a five-point scale ranging from 'very good' to 'very poor'. An arithmetic mean score was then computed where a response of 'very good' was given a score of five and a response of 'very poor' a score of one. The twenty-one dimensions were then collapsed into six groups, the mean scores for which are shown in Table 6.7.

Table 6.7 Boss rating

Variable	All	Match	USM
Feedback	3.67	3.54	3.80
	(0.91)	(0.90)	(0.91)
Support	4.08	4.17	4.00
	(0.90)	(0.86)	(0.94)
Orientation	3.46	3.38	3.55
	(0.89)	(0.84)	(0.94)
Innovation	4.09	4.04	4.14
	(0.76)	(0.68)	(0.84)
Performance	4.13	4.06	4.20
	(0.72)	(0.70)	(0.74)
Communication	3.81	3.79	3.84
	(0.78)	(0.68)	(0.87)
Average rating	3.88	3.83	3.92
	(0.62)	(0.56)	(0.68)

The table shows that while the USM bosses score more highly than the Match bosses in six out of the seven dimensions the differences between the two groups are not significant in any single dimension.

Table 6.8 is in two parts. The upper half presents the simple correlation coefficient for organizational characteristics and job satisfaction. It shows in the final row that, for managers as a whole, there was a highly significantly positive correlation between the levels of job satisfaction of managers and those organizations classified by their owners as *innovation* orientated – defined as 'dominated by its need to develop new items and products'.

Much more surprisingly we find that those organizations classified by their owners as *crisis* orientated and those classified as *rules* orientated also appeared to have managers with high levels of job satisfaction. As will be shown later this can be partly explained by differences between the managers in the USM and match groups.

The lower section of Table 6.8 shows the zero-order correlation coefficients between each of the dimensions of boss ratings and job satisfaction. It shows, not surprisingly, that there is a strong positive association between the managers' job satisfaction score and the esteem in which the boss is held. The high positive correlations between each of the boss ratings dimensions suggest that bosses who score highly on one dimension also score highly on others.

In summary, therefore, our univariate results show that there is some association between the characteristics of an organization and the job satisfaction expressed by managers. The extent to which this is related to, or independent of, remuneration and the operations of the managerial labour market more generally can only be determined through multivariate analyses.

Managers' job satisfaction: multivariate results

Table 6.9 presents the satisfaction model results described in equations (6.11) and (6.12). As with the salary models presented earlier in Table 6.5, because of the small sample sizes and collinearity between the explanatory variables, only the results of a reduced form model are shown. Using the standard F-test methodology, once the variables shown in the table had been entered into the equation, none of the excluded variables, either individually or as a group, were significant at 10 per cent confidence levels. Again, as in Table 6.5, a pooled estimate is provided along with the un-restricted estimates of the USM and match groups and the coefficient differences derived from interaction tests and their individual t-values. The F-value at the bottom of the difference column indicates the overall significance of the coefficient differences and as explained earlier is formally equivalent to a Chow test.

Table 6.8 Correlation coefficients

Section A: Organizational characteristics

	Market	Crisis	Cost	People	Innovation	Security	Rules	Leader
Market	–							
Crisis	0.15	–						
Cost	0.01	-0.02	–					
People	0.15	-0.10	0.18	–				
Innovation	0.32	0.17	0.07	0.08	–			
Security	0.30	0.14	0.05	0.08	0.43	–		
Rules	-0.09	0.18	0.16	0.20	0.08	0.07	–	
Leader	0.23	0.18	-0.06	-0.03	0.24	0.36	0.06	–
Satisfaction	0.09	0.24	0.13	-0.05	0.38	0.16	0.21	0.08

Section B: Boss rating

	Feedback	Support	Orientation	Innovation	Performance	Communication	Average
Feedback	–						
Support	0.47	–					
Orientation	0.65	0.54	–				
Innovation	0.39	0.35	0.47	–			
Performance	0.40	0.36	0.54	0.53	–		
Communication	0.56	0.50	0.51	0.38	0.58	–	
Average	0.78	0.72	0.83	0.67	0.73	0.77	–
Satisfaction	0.32	0.05	0.39	0.26	0.24	0.32	0.35

Table 6.9 shows that 36 per cent of the variation in managers job satisfaction levels (in terms of adjusted R^2) can be explained in terms of the ten included variables.

All the variables in Table 6.9 have been defined in previous tables and can also be found in Appendix 6.1. The variable $(w-\hat{w})$, as expected, shows that those managers that are relatively overpaid (underpaid) are more satisfied (dissatisfied). Hence there is a positive, but insignificant, coefficient on $(w-\hat{w})$. The *Qual* variable shows that managers with degrees or professional qualifications are less satisfied in their current job than those with lower educational qualifications. This finding is, however, not statistically significant at the 10 per cent level. The *Promote* variable shows, again not surprisingly, those managers that expect to be promoted within the next two years are more satisfied but again not significantly so.

The *Man* variable shows those current managers who moved from a previous managerial post to their current post (either internally within the firm or externally) are currently more satisfied than those moving to a managerial post for the first time. This is clearly the case for USM managers, whereas for match managers there is no clear impact of prior managerial experience upon current job satisfaction.

The *FS* variable, it will be recalled from Figure 6.1, may be considered to be a workload or responsibility measure (log firm size/status). In the current equation it suggests that *FS* is positively related to job satisfaction. For USM managers there is, however, a weak negative relationship, compared with a significantly positive relationship for match managers.

The *Sex* variable suggests that for both USM and match managers, females are likely to indicate higher levels of job satisfaction than male managers, contrasting with the observations of Nicholson and West (1988, p. 206) who say '. . . women see themselves as discriminated against by organisational career policies'.

Of the remaining five variables, two relate to the characteristics of the organization (as perceived by the owner) and three relate to how the manager perceives either his or her boss. The two organization related variables included are *Rules organization* and *Innovative organization*. The former is defined as 'dominated by its concern with administration through policies and procedures'. It will be recalled that owners had five options in responding to this ranging from, at one extreme 'very much like this' to 'not at all like this'.

Perhaps somewhat surprisingly it can be seen from Table 6.9 that managers, particularly those in USM companies, would appear to be more satisfied in those types defined by their owners as being *Rules organizations*. Rather less surprisingly managers also have higher levels of job satisfaction in those firms which owners regard as *Innovative organization*,

Table 6.9 Satisfaction model results

Variable name	All	USM	Match	Difference
$(w-\hat{w})$	0.0091	0.0048	0.0136	− 0.0088
	(1.03)	(0.42)	(0.70)	(0.39)
Qual	− 0.2486	− 0.3639	− 0.3900	0.0261
	(1.29)	(1.25)	(1.38)	(0.06)
Promote	0.2642	0.2714	0.7791	− 0.5077
	(1.02)	(0.78)	(1.81)	(0.91)
Man	0.3600	0.6361	− 0.0373	0.6734
	(1.61)	(1.88)	(0.13)	(1.49)
FS	0.0756	− 0.1179	0.3084	− 0.4263
	(1.08)	(1.22)	(2.49)	(2.69)
Sex	− 0.5402	− 0.4664	− 0.6482	0.1819
	(2.03)	(1.11)	(1.78)	(0.33)
Rules organization	0.1267	− 0.0085	0.2164	− 0.2249
	(1.77)	(0.07)	(2.20)	(1.50)
Goal orientated boss	0.4592	0.5946	0.3505	0.2441
	(3.40)	(3.17)	(1.75)	(0.89)
Innovative organization	0.2568	0.2811	0.3278	− 0.0467
	(3.53)	(2.42)	(3.40)	(0.31)
Communicative boss	0.3359	0.3246	0.2917	0.0329
	(2.28)	(1.73)	(1.11)	(0.01)
Supportive boss	− 0.2868	− 0.5418	− 0.0492	− 0.4927
	(2.14)	(2.79)	(0.26)	(1.82)
Constant	5.3833	7.2960	3.8411	3.4549
	(8.68)	(7.56)	(4.49)	(2.68)
$\bar{R}^2$	36%	29%	42%	
F	5.98	2.81	4.06	1.43
	11,85	11,37	11,36	12,73

Note: Figures in parenthesis are 't' statistics.

defined as 'dominated by its need to develop new items and products'. For both USM and match managers this appears to be an organizational type clearly yielding significantly positive levels of job satisfaction.

The three included variables relating to the managers boss are *goal orientated*, *communicative* and *supportive*.

The *goal orientated* variable focuses upon the extent to which the manager feels his/her boss spends time helping, planning out work and anticipating future difficulties with subordinates. This has a significant coefficient for all cases and appears of particular importance in explaining job satisfaction among USM managers.

The *communicative* variable combines the extent to which subordinates perceive bosses communicate by informing their subordinates, how well they run meetings, listen and how well they respond to criticism. For all managers the coefficient is significant, although it is not in the separate equations for USM and match managers.

Finally the *supportive* variable is also included, but with a negative sign. This variable is designed to capture the extent to which the boss is viewed by subordinates as a 'nice person'. Specifically it asks about the extent to which he/she is sympathetic and approachable, friendly and supportive to subordinates. The implication of the negative sign is that these qualities are not appreciated by subordinates, probably on the grounds that they are a substitute for other competence-related qualities. It is particularly interesting to note that it is the USM managers where the coefficient is significantly negative, suggesting that the 'niceness' of the boss is not a valued attribute among this group of managers.

Overall the differences between the USM and match models are *FS* (which is a much more important influence upon satisfaction for the match firm managers than for the USM managers), *supportive* (which has a significantly negative impact upon satisfaction only for the USM managers) and Constant (which indicates that even after allowing for the other factors USM managers are more satisfied in their current job). Previously having been a manager, *Man*, is more important for USM managers satisfaction but not for the match group. Similarly, *rules* is positively and statistically significantly associated with satisfaction only for the match group and the difference is nearly significant.

As with the wage model, we can explain significantly more of the variance in match managers satisfaction than we can in respect of the USM group.

ANTICIPATED FIRM MOVES

This section attempts to provide an explanation of whether or not a manager expects to move jobs over the next two years. In asking this question we recognize that a stated intention to move does not, by any means, always result in an actual move over that time. Nicholson and West (1988, p. 91) for example show 'only 28 per cent of managers who expected promotion achieved it, and the proportion is identical for employer change'. Their study was over a one-year period.

Despite these reservations, expected future job changes have been used in several studies. For example Cannings and Montmarquette (1991) ask managers in a large Canadian company for their subjective view of whether or not they were likely to be promoted in the next three years. Cannings (1991) also examines this issue by asking respondents about the pay increase which they would expect to receive to move to another firm with similar promotion prospects.

Ultimately the labour market adjusts through the actual movement of individuals from one firm to another rather than statements of prospective movement. This means that while expressed levels of job satisfaction do provide, among other things, an indicator of likely movement (Freeman 1978) our interest in the managerial labour market means that it is job moves that are our prime interest. Ideally we would like data on actual job moves but, in the absence of such information, expected job change data are used.

Table 6.10 shows that of the ninety-seven managers, some 66 per cent expect to be in the same post in the same firm in two years time. A further fifteen managers expect to be promoted within the firm while the remaining eighteen individuals expect to have moved firms within the next two years. While nine managers in both the USM and Match groups expect to move firms, twice as many USM managers (ten individuals) expect to be promoted internally than is the case for the match group (five individuals). This pattern is to be expected since the USM firms, being rapidly growing organizations which operate an internal labour market (ILM), are likely to create a significantly larger number of new managerial posts than are the match firms.

Table 6.10 Expectations in two years

	All	Match	USM
In same job	64 (66.0%)	34 (70.8%)	30 (61.2%)
Promote internal	15 (15.5%)	5 (10.4%)	10 (20.4%)
Move firms	18 (18.6%)	9 (18.8%)	9 (18.4%)
Total	97 (100.0%)	48 (100.0%)	49 (100.0%)

Modelling anticipated job moves

The decision by a manager to move or to stay in his/her present job is modelled as a discrete decision in which *stay* is given a zero value and *move* is given a value of unity.

(Stay/Move)

$$(0/1)u = \alpha + \sum_{i=1}^{i}\beta_i D_i + \sum_{j=i+1}^{j}\beta_j i_j S + \beta_{j+1}(w-\hat{w}) + \beta_{j+2}(Sat-\hat{Sat}) + e \quad (6.13)$$

$$(0/1)m = \alpha + \sum_{i=1}^{i}\beta_i D_i + \sum_{j=i+1}^{j}\beta_j S_j + \beta_{j+1}(w-\hat{w}) + \beta_{j+2}(Sat-\hat{Sat}) + e \quad (6.14)$$

Equations (6.13) and (6.14) model the decision for the USM and match managers respectively. After including *promote* in the model (those that expect to be promoted internally and therefore don't expect to move), it, in effect, examines the different probabilities of moving for those who do not expect to be promoted internally. Given this, both $(Sat-\hat{Sat})$ and $(w-\hat{w})$ are expected to be negatively related to moving firms, i.e. a manager who is either or both relatively higher paid or highly satisfied is less likely to move even though he/she does not expect to be promoted internally.

The same type of reduced form model is used as before, though in this case it is a Logit model where the dependent variable is set to unity if the individual expects to move firms within the next two years and to zero otherwise.

The results are shown in Table 6.11. It shows that highly qualified managers are significantly more likely to suggest they will leave if they do not expect to be promoted (and the relationship is slightly stronger for the USM group). The male USM managers who are not expecting to be promoted are more likely to state they will leave (positive coefficient) while the reverse is the case for the match group (negative coefficient) – though the difference in the coefficients is below conventional significance levels. The larger the firm and/or the higher the managerial status, the less likely it is that a manager will be stating an expectation of leaving. However, this is only true for the match group – for the USM managers *FS* is not related to anticipated firm moves.

With both $(Sat-\hat{Sat})$ and $(w-\hat{w})$ for USM managers the coefficients are in the expected direction (negative) and both significant or nearly so. For the match group, however, both coefficients are positive – though only the $(Sat-\hat{Sat})$ coefficient is significant. The difference between the two groups is also significant for the $(Sat-\hat{Sat})$ variable. It suggests the presence of relatively unsatisfied managers not intending to move and relatively satisfied managers expecting to move from match firms (even after allowing for deviations from expected market salary levels).

The role of tenure follows an inverted U pattern for both groups – though it is a slightly stronger relationship with the USM managers. Thus those individuals with short and long periods of tenure are the least likely to move, whereas those in the mid-range are most likely to indicate a move.

Table 6.11 Probability of moving firms model

Variable	All	USM	Match	Difference
$(Sat–\hat{Sat})$	– 0.0247	– 0.8101	0.6413	1.4513
	(0.13)	(1.70)	(1.68)	(2.38)
$(w–\hat{w})$	– 0.0095	– 0.0346	0.0037	– 0.0382
	(0.50)	(1.20)	(0.12)	(0.92)
Qual	0.6476	1.1856	0.9521	0.2334
	(2.04)	(1.83)	(1.58)	(0.26)
Sex	– 0.1102	0.4380	– 0.3324	0.7704
	(0.28)	(0.49)	(0.56)	(0.72)
FS	– 0.1156	0.0028	– 0.6786	0.6814
	(0.96)	(0.01)	(1.69)	(1.46)
Tenure	0.2733	0.9217	0.3635	0.7704
	(1.66)	(1.58)	(1.34)	(0.72)
$Tenure^2$	– 0.0200	– 0.0898	– 0.0253	0.5582
	(1.41)	(1.39)	(1.15)	(0.87)
Man	– 0.4464	– 0.5426	– 0.8042	0.2615
	(1.31)	(0.77)	(1.25)	(0.27)
Promote	– 4.2714	– 4.3725	– 4.5993	0.2268
	(0.35)	(0.42)	(0.32)	(0.01)
Constant	4.2714	2.2790	5.6385	– 3.3595
	(8.49)	(1.45)	(4.85)	(1.72)

Note: Figures in parenthesis are 't' statistics.

Those individuals previously holding managerial posts are less likely to move – though the relationship is slightly stronger for the match than for the USM group.

The significant difference in the constants suggests that USM managers that are not expected to be promoted within the next two years are less likely to move firms.

CONCLUDING REMARKS

The central question with which this chapter is concerned is whether there are real differences between managers currently employed in USM and match firms. In passing, we also point to those respects in which managers in small firms appear to differ from their large-firm counterparts.

To achieve the main objective the chapter has examined three key dimensions of the labour market for small-firm managers. It examined the salary/remuneration of the group, their job satisfaction and their self-assessed likelihood of moving to another job during the next two years.

Prior to undertaking this multivariate analysis, some more general findings were presented. We showed that, while the average age of USM and match managers was almost identical, there did appear to be several significant differences within each of the groups.

In examining their prior job history it appears that those managers currently employed in USM firms, and who were externally recruited, were more likely to have switched sectors than managers currently employed in match firms. It also appears that USM managers are more likely to have had prior employment in a large firm than current USM managers.

There also appears to be evidence to suggest that managers currently employed in USM firms are better qualified than those in match firms. Interestingly the USM managers also appear to be more satisfied in their current job than match managers. This finding is particularly noteworthy given the fact that in their prior jobs there appears to be no difference whatsoever in the satisfaction levels expressed by both groups of managers.

We have already pointed to the fact that there is virtually no difference in age between managers in USM firms and in match firms. A second important, yet negative, finding is that formal training, either in the current or prior jobs, does not appear to differ between USM and match managers. Nevertheless, as we saw, there are major differences in the salaries paid to the two groups of managers. It therefore appears that formal training within the firm is not related to managerial salaries in the small-firm sector.

In our multivariate examination of remuneration for USM and match managers we found that on average the match manager was paid approximately £11,500 per year less than the USM manager. Our central finding, however, is that there is no evidence that the estimating equations for the two groups differ significantly. In other words an identical individual with an identical career history and qualifications working in the same locational sector would expect to get paid the same salary whether they worked for a USM or for a match company (provided, of course, that the firms were of similar size). It suggests therefore that the segmentation of the managerial labour market is more related to factors such as firm size and the different job history and personal qualities of individuals rather than whether or not a firm is quoted on the Unlisted Securities Market. In this sense it constitutes a further justification for the use of the USM/match sampling frame.

In our examination of current job satisfaction the univariate analysis showed that managers currently employed in USM firms are more satisfied than those currently in match firms, but these differences were not apparent in the prior jobs of both groups of managers. The multivariate examination of factors influencing these levels of job satisfaction indicate the importance of firm size and responsibility levels, the relationship between the manager and his/her boss and the culture of the organization. It is clear that, in general, USM managers have a higher regard for their boss than is the case for match managers. Indeed it may not be unduly stretching our findings to suggest that the USM managers place a particularly low rating on the 'niceness' of their boss, with their focus being much more heavily upon the ability of their boss to do an effective job for the organization.

A second finding is that organizational culture (albeit defined by the owners) can also be important in determining levels of job satisfaction of managers. The particular significance here is that managers appear to enjoy working in those firms which the owner regards as being highly innovative.

Anticipated job moves could be considered to be another measure of job satisfaction. In our formal examination of whether or not managers expected to move we found a negative relationship with satisfaction levels for USM firms and a positive relationship for match firms. This suggests that for the match group there are a number of (relatively) dissatisfied managers who are not expecting to move and a number of satisfied managers who are expecting to move. We also found an inverted U-shaped relationship between tenure and anticipated job moves, suggesting that those individuals least likely to move were those who had either recently joined the firm or those who had been there for many years.

Overall these findings suggest that individuals who are better qualified and who seek better paid work do gravitate towards USM companies. Such individuals are willing to switch sectors and appear to place much greater emphasis upon the ability of their boss to undertake his/her work in an innovative manner than is the case for match managers.

With the exception of data provided by owners on the characteristics of the organization, this chapter has focused exclusively upon the responses of managers. To obtain a complete picture of the managerial labour market in small firms requires the perspective provided by owners. It is to that group that we now turn.

NOTES

1   In addition, interaction tests were undertaken for determining whether any of the individual coefficients were statistically significantly different for the two groups.
2   Several other model specifications containing some or all of the additional variables listed in the appendix were tried. However, using the standard F-test methodology, none of these alternative models were as efficient as the model presented in this chapter. In addition, all regression results presented are after White's (1980) adjustments for an unknown form of heteroscedasticity.
3   Ramsey's (1969) RESET procedure for detecting an unknown form functional misspecification was undertaken for each of the estimated models presented.

The resulting test statistics indicated, however, that the null hypothesis of no misspecification could not be rejected at 5 per cent confidence levels.

4   Though the estimated Probit function was itself highly significant ($p < 0.01$), the inclusion of the estimated scores (Z_i s) into the wage model equations (6.7) and (6.8) did not materially alter either the overall significance levels of the models or the magnitudes of any of the individual coefficients. In neither equation were the estimated coefficients on the Z_i s individually significant and, hence, though some selectivity bias is present, we do not consider it necessary to adjust our previous wage model results.

Appendix 6.1: Variables extracted from interview data

1. Current salary (*salary*)
2. Age of manager (*age*)
3. Years of managerial experience (*exp*)
4. Period in current post (*tenure*)
5. A dummy variable coded 1 if the manager had no formal educational qualifications beyond O levels/CSEs and 0 otherwise (*qual0*)
6. A dummy variable coded 1 if the manager's highest formal qualification was a degree or higher degree and 0 otherwise (*qual1*)
7. A dummy variable coded 1 if the manager's highest formal qualification was of a post-graduate professional nature and 0 otherwise (*qual2*)
8. A dummy variable coded 1 if the manager had some form of formal educational qualification but was not any of the above and 0 otherwise (*qual3*)
9. A dummy variable coded 1 if the manager was male and 0 otherwise (*sex*)
10. A dummy variable coded 1 if the manager had received a significant amount of training since being appointed to his/her current job (*train*)
11. The number of levels from the top of the firm that the manager's current job occupied (*status*)
12. Current firm size in terms of employment (*fsize*)
13. Employment growth in the previous two years (*psize*)
14. The expected growth in sales turnover in the coming year (*sales*)
15. The number of establishments/sites in the UK (*sites*)
16. A dummy variable coded 1 if the manager received no fringe benefits in addition to a fixed salary and 0 otherwise (*none*)
17. A dummy variable coded 1 if the manager had exclusive use of a company car and 0 otherwise (*car*)
18. A dummy variable coded 1 if the manager was a member of a share-based profit sharing scheme approved under the Finance Acts or an executive share option scheme and 0 otherwise (*ps*)

19   A dummy variable coded 1 if the manager had the benefit of a private and non-contributory health care/insurance scheme and 0 otherwise (*ph*)

20   A dummy variable coded 1 if the manager received any other fringe benefits not included in the above (primarily private pension plans, profit-related pay and other forms of annual cash bonus) and 0 otherwise (*other*)

21   A dummy variable coded 1 if the manager's current post was primarily of an accounting/finance nature and 0 otherwise (*func*)

22   A series of five dummy variables coded 1 if the firm operated within the financial services (*ind1*), other non-manual professional services (*ind2*), other service, printing and retail (*ind3*), electronics and computing (*ind4*) and other manufacturing (*ind5*) sectors and 0 otherwise

23   A dummy variable coded 1 if the firm was located in the London and south-east area and 0 otherwise (*location*)

24   Level of satisfaction experienced in current job, ranging from 0 to 10 (*sat*)

25   A dummy variable coded 1 if the manager anticipated moving to another firm within the next 2 years and 0 otherwise (*move*)

26   A dummy variable coded 1 if the manager anticipated being promoted within the next 2 years and 0 otherwise (*promote*)

27   A dummy variable coded 1 if the manager's previous post was also a managerial post and 0 otherwise (*man*)

28   A dummy variable coded 1 if the manager's previous job was with the same firm and 0 otherwise (*int*)

29   A dummy variable coded 1 if the manager previously worked for a firm operating in the same industrial sector as his/her current firm and 0 otherwise (*sector*)

30   A dummy variable coded 1 if the manager was previously employed in a firm with more than 500 employees and 0 otherwise (*big*)

31   A dummy variable coded 1 if the manager received training in his/her previous post and 0 otherwise (*pt*)

32   The period in years since the manager's current firm became incorporated (*firmage*)

33   A total of eight individual organizational characteristics as perceived by the firm's current owners, each dimension coded from 1 to 5. See text for details

34   A total of twenty-one boss ratings, as perceived by the manager, each dimension coded 1 to 5. See text for details

In addition to the above, the following new variables were created and used in the empirical analysis:

(a) *qual* = a dummy variable coded 1 if *qual1* or *qual2* = 1 and 0 otherwise
(b) *fs* = ln (*fsize*)/*status*
(c) *fb* = a dummy variable coded 1 if *ps* and *BUPA* and *car* = 1 and 0 otherwise
(d) *age2* = *age* squared
(e) *tenure2* = *tenure* squared
(f) *exp2* = *exp* squared.

7 Owners and firm size

INTRODUCTION

Chapters 2 and 3 reviewed several approaches to understanding the behaviour of firms. In this chapter, we report the results of our attempt to empirically apply these approaches to the sample of firms described in Chapter 5 by analysing the views of small business owners. In this sense it provides a contrast to Chapter 6 where the data provided came almost exclusively from managers.

A central theme of this text is that a key component in the labour market for both owners and managers is the performance of firms. In the larger-firm sector if the market for 'corporate control' is efficient then poorly performing owners/managers will be replaced. Control is exercised by external shareholders, creditors (in particular, the banking institutions) or other external parties in the form of takeover bids.

While mechanisms for corporate control exist in small and medium-sized firms, they are less effective than for large firms. The closely held nature of small firms, and their general lack of visibility, means they can be X-inefficient without attracting the attention of outsiders because the costs of any 'shirking' are borne solely by the owner-manager(s).

Ultimately, of course managerial and/or ownership change occurs in poorly performing small firms through the closure of the firm. Change also occurs in growing firms via the employment of new managers, so as to facilitate further growth. Thus firm performance, both successful and unsuccessful, is linked to managerial/owner labour markets.

In this chapter the index of performance we consider is the size of the organization. Chapter 4 showed labour market segmentation to be characteristic of large organizations. Small and large firms offer very different career structures and demand very different skills from their management. The roles of owners are also likely to be substantially different for the two 'sizes' of firm. Thus to understand the workings of the labour markets for owner/managers there is a clear need to understand some of the key determinants of firm size. While the economics literature on the performance of smaller firms is well established (see Storey *et al.* 1987), the strategy and organizational literature appears to be less well developed.

As Chapter 5 shows the firms listed on the USM are very much larger than the match firms, in terms of employment, for a given age and can therefore be classified as 'good performers'. However, even between and within each of these two groupings the influences upon firm size is also examined. These influences cover the four broad headings of founding strategy, management expertise and recruitment, team building and recruitment, and organizational characteristics. Each topic is considered independently and related to current firm size. Finally a synthesis of these issues is presented.

OWNER MOTIVATIONS AND CHARACTERISTICS

This section relates current firm size to the founding strategy and personal characteristics of the owner.

Owner motivations

There are a wide variety of factors which influence an individual to establish a business. As shown in Chapter 4, these motivating factors can be crudely categorized as being either positive or negative (Curran 1986). A negative motivation is defined as one where the individual felt pushed by external pressures into starting a business: an obvious example being unemployment. In contrast, positive motivations are those where the owner felt attracted into firm ownership by, for example, the perception of a market opportunity or the wish to be independent. It is hypothesized that owners starting a business for positive reasons would be expected to perform better than those established for negative reasons.

To test this, owners were asked to detail in their own words how their firms had come into existence. From these verbatim statements each response was coded and then subsequently classified as being a positive, negative or neutral motivation factor: positive factors being coded as +1, negative factors as −1, and neutral factors as 0.

Two approaches to analysing this variable were tried. First a motivation score was calculated for each respondent, ranging from a possible +4 for owners having four separate motivations, all of which were positive, to a possible −4 for owners having identified four separate motivations, all of which were negative.

Second, all positive total scores were recoded to +1 and negative total scores to −1. Hence a variable ranging from +1 to −1 was created. The results of the analysis showed that the two forms of the variable produced similar results and, given that the second form is easier to understand and present, it forms the basis of the following analysis.

Table 7.1 Motivations for firm creation

	USM		Match		All		Chi-square	Significance
	No.	%	No.	%	No.	%		
Positive	30	56	29	58	59	56		
Neutral	14	26	8	16	22	21	1.8936	0.3880
Negative	10	19	13	26	23	22		

Table 7.1 analyses the positive, negative and neutral motivations for starting up a firm, distinguishing between USM and match firms. For both groups positive factors were the overriding motivating force, with 56 per cent and 58 per cent of USM and match firm owners respectively having positive total motivation scores, there being no significant difference between the two groups of firms in this respect.

Motivation score is also unrelated to size, defined as total employment. This is the case for the sample as a whole and for both the USM and the match firms. Given the general insignificance of the results, they are not reported here in detail.

The absence of a relationship may reflect the research method employed, since the questions are asked of founders after many years of presumably relatively successful performance (all firms in the sample are 'successful' in terms of having survived for a number of years). It may also reflect the crude 'scoring' system used. Nevertheless the absence of any clear association is somewhat surprising.

Entrepreneurial characteristics

Chapter 4 pointed out that many empirical studies have demonstrated that the performance of new and small firms are related to the personal characteristics of the owner (Kalleberg and Leicht 1991, Bates 1990). These characteristics may broadly be categorized as the human capital which the individual(s) bring to the business. It was hypothesized that the greater the stock of human capital, the better will be the performance of the firm.

Six components of human capital are now specified. These are age, gender, educational qualifications, other business interests in addition to that of the sampled firm, employment status prior to setting the business up and whether or not the firm was operated on a part-time basis at any time.

It is hypothesized that firm performance will be positively related to other business interests, education qualifications and part-time business experience, on the grounds that each demonstrate either experience or formal qualifications which are likely to be associated with higher performance. Empirical support for this is provided by Bates (1991) who shows that founders with degrees are less likely to fail in business, while prior self-employment experience is shown to be beneficial by Kalleberg and Leicht.

The impact on firms of performance, gender and age in prior studies has been shown to be indeterminate, but for the present analysis it is assumed that an unemployed individual is less likely to form a fast-growth business since unemployment is disproportionately concentrated among socially disadvantaged groups which combine low levels of wealth, limited job experience and educational attainment.

Table 7.2 presents summary statistics for each variable. The age and gender profiles show little difference between USM and match firms. More than 94 per cent of founders were male for both groups and their average age was approximately 34 years when the business started. Similarly, the two groups of founders currently have approximately the same number of outside business interests. Founders of USM firms with outside interests owned on average 4.1 other businesses, while the match founders averaged 3.2. Both groups of founders were more likely to own other businesses than was the case in our earlier work (Storey *et al.* 1987).

There are, however, several aspects in which the groups differ. In terms of formal educational and/or professional qualifications, owners were asked to give details of the highest qualification gained. Owners of USM firms were less likely to have obtained only degree level qualifications than match firm owners, although USM owners are slightly more likely to have obtained post-graduate and/or professional qualifications. In addition, while USM owners have more pre-degree qualifications than match owners, they also are more likely to have no formal qualifications at all. Overall match firm owners appear to be more highly qualified than USM owners.

Table 7.2 shows a difference in the employment status of USM and match founders prior to start-up. Nearly a quarter of match firm owners were unemployed prior to start up, compared with less than 10 per cent of USM owners. It suggests match firm owners may have been more likely to have 'negative' reasons for starting up a firm than USM owners. In this sense it contrasts with our earlier more general findings on motivation which suggested no difference between the two groups according to overall motivations at start up. Marlow and Storey (1992) reconcile these findings by showing that a number of founders who were unemployed or likely to be unemployed, did not regard themselves as being 'pushed' into starting a

Table 7.2 Founder characteristics and firm type: summary statistics for the characteristics of owners

	USM		Match		All		Chi-square	Significance
	No.	%	No.	%	No.	%		
Gender								
Male	53	98	47	94	100	96	0.35	0.56
Female	1	2	3	6	4	4		
Qualifications								
None	19	35	15	30	34	33		
Pre-degree	13	24	5	10	18	17	8.89	0.03
Degree	12	22	24	48	36	35		
Post-grad and professional	10	19	6	12	16	15		
Other business interests								
Yes	21	39	19	38	40	38	0.00	1.00
No	33	61	31	62	64	61		
Unemployed								
Yes	5	9	12	24	17	16	3.12	0.08
No	49	91	38	76	87	83		
Part-time business								
Yes	4	7	12	24	16	15	4.29	0.04
No	50	93	38	76	88	84		

	Mean	Median	Std dev.	N
Age of owner				
USM	33.94	35.00	8.78	53
Match	33.88	32.00	8.03	49
All	33.91	33.00	8.39	102

business, since they intended to start the business in any case. Conversely others saw themselves as being 'pushed' even though they were not unemployed.

A higher proportion of match firms were run as a part-time business before becoming full time, than was the case for USM firms. It suggests match firm owners were less likely to risk setting up immediately as a full-time concern, preferring to 'test the water' first. Conversely, these results may suggest that USM owners are either more 'certain' of success and/or more 'risk-taking' than their match counterparts.

Overall, while the composition of the two groups of founders are similar in respect of gender, age and outside business interests, they differ in terms of educational qualifications, employment status and setting up the business as a part-time concern prior to commencing on a full-time basis.

Moving on to consider if personal characteristics of founders are related to current firm size in terms of employment, Table 7.3 presents only those

Table 7.3 Founder characteristics and current firm size

Size		*Mean*	*Std dev.*	*N*	*t-statistics*
Other business interests					
All	Yes	238.92	317.78	39	− 1.74*
	No	146.44	221.07	64	
USM	Yes	395.90	371.45	20	− 1.58
	No	257.94	262.78	33	
Match	Yes	73.68	106.55	19	− 2.30**
	No	27.74	27.18	31	
Unemployed					
All	Yes	57.88	102.02	17	− 2.15**
	No	205.88	279.63	86	
USM	Yes	138.80	163.46	5	− 1.30
	No	327.83	319.56	48	
Match	Yes	24.17	34.73	12	− 1.17
	No	51.84	79.03	38	
Part-time business					
All	Yes	69.81	126.44	16	1.86*
	No	201.99	278.03	87	
USM	Yes	195.25	221.98	4	0.76
	No	319.37	318.31	49	
Match	Yes	28.00	27.09	12	0.95
	No	50.63	80.31	38	

Notes: * Significant at 10%
      ** Significant at 5%

relationships where a statistically significant relationship was found. From the table it can be seen that match firms whose owners currently had other business interests were significantly larger than those firms whose owners had no other business interests. More interestingly, firms whose founders were employed prior to start-up are now significantly larger than those whose owners were unemployed prior to start up. While this finding was significant for the full sample, it was insignificant for the individual samples of USM and match firms. Finally, firms which were initially operated on a part-time basis were significantly smaller than those which had always operated on a full-time basis. Again this is true for the sample as a whole, but not for the individual groups.

Univariate analysis in these circumstances is unsatisfactory since current firm size is clearly related to more than a single variable. Table 7.4 therefore reports the regression results relating firm performance to entre-preneurial and firm characteristic variables. The form of each of the variables used are described in Appendix 7.1.

A stepwise technique is used, and because of skewness in the distri-bution of the firm performance variable *size*, the natural log transformation was used.

Due to differences in the relationship between owner characteristics and firm performance among USM and match firms, separate regressions are reported for both groups of firms and for the full sample. All full sample regressions include the variable *USM* which is coded 1 if the firm is a USM firm and 0 if the firm is a match.

The stepwise regression of *ln(size)* on the entrepreneurial and firm-specific variables for the full sample shown in Table 7.4 indicate the coefficients of the variables *USM* and *unemployed* are significant at the 5 per cent level of confidence, while the variables *bus ints* and *part-time* are significant at the 10 per cent level of confidence employing two-tail tests. The significance of the variable *USM* indicates that USM firms are very much larger than match firms. Indeed, the *USM* variable alone explains over 50 per cent of the difference in size between the sampled firms. The positive relationship between the size of the firm and *unemployed* suggests that firms whose founders were in employment immediately prior to starting their firm are larger than those whose owners were unemployed. In addition, the significance of the variables *bus ints* and *part-time* suggests that firms whose owners currently have other business interests, and firms which were never operated as a part-time concern at any time, are larger in terms of the numbers employed.

Separate regressions for USM and match firms yield somewhat different results. For both USM and match firms *bus ints* is significantly and positively related to *size*. However, *unemployed* and *part-time* are no longer significant in

Table 7.4 Stepwise regressions of entrepreneurial and firm-specific characteristics on size (ln (*size*))

	USM	Unemployed	Bus. ints	Part-time	Firm age	Constant	N	$\overline{R}^2$
All	1.8642	0.6898	0.3860	-0.4548		2.6692	101	0.5778
	(9.57)	(2.67)	(1.93)	(-1.69)		(11.09)		
USM			0.5937		-0.0731	5.9141	52	0.1390
			(2.21)		(-2.64)	(16.73)		
Match			0.6382		0.0585	2.3513	49	0.1769
			(2.51)		(2.42)	(7.9)		

Note: Figures in parenthesis are 't' statistics.

either the USM or match firm regressions. This is probably due to the reduction in sample sizes for the individual regressions, as both variables, while having insignificant *t*-statistics, retain the same signs as in the full regression.

Firm age is a significant variable in both the USM and match firm regressions, but it has opposite signs in each equation, hence its lack of significance in the full sample regression. For USM firms, firm age is negatively related to firm size, whereas for match firms, the relationship is positive. We have no satisfactory explanation for this finding.

Overall, these results suggest current firm size is related to whether an owner currently has other business interests, his/her employment status prior to start-up, whether the firm was operated as a part-time business at any time and the age of the firm. These findings, in the main, apply to both USM and match firms, with the exception of the age of the firm, whose relationship to size differs depending whether the firm is USM or match.

OWNER-MANAGER EXPERTISE

Firm growth eventually requires the original skills of the founder(s) to be complemented and supplemented by others. Even so, the original skills of the start-up team have an important influence on the resulting portfolio of managerial skills. This section considers the managerial skills when the firm was first established, the current managerial skills and how any changes in skills were brought about.

Management expertise

Table 7.5 (a) examines the managerial skills of the owners *at start-up*. The skills are defined across six dimensions of functional expertise; production, finance, marketing, personnel, research and development and general management. Each owner respondent was asked to assess the extent of the expertise of the firm both at start-up and at the time of the interview in each of the six areas. Five options were provided – considerable, good, moderate, some and none. These responses were coded from 5 for considerable expertise to 1 for no expertise.

The *All* column of Table 7.5 shows the equally weighted average score for all firms. This is preceded by scores for USM and match firms separately. The percentage column shows those firms whose owners considered them to have 'considerable' expertise in each functional area. Finally, the table presents chi-square statistics testing for differences between USM and match firm owners according to their score.

Taking all firms in the sample, start-up expertise was judged to be

Table 7.5 Expertise within the business

	USM		Match		All		Chi-square
	Score	%	Score	%	Score	%	
(a) *Start-up*							
Production	2.93	22	2.70	18	2.83	20	1.8775
Finance	2.82	9	2.62	6	2.72	8	3.1394
Marketing	2.98	18	2.84	24	2.91	21	5.7355
Personnel	2.35	7	2.80	8	2.57	8	8.0590*
R&D	2.22	11	1.74	6	1.99	9	6.8181
General management	2.81	11	2.94	10	2.88	11	2.1725
(b) *Current*							
Production	4.17	59	3.78	44	3.98	52	6.2083
Finance	4.63	65	4.12	36	4.38	51	11.8403**
Marketing	4.32	55	3.84	42	4.09	49	6.0127
Personnel	3.57	18	3.68	20	3.63	19	3.8779
R&D	3.24	35	2.42	8	2.85	22	12.1903**
General management	4.28	48	3.90	26	4.10	37	6.9975

Notes: * denotes significance at 0.1 levels of confidence.
      ** denotes significance at 0.05 levels of confidence.

greatest in marketing, general management and production. These rankings are altered slightly when the USM and match firms are considered separately, with USM firms scoring highest in the areas of marketing, followed by production and general management. Match firms judge their expertise at start-up to be highest in general management, followed by marketing and personnel. The importance of marketing expertise at start up confirms our earlier work on this matter (Storey *et al.* 1989).

When the percentage of firms ranking their expertise in the functional areas as 'considerable' are analysed, a larger percentage of USM firms rate their production expertise as being considerable, while for the match firms, marketing expertise gains the largest percentage of considerable ratings. The chi-square statistics indicate that for each of the functional areas, there is little difference between the ratings given by USM firms and match firms at start-up, with the exception of personnel. Here, match firms considered themselves to be significantly more expert in such areas, with 42 per cent of match firms considering themselves to have 'Good' or considerable expertise, compared with only 20.4 per cent of USM firms.

It can be seen from section (b) of Table 7.5 that firms considered themselves to be *currently* most expert in the area of finance, followed by general management and marketing. Owners of USM firms considered themselves to be marginally more expert in virtually all managerial functional areas than match firm owners. In particular, USM owners rated their current expertise in finance significantly higher than match owners, with 65 per cent of USM owners considering their firms to have considerable expertise in finance compared with only 36 per cent of match firms. This is not surprising, given the more stringent reporting requirements associated with a listing on the UK Unlisted Securities Market.

Expertise in R&D management was also considered to be significantly higher in USM firms than in match firms, with 35 per cent of USM owners rating their management expertise in this area as considerable compared with only 8 per cent of match owners.

Not surprisingly current managerial expertise is judged to be higher than at start-up. Both USM and match firm owners felt expertise had increased most in finance and least in R&D, but the average increase in 'score' across areas of expertise was higher at 1.18 for USM firms, compared with 1.02 for match firms. No differences exist between functional area scores for USM and match firms.

In fact Table 7.5 shows some interesting similarities in the relative rankings of managerial expertise across the functional areas. It has already been noted that while financial expertise was rarely 'on board' at start-up this functional area is now generally regarded as being currently the strongest area. At the other extreme are the personnel and R&D functions. Managerial expertise here was deemed to be weakest at start-up and currently continues to be viewed as weak. R&D management, in particular, is viewed as markedly weaker in the match than in the USM firms.

We now relate *size* in terms of employment, to three measures of management competence (expertise at start-up, current expertise and changes in expertise since start-up). Pearson's correlation coefficients, for significant associations only, are shown in Table 7.6.

Part (a) of the table relates firm performance measures to current expertise. For the full sample of firms, *size* is positively related to finance and marketing expertise, although these relationships lose significance when the separate samples of USM and match firms are considered.

Table 7.6 (b) presents significant correlations between firm performance and changes in expertise. For USM firms, *size* is positively related to increased expertise in personnel, possibly reflected in the formal establishment of a new department.

Stepwise regressions relating current *size* to start-up and current expertise and changes in the levels of expertise are shown in Table 7.7. A full description of the variables used in these regressions is included in Appendix 7.1.

Table 7.6 (a) Pearson correlations of expertise within business with size

Current expertise	USM		Match		All	
	Coeff	*N*	*Coeff*	*N*	*Coeff*	*N*
Finance	0.1201	53	0.1069	50	0.2312*	103
Marketing	0.2822	53	0.0778	50	0.2521*	103

Note: * denotes significance at 0.05 levels of confidence.

Table 7.6 (b) Change in expertise from start-up to current

	USM		Match		All	
	Coeff	*N*	*Coeff*	*N*	*Coeff*	*N*
Personnel	0.3487*	53	0.0504	50	0.2900*	103

Note: * denotes significance at 0.05 levels of confidence.

Current firm *size* for all firms is positively and significantly related to start-up expertise in marketing, current expertise in production and the change in expertise in personnel. This reflects the findings for USM firms where very similar results were obtained.

Indeed marketing is the *only* functional area of expertise, at start-up, which is positively and significantly related to current firm size. The increase in personnel expertise probably reflects the greater formality of personnel matters as numbers of employees increase.

Explaining *size* in match firms produced rather different results. The only variables included here were current expertise in production and finance. No start-up functional expertise variables were found to be significant.

Overall both USM and match firms emphasized their start-up expertise was in marketing and general management. Currently, however, there were few differences between the two groups of firms in terms of functional expertise, although both now place much greater emphasis on finance expertise. Since start-up, however, expertise has been deemed to have increased, particularly in respect of USM firms.

Increasing managerial expertise

This subsection considers how managerial expertise increased after start-up. Three methods are identified. First, the owner and the original management team may develop the required skills themselves. Secondly,

Table 7.7 Stepwise regression of levels of expertise at start-up, at time of interview and changes in expertise, on size (ln (*size*))

	Start-up marketing	Current prodn	Current finance	Change personnel	USM	Constant	N	$\bar{R}^2$
All	0.1697	0.1139		0.2576	1.9052	2.0942	103	0.5861
	(2.63)	(1.74)		(3.52)	(10.31)	(5.97)		
USM	0.2018			0.3372		4.2797	53	0.1805
	(2.08)			(3.43)		(11.91)		
Match		0.2292	0.2960			1.1479	50	0.1688
		(2.71)	(2.09)			(1.71)		

Note: Figures in parenthesis are 't' statistics.

outsiders with the necessary managerial skills may be recruited. Thirdly, individuals in non-managerial positions may be promoted into managerial positions. For each functional area owners were asked to identify the method, or combination of methods, by which expertise was acquired.

Table 7.8 shows USM firms were markedly more likely to have recruited managers from outside than were match firms, for all functional areas except for general management and personnel. In contrast, match firms were more likely to develop the skills of the start-up team, with only finance expertise being more likely to have been recruited from outside the firm. Both sets of firms seemed to make approximately equal use of in-house promotion to increase their expertise. These results confirm the findings in Chapter 6 derived from interviews with managers currently within the firm. For example Table 6.1.(c) showed that current USM and match managers differed significantly in that the former were much more likely to have been externally recruited.

Examining how this varies between the functional areas, Table 7.8 shows that the recruitment of outsiders was used by USM firms significantly more than by match firms in the areas of production, finance and R&D. Conversely match firms were more likely to have developed the skills of the start-up team in personnel.

Comparing in-house promotion across the functional areas also yields some interesting insights, when compared with the role of the start-up team. For match firms the start-up team is significantly more likely to be referred to in the areas of increasing expertise in production, finance, marketing, personnel and R&D. Only in the area of general management is promotion of outsiders referred to almost as frequently as the start-up team.

Among match firms the promotion of in-house staff to managerial positions is mentioned almost as frequently as the recruitment of outsiders in all functional areas with the exception of finance.

In two functional areas there are some particularly interesting patterns – personnel and R&D. In personnel it has already been noted that the start-up team was much more likely to develop this function in match than in USM firms. The second interesting point is that this is the only functional area, for USM firms, where in-house promotion is virtually as important as recruitment of outsiders. R&D shows a very different pattern. This is the *least* likely functional area to be developed by the start-up team in USM firms, but managers in this area are more than twice as likely to be recruited from outside or be promoted in-house in USM firms as in match firms.

Relating recruitment method to *size*, Table 7.9 yields several significant relationships. In the area of finance, match firms which increased expertise via the recruitment of outside personnel were significantly larger than match firms which used other methods for supplementing financial expertise. This was also the case for all firms taken together.

Table 7.8 Method of increasing expertise

	USM No.	USM %	Match No.	Match %	All No.	All %	Chi-square	Significance
Production								
Developed by start-up team	20	37	23	46	43	41	0.5301	0.4666
Recruitment of outsiders	33	61	19	38	52	50	4.6607	0.0309*
Promoted in-house	25	46	15	30	40	38	2.2651	0.1323
Finance								
Developed by start-up team	14	26	20	40	34	33	1.7411	0.1870
Recruitment of outsiders	49	91	33	66	82	79	8.1012	0.0044*
Promoted in-house	11	20	11	22	22	21	0.0000	1.0000
Marketing								
Developed by start-up team	23	43	23	46	46	44	0.0231	0.8792
Recruitment of outsiders	33	61	22	44	55	53	2.4026	0.1211
Promoted in-house	14	26	17	34	31	30	0.4690	0.4934
Personnel								
Developed by start-up team	16	30	24	48	40	39	2.9662	0.0850*
Recruitment of outsiders	19	35	15	30	34	33	0.1253	0.7233
Promoted in-house	18	33	13	26	31	30	0.3628	0.5469
R&D								
Developed by start-up team	19	18	15	30	34	33	0.1253	0.7233
Recruitment of outsiders	23	43	9	18	32	31	6.2617	0.0123*
Promoted in-house	15	28	7	14	22	21	2.1864	0.1392
General management								
Developed by start-up team	32	59	27	54	59	57	0.1175	0.7317
Recruitment of outsiders	32	59	24	48	56	54	0.9100	0.3401
Promoted in-house	25	46	24	48	49	47	0.0000	1.0000

Note: * Significance at 0.10 levels of confidence.

Table 7.9 Methods of increasing expertise by employment size of firms

		Yes			No			T-stat
		Mean	Std dev.	N	Mean	Std dev.	N	
Finance								
Match	Recruitment of outsiders	58.33	85.18	33	19.71	12.43	17	−1.85*
All	Recruitment of outsiders	213.73	285.62	81	62.64	98.23	22	−2.43**
Marketing								
USM	Recruitment of outsiders	388.25	363.75	32	190.76	153.62	21	−2.35**
	Promoted in-house	173.08	163.07	13	354.50	336.89	40	1.86*
Match	Recruitment of outsiders	71.23	101.77	22	24.75	16.38	28	−2.38**
	Promoted in-house	68.47	110.36	17	33.21	36.46	33	−1.68*
All	Recruitment of outsiders	259.09	325.91	54	95.90	129.00	49	−3.28**
	Promoted in-house	113.80	143.19	30	209.26	296.63	73	1.68*
Personnel								
Match	Promoted in-house	81.00	123.61	13	32.62	35.55	37	−2.17**
All	Recruitment of outsiders	243.73	362.41	34	150.77	195.26	69	−1.69*
R&D								
Match	Recruitment of outsiders	107.33	143.25	9	31.56	33.47	41	−3.12**
	Promoted in-house	126.43	157.98	7	31.98	33.77	43	−3.61**
All	Recruitment of outsiders	292.44	315.77	32	131.44	222.35	71	−2.97**
General management								
Match	Recruitment of outsiders	66.83	96.23	24	25.23	25.92	26	−2.12**
All	Recruitment of outsiders	234.02	308.86	55	121.23	187.16	48	−2.20**

Notes: * denotes significance at 0.10 levels of confidence.
** denotes significance at 0.05 levels of confidence.

Both USM and match firms which recruited outsiders in marketing were significantly larger than those using other methods. Conversely USM firms using in-house promotion of marketing staff were significantly smaller, whereas the reverse was the case for match firms.

In personnel, match firms promoting in-house were larger than others. Match firms which recruited outsiders or promoted in-house in R&D were significantly larger than firms whose expertise was developed by the start-up team or which did not increase their expertise in this area. Lastly, match firms recruiting outsiders into general management were larger than other match firms.

Overall, the results suggest that the method of increasing expertise in the six functional areas is associated with the current size of both the match firms and USM firms. The strongest associations are found among match firms where the recruitment of outsiders is consistently associated with larger size.

Table 7.10 presents the results of stepwise regressions of current *size* on the method of recruitment in the six functional areas. All variables are dummy variables, coded 1 if the method of increasing expertise was used in the particular area and 0 otherwise. For example, the variable *start-up team finance* is coded 1 if expertise in the finance area was gained by developing the knowledge of the start-up team and 0 if not. Hence, three dummy variables are used to describe the methods employed to increase expertise in each of the six function areas. In addition, the variable USM is included in the full sample regressions. Appendix 7.1 again provides a full description of the variables employed.

The results of the *size* regression for all firms indicate external recruitment in marketing and R&D is associated with currently larger firms. However, the results of the separate regressions for USM and match firms are quite different. For USM firms, external recruitment in marketing is positively related to *size*, while promotion in-house in marketing has a negative sign. This confirms the univariate findings, suggesting that the currently largest USM firms recruited their marketing expertise externally, and were least likely to promote internally.

For match firms, none of these variables are significant. Instead the variables found to be related to *size* are external recruitment in general management and internal promotion in R&D.

Overall, the methods of increasing managerial expertise in the six functional areas appear to differ between USM and match firms. In general, USM firms tend to increase expertise via the recruitment of experienced outsiders, whereas match firms are more likely to develop the skills of the start-up team. The results of the *t*-tests and regression analysis suggest that, generally, the recruitment of outsiders results in higher performance. This

Table 7.10 Stepwise regression of method of increasing expertise by size (ln (size))

	Outsiders marketing	Outsiders R&D	Outsiders Gen. man.	Promoted marketing	Promoted R&D	USM	Constant	N	$\bar{R}^2$
All	0.5073 (2.67)	0.4626 (2.20)				1.8569 (9.64)	2.9271 (18.63)	103	0.5726
USM	0.6099 (2.35)			−0.7388 (−2.51)			5.1040 (23.94)	53	0.1568
Match			0.5876 (2.33)		0.8569 (2.36)		2.8315 (16.26)	50	0.1902

appears to be strongest in explaining current *size* among match firms. It also suggests that the areas of managerial responsibility adopted by the start-up team do not materially influence performance. However, no method emerges that is uniformly superior to all others.

THE DEVELOPMENT OF THE MANAGERIAL TEAM

The previous section considered three ways in which managerial skills were assembled. This section analyses the qualities sought when individual managers were appointed, the recruitment procedures used and the reasons given by owners for why managers joined the enterprise. The influence of management training is also considered. The term 'manager' is defined to include any individual who is responsible for the management of others, but who is not a significant shareholder in the business. Thus this individual may be called a director, but we do *not* include the cases where the new director becomes a major shareholder in the business.

The analysis is based upon the owners descriptions of the first and last two managerial appointments made by the firm. Again the prime focus is to consider firm performance, but on this occasion to also link it to the choice of managerial qualities claimed to be sought by founders.

Management qualities

The qualities sought by owners from new managers have been grouped into four categories; personal skills, experience/ knowledge, qualifications/ expertise and personal qualities. The data are derived from the responses of the owners to open-ended questions on this topic. While judgement has to be exercised when categorizing open-ended responses, the four categories cover the bulk of the responses given.

The first group of responses relate to the personal 'skills' of the management. Included in the group are owners who said they sought from their managers 'get up and go', 'flair', 'personal empathy', 'public presence', 'ability to get things done', etc.

The second category contains responses which emphasized the need for managers to have experience and knowledge, particularly the need for knowledge of the industry and for the market and a proven track record. Owners responding in such a manner tended to require the possession of a fairly narrow range of skills, which focused tightly upon the particular requirements of their business and/or industry, rather than upon more general managerial experience. Frequently respondents wished to employ personnel who had a knowledge of the industry and its operations, so avoiding the need for additional training.

The third category includes requirements relating to formal qualifications and technical expertise from managers. Here the emphasis is on knowledge and expertise gained from formal academic, professional and technical qualifications, rather than on experience alone.

The final category relates to the personal qualities of managers. Examples include responses such as 'easy to get along with', 'would fit in with the present set-up', 'loyalty', 'reliable', etc. In contrast with responses in the first category, which emphasized 'flair' and 'get up and go', this category emphasized the need for managers to fit into the organization.

Table 7.11 shows that USM and match firms founders are equally likely to emphasize personal skills (*peskill*) in their first two and last two managerial appointments. For the first two appointments, both groups of firms rank this requirement as being the most important. However, these qualities are referred to much less frequently in discussing the last two managerial appointments. This suggests that at start-up, firms place greater emphasis upon flair and energy among their new managers, whereas with more recent appointments the skills of managing an established organization are in greater demand.

The requirement for managers to have experience of the industry/market (*expkn*) is also equally characteristic of USM and match firms when making the first managerial appointments. This changes for more recent managerial appointments, where USM owners are more likely to stress the need for experience and knowledge than match firm owners.

Both groups of firms place similar emphasis on the need for their first

Table 7.11 Qualities and skills required in managerial appointments

	USM		Match		All		Chi-square	Significant
	No.	%	No.	%	No.	%		
First two managers								
Peskill	31	58	29	58	60	58	0.0000	1.0000
Expkn	25	46	26	52	51	49	0.1483	0.7002
Qualexp	29	54	27	54	56	54	0.0000	1.0000
Perqual	16	30	25	50	41	39	3.6983	0.0545*
Last two managers								
Peskill	20	37	20	40	40	38	0.0118	0.9135
Expkn	38	70	24	48	62	60	4.5072	0.0338*
Qualexp	27	50	18	36	45	43	1.5418	0.2143
Perqual	17	31	21	42	38	36	0.8266	0.3632

Notes: * significant at 5%

managerial appointments to have formal qualifications and expertise (*qualexp*). However, USM firms place greater emphasis on such qualities in their last appointments (50 per cent) than match firms (36 per cent), although this difference is not statistically significant. Formal qualifications are ranked by USM firms as second only to experience and knowledge when making their last appointments, whereas match firms place least emphasis on this quality.

The personal qualities (*perqual*) of the first two managerial appointments are mentioned by 50 per cent of match firm owners, but by only 30 per cent of USM firm owners. This may be because match firm owners are more concerned with creating an informal 'friendly' atmosphere as a means of improving the performance of the firm. Match firms continue to stress these qualities in their last two managerial appointments. In contrast, USM firms are least likely to refer to personal qualities when discussing either their first or last managerial appointments.

Both groups of firms change the emphasis of their managerial appointments as the firm develops. For their first managerial appointments, owners consider personal skills, qualifications and expertise to be more important than experience and knowledge, whereas for the last appointments, experience and knowledge are given greater emphasis.

Several differences therefore exist between USM and match firms in the qualities sought by founders in their managerial appointments. In their first two appointments, match firm owners are much more likely to refer to the personal qualities of managers than USM founders. The latter stress the need for personal skills and qualifications and expertise above other qualities in their managers.

In discussing more recent appointments USM founders place emphasis on experience and knowledge, and a lower priority on personal qualities, such as the ability to fit into the organization, loyalty and reliability. Match firm owners responses are almost equally distributed, but they place least emphasis on formal qualifications and expertise.

Univariate statistical analysis relating *size* to the qualities sought from either the first or the last two managers reveal few significant relationships and so are not tabulated here.

These results are disappointing and suggest either that the qualities sought in managerial appointments do not influence the eventual performance of the firm, or that the mode of analysis is inappropriate. The obvious reasons for this could be the inability of owners to adequately remember, or be truthful about, these qualities. The crude, four grouping, classification may also fail to adequately reflect the diversity and subtlety of response to this question.

To explain *size*, in a multivariate framework, in terms of the qualities required of managerial appointments, eight dummy variables were created.

Peskill1 was coded 1 if owners emphasized the need for personal skills in their first two appointments and 0 otherwise. Similarly, the variables *expkn1*, *qualexp1* and *perqual1* represented experience and knowledge, qualifications and expertise, and personal qualities sought in the first managerial appointments, respectively. In terms of the last two appointments, the dummy variables *peskill2*, *expkn2*, *qualexp2* and *perqual2* were created. A full description of the variables employed is provided in Appendix 7.1. Stepwise regressions of the variables on the log forms of *size* are shown in Table 7.12.

Table 7.12 Stepwise regression of qualities and skills required in managers on size (ln (*size*))

	First managers expkn	Last managers peskill	USM	C	N	$\bar{R}^2$
All	0.4569		2.0882	2.9960	103	0.5405
	(2.39)		(10.92)	(17.71)		
Match	0.5602	0.5527		2.7211	50	0.1497
	(2.18)	(2.11)		(13.40)		

First, the regression of managerial qualities on the log of *size* for the sample of all firms indicates that the only variable of significance is *expkn1* – the need for experience and knowledge in the first managerial appoint- ments. However, separate regressions for USM and match firms reveal this variable is only significant for match firms. In addition, the need for personal skills in the last managerial appointments (*peskill2*) is significant for the match firms. No variables were found to have statistical significance for USM firms.

Overall, these results provide little support for the notion that the qualities sought in managerial appointments as we have chosen to identify and analyse them are associated with firm performance. Although the analysis indicated that, in terms of first managerial appointments, some relationships were of significance, few consistent relationships emerged.

Mode of recruitment

This subsection examines whether USM firms recruited their managers in different ways from match firms and whether this has changed between the recruitment of the first two and the last two appointments. Five general modes of recruitment are shown in Table 7.13 – personal approaches, internal appointments, general advertising, recruitment by others and appointment due to the reorganization of the business.

Table 7.13 How managers were recruited

	USM No.	USM %	Match No.	Match %	All No.	All %	Chi-square	Significance
First two managers								
Personal approach	31	57	29	58	60	58	0.0000	1.0000
Internal appointment	7	13	22	44	29	28	10.9410	0.0009*
Advertised	12	22	13	26	25	24	0.0488	0.8252
Recruited by agencies	12	22	8	16	20	19	0.3035	0.5786
Reorganization	1	2	0	0	1	1	0.0000	1.0000
Last two managers								
Personal approach	23	43	17	34	40	39	0.4875	0.4850
Internal appointment	13	24	10	20	23	22	0.0696	0.7920
Advertisement	7	13	13	26	20	19	2.0635	0.1509
Recruitment by agencies	29	54	11	22	40	39	9.7262	0.0018*
Reorganization	4	7	0	0	4	4	2.1093	0.1464

Notes: * significant at 5%

At start-up both USM and match firms relied heavily on personal contacts for their managerial appointments. Here owners frequently approached individuals known to them from a work situation. Often that person worked with the founder in the same firm, but in other instances it was someone whom the founder encountered working for another firm – for example a salesman. Less frequently, certainly for USM firms, is the use of family members. Informal recruitment continues to be dominant for match firms even for more recent managerial appointments, whereas USM firms have moved to more formalized procedures.

There are two statistically significant differences between the methods used for recruiting USM and match managers. For the first two appointments, the significant difference is that 44 per cent of match firms appoint from within the firm, compared with only 13 per cent of USM firms. For the last two appointments 54 per cent of USM firms used external recruitment agencies, compared with only 22 per cent of match firms. The much greater use of internal appointments among match firms for their first managerial appointments supports our findings from answers to other questions. It also suggests the appointment of a manager from 'outside' in the early years of a firm is a key difference between a USM and a match firm. The currently greater use of external agencies by USM firms is more expected since it reflects the greater formality of larger organizations.

To relate firm performance to the methods of managerial recruitment, *t*-tests were conducted. Few significant results were obtained, so the results are not tabulated but are discussed briefly.

Relating current firm *size* to the method of recruiting the first two managers, it appears that firms which recruited via internal appointments were significantly smaller than those using other methods.[1] Secondly, all firms using external agencies were significantly larger than those using other methods.[2] However, no significant difference was apparent when considering the separate samples of USM and match firms.

Turning now to the last two managerial appointments, USM firms appointing from within the firm were significantly smaller than other USM firms.[3] Finally, for the full sample of firms, those using external agencies to recruit their last managers were significantly larger than others,[4] although for the separate samples of USM and match firms, this difference was insignificant.

Overall, the univariate analysis indicates that the method of recruitment has only a modest impact on the firm performance. This finding is supported by the stepwise regression attempting to explain log of *size* using the method of recruitment variables, as presented in Table 7.14. Dummy variables were created for both first and last managerial appointments and coded 1 if the particular method of recruitment was employed, 0 if not. For example, the variable *last managers internal* is coded 1 if the last managers were recruited internally and 0 if not. A full description of the variables is given in Appendix 7.1.

Table 7.14 shows that for the full sample of firms *size* is unrelated to any recruitment variables. This is also the case for match firms separately, although for USM firms, the use of internal promotion to appoint the last managers is negatively related to *size*.

Overall, this subsection suggests USM and match firms are broadly similar in terms of the methods used to recruit managers, although match firms make significantly greater use of the internal promotion as a means of recruiting their first two managers, and USM firms use external agencies

Table 7.14 Stepwise regression of managers on employment size of firm

	Last manager internal	USM	Constant	N	$\bar{R}^2$
All		2.0575	3.2333	103	0.5191
		(10.541)	(23.094)		
USM	−0.8446		5.4982	53	0.1163
	(−2.801)		(36.810)		

more when making their later appointments. The *t*-tests and regression analyses suggest that smaller (slower growing) firms were more likely to appoint managers from within the firm and less likely to use external recruitment agencies. These observations are broadly consistent with the results obtained from the questionnaire responses of the managers analysed in Chapter 6, where it was found that a much higher proportion of the managers interviewed in the match firms had been internally promoted.

Reasons for joining the company

This subsection reports owners' perceptions of the reasons why managers joined their firms. To obtain this information owners were asked why they felt that their first two, and their last two, managers had joined the firm. Owners responses were then grouped into seven broad categories – the attractions of the company, the attractions of the people, the attractions of the job, the remuneration package offered, disenchantment with his/her previous job, a career step and non-work factors – with an eighth 'other' category. The data are presented in Table 7.15.

The first category refers to the attractions of the company itself, such as where the owner believed that the small size of the company and its prospects for growth were what attracted the managers. The second category relates to responses where the attractions of the people currently employed, rather than the company itself, were considered to be the primary factor. The third category refers to specific attractions of the job and/or tasks to be carried out, as the major attraction. The fourth category refers to cases where the remuneration package offered by the firm was considered to be the prime attraction to the manager. The fifth category includes cases in which the manager was believed to be disenchanted with his/her previous job, usually through boredom or from fear of job loss due to takeover/bankruptcy. Responses referring to the importance of the job as a career step, rather than as an end in itself, form the sixth category. Finally, the non-work factors include responses which were unrelated to the company or the job, such as references to the area of location, family commitments, etc.

The USM owners felt that the first two managers appointed had joined the firm primarily because of the attractiveness of the company, whereas match firm owners were more likely to refer to the attractions of the job rather than to the firm. Owners of USM firms also believed that the remuneration package offered was more important than did match firm owners. No other differences were observed, and none of those identified above are significant at the 0.05 level.

Both USM and match firm owners felt the attractions of the company

Table 7.15 Reasons for joining the firm

	USM		Match		All		Chi-square	Significance
	No.	%	No.	%	No.	%		
First managers								
Attractions of company	29	54	19	38	48	46	1.9830	0.1591
Attractions of people	10	19	5	10	15	14	0.9142	0.3390
Attractions of job	18	33	26	52	44	42	2.9808	0.0843
Remuneration package	10	19	5	10	15	14	0.9142	0.3390
Disenchantment	8	15	13	26	21	20	1.3812	0.2399
Career step	10	19	8	16	18	17	0.0064	0.9364
Non-work factors	8	15	8	16	16	15	0.0000	1.0000
Others	7	13	4	8	11	11	0.2532	0.6148
Last two managers								
Attractions of company	30	56	14	28	44	42	6.9868	0.0082*
Attractions of people	5	9	6	12	11	11	0.0182	0.8926
Attractions of job	16	30	13	26	29	28	0.0375	0.8465
Remuneration package	12	22	11	22	23	22	0.0000	1.0000
Disenchantment	8	15	9	18	17	16	0.0301	0.8622
Career step	15	28	10	20	25	24	0.4869	0.4853
Non-work factors	9	17	5	10	14	14	0.5009	0.4791
Others	8	15	5	10	13	13	0.1981	0.6563

Notes: * significant at 1%

were the key factor in the decisions of the last two managers to be appointed. However, a much higher percentage (55.6 per cent) of USM firms felt this was the key factor compared to only 28 per cent of match firm owners. This was presumably because of the higher profile of companies quoted on the USM, compared with unquoted companies.

A comparison between the factors which owners thought influenced the first two managers to join the firm, compared with the last two indicates broad similarity for USM firms. The only slight difference is that among USM owners less emphasis was placed by the last two managers on the attractions of the current management team and rather more on viewing the job as a career step. For match firms there is a quite striking change with many fewer owners referring to the attractions of the job as influencing the more recent managerial appointments to join the firm. Rather more refer to the career step and the attractions of the remuneration package than was the case for the first two managerial appointments.

The perceptions of owners as to why managers joined the firm can be related to firm *size*. Few significant relationships were found and so the results are reported in the text rather than tabulated in full. It appears that those firms whose first and last two managers were thought to be attracted by aspects of the company were significantly larger than firms citing other reasons. This relationship held for both USM and match firms, but was only significant for the USM firm's last two, but not their first two, managers. Finally, match firms whose owners believed the attractions of the job were the key factor for the first two managers are significantly smaller than other match firms.[5]

Stepwise regressions relating firm performance to the reasons for joining the firm are presented in Table 7.16. Dummy variables are again created and coded 1 where an owner stated a particular category of reason for his/her first or last managers joining the company and 0 otherwise. The variables are fully described in Appendix 7.1.

The regression on *size* for all firms indicates this is negatively related to owner mentions of the remuneration package for the first two managers and positively related to mentions of the attractiveness of the company for last two managers. It suggests owners of relatively larger firms perceive the remuneration package to be of less importance for the first managers joining a firm than owners of relatively smaller firms. Not surprisingly, larger firm owners emphasize the profile of their company in attracting more recent managers.

For USM firms, only the attractiveness of the company for the last two managers is significantly related to *size*, confirming the results of the *t*-tests. For match firms, owners were significantly more likely to refer to the attractions of the people within the company.

Overall, owners' appear to think that managers joined their firms because of the attractions of the company and the attractions associated with the job. For the first two managerial appointments, USM owners

Table 7.16 Stepwise regression of reasons for joining firm on performance (ln (*size*))

	Remun 1	Attpeop1	Attco2	USM	Constant	N	$\bar{R}^2$
All	−0.5543		0.4921	1.9659	3.1512	103	0.5619
	(−2.07)	(2.48)	(9.98)	(21.24)			
USM			0.6941		4.8981	53	0.1022
			(2.63)		(24.67)		
Match		0.9720			3.1363	50	0.0725
		(2.20)			(22.43)		

stressed the attractions of the company, while match owners emphasized the attractions of the job. For the last two managerial appointments, all firm owners considered the attractions of the company to be the prime attraction, although more USM owners considered this to be the major factor.

This suggests USM owners consider their firms offer a more prestigious package, in terms of status and in the satisfaction from contributing to the success of a quoted company. The significant factor in both the univariate and multivariate analyses was the relationship between firm size and the attractiveness of the company for the last two managers for USM firms.

Management training and fringe benefits

This subsection examines the relationship between firm *size* and the provision of both management training and fringe benefits to managers.

In principle the provision of management training should lead to improved firm performance, but it may be that only successful firms can afford to provide training for their managers. Hence, given the problem of interpreting causality, only tests for associations between training and firm size will be presented.

Owners were asked to detail the type of training made available to their first two and last two managerial appointments. Such training was classified as being either in-house or external. Hence, three dummy training variables were derived – *notrain* is coded 1 if no training was provided, *in-house* is coded 1 if the firm provided in-house training to its managers, and *external* is coded 1 if external training was provided. Obviously, firms may provide a mix of in-house and external training and this coding scheme allows for this possibility.

Table 7.17 indicates there are significant differences between USM and match firms in respect of training and the type of training provided to managers. Surprisingly, a significantly greater percentage of USM firms (41 per cent) provided no training at all to their first and last two managerial appointments, compared with only 22 per cent of match firms. This may be

Table 7.17 Provision of training

	USM		Match		All		Chi-square	Significance
	No.	%	No.	%	No.	%		
No training	22	41	11	22	33	32	3.3885	0.0657
In-house training	17	32	25	50	42	40	2.9688	0.0849
External training	27	50	32	64	59	57	1.5418	0.2143

because, although USM and match firms place equal emphasis on the need for educational qualifications, USM firms recruit more highly qualified/skilled personnel than their match counterparts. They may view this as reducing the need to provide further training. Certainly, the analyses presented in Chapter 6 which showed that the USM firm managers interviewed were more highly qualified and had more managerial and large-firm experience, seems to point to such a conclusion.

Match firms were more likely to provide both external and in-house training for their managers than USM firms. As noted above, this may be because of the lower level of skills possessed by the match firm managerial appointments.

Relating firm *size* to the provision and type of training given to first and last two managerial appointments reveals few significant relationships. Nevertheless it is very interesting that USM firms which provided training were found to be significantly larger than those USM firms which did not.[6]

These results were largely supported by a stepwise regression of performance on the variables *notrain*, *in-house* and *external*. Table 7.18 shows that *size* is positively related to the provision of in-house training for USM firms.

In general, *size* is unrelated to the provision of training. Given that the majority of match firms provide some training, the most obvious conclusion is that management training and firm performance are unrelated. The results relating to USM firms suggest it is the larger firms which provide training in the form of in-house courses. This lack of a relationship between training and firm performance is interesting when placed alongside our findings in Chapter 6 that the provision of training did not seem to influence managerial salaries. If there is no effect either on firm performance or salary it suggests that the nature of training provision is ineffective.

Finally, the provision of fringe benefits provided by the firm to its first two and last two managerial appointments is considered. Here firm *size* is assumed to influence the type of fringe benefits provided rather than vice versa. However, the differences between USM and match firms in their

Table 7.18 Stepwise regression of provision of training on size (ln (*size*))

	Notrain	External	In-house	USM	Constant	N	$\bar{R}^2$
All				2.0575 (10.54)	3.2335 (23.09)	103	0.5191
USM			0.5923 (2.07)		5.1010 (31.40)	53	0.0591

provision of fringe benefits is of interest and hence univariate analyses of these factors are presented.

Owners were asked whether their first two and last two managers were provided with any of the following fringe benefits – a company car, a profit sharing scheme, a share option scheme, a bonus scheme, BUPA or similar health insurance scheme – and asked to identify any other benefits provided. From the 'other' responses, a further two fringe benefits were identified – a company pension scheme and disability insurance. Accordingly, seven dummy variables were created, denoting provision of the above fringe benefits.

Table 7.19 indicates that, for USM firms, the most frequently provided fringe benefit was the company car, provided by 98 per cent of firms, while for match firms, a bonus scheme was provided by 72 per cent of firms. There are several significant differences between USM and match firms in terms of the type of fringe benefits provided: USM firms are significantly more likely to provide a company car, share option schemes, health insurance, a company pension scheme and to a lesser extent, a profit sharing scheme.

These findings are broadly in line with those found by asking existing managers as reported in Chapter 6. There, it will be recalled, current managers were asked about the fringe benefits which they receive. In Table 6.4 88 per cent of USM managers reported having a company car compared with 69 per cent of match managers – slightly below those reported by owners for the first and last two managerial appointments. Despite the differences in individuals about which it is asked, the findings are broadly similar.

Overall, the results indicate that the majority of both USM and match firms provide some fringe benefits to their managers, but that managers in USM firms are much more likely to be in receipt of most forms of benefit than are their match counterparts.

Table 7.19 Fringe benefits

	USM		Match		All		Chi-square	Significance
	No.	%	No.	%	No.	%		
Company car	53	98	30	60	83	80	21.1373	0.0000
Profit sharing scheme	38	70	26	52	64	61	2.9662	0.0850
Share option scheme	43	80	14	28	57	55	25.8942	0.0000
Bonus scheme	32	59	36	72	68	65	1.3416	0.2468
BUPA	49	91	25	50	74	71	19.0563	0.0000
Pension scheme	11	20	1	2	12	11	6.8781	0.0087
Disability insurance	19	35	18	36	37	36	0.0000	1.0000

Relating firm size to fringe benefits revealed several significant differences. Overall, firms providing company cars were significantly larger than those firms which did not,[7] a finding that was largely due to the fact that all but one of the USM firms provided company cars. Firms with profit sharing schemes were significantly larger than those without such schemes, although these differences were not significant for the separate samples of USM and match firms. In addition, USM firms providing share option schemes were significantly larger than those that did not provide such schemes.[8] With respect to the provision of health insurance schemes, match firms were significantly larger than those which did not.[9]

In summary, the provision of one or more fringe benefits is the norm in the majority of firms. In line with prior expectations, it is the currently larger firms which are most likely to provide such benefits. Nevertheless, since we are examining the provision of fringe benefits for both the first two and the last two managerial appointments it does suggest that the provision of these benefits was characteristic of the larger firms even in their early years of life.

FIRM SIZE: A GENERAL ANALYSIS AND SYNTHESIS

The previous sections of this chapter have separately considered the performance of the firm – its current size – and its relationship to each of eight key areas of interest:

1 Owner motivations
2 Entrepreneurial characteristics
3 Managerial expertise
4 Methods of increasing expertise
5 Management recruitment
6 Management qualities
7 Management training
8 Firm characteristics

The purpose of this section is to reach an understanding of the *relative* importance of *each* area in explaining firm performance. To achieve this a stepwise regression analysis is performed to explain *size* using all the explanatory variables from the previous sections. In addition, a logit analysis is conducted to determine if there are significant differences between USM and match firms.

Table 7.20 (a) shows the 'best' equation which explains current *size* for all firms, section (b) provides the equation for USM firms only and section (c) provides the equation for match firms only.

It can be seen from Table 7.20 that the explanatory power of the

Table 7.20 Stepwise regression of all variables on size

		β	t-stat
(a)	*All firms*		
	Bus ints	0.2724	1.875
	Unemployed	0.9067	4.557
	SU finance	− 0.1597	− 2.618
	SU gen man	0.2931	4.462
	Change personnel	0.3118	5.492
	SU team gen man	− 0.3808	− 2.636
	Outsiders' production	− 0.3147	− 2.129
	Outsiders' finance	0.5767	3.285
	Outsiders' marketing	0.4662	3.151
	Outsiders' R&D	0.3682	2.337
	Promoted marketing	− 0.3096	− 1.922
	Perapp2	0.6386	4.194
	Advert1	0.4450	2.804
	Attjob2	− 0.3438	− 2.148
	Remun1	− 0.6654	− 3.471
	Career2	− 0.3616	− 2.116
	Expkn1	0.4215	3.012
	USM	1.7256	11.468
	Constant	1.1636	3.432
	$N = 101$	$\bar{R}^2 = 0.8002$	
(b)	*USM firms*		
	Bus ints	1.2044	7.793
	Age	− 0.0323	− 3.297
	Change personnel	0.5278	7.976
	Change gen man	− 0.3162	− 5.154
	SU team gen man	− 0.3961	− 2.797
	Outsiders' gen man	0.5059	3.105
	Promoted gen man	− 1.0621	− 6.417
	Perapp2	0.4697	3.010
	Intern2	− 0.7022	− 3.846
	Recruit1	− 0.4838	− 2.301
	Reorg2	1.1126	3.434
	Career1	0.5397	2.980
	Non work2	− 0.4570	− 2.493
	Expkn1	0.9858	6.400
	Peskill1	− 0.8314	− 5.145
	Firm age	− 0.1235	− 6.070
	Constant	7.6702	13.050
	$N = 52$	$\bar{R}^2 = 0.7937$	

Table 7.20 Continued

		β	t-stat
(c)	*Match firms*		
	Change personnel	0.2038	2.002
	Change gen man	− 0.2633	− 2.976
	Current production	0.1205	1.799
	Current finance	0.4391	3.902
	SU team production	0.5634	2.362
	SU team finance	− 0.8893	− 3.882
	Outsiders gen man	0.7437	4.025
	Promoted R&D	0.7282	2.611
	Attjob1	− 0.4093	− 2.301
	Expkn1	0.4428	2.367
	Constant	0.6356	1.260
	N = 49	$\overline{R}^2 = 0.6336$	

regression equations is high. The value of $\overline{R}^2$ in both section (a) and section (b) is approximately 0.8, while that for section (c) is 0.63.

An examination of sections (a) (b) and (c) of Table 7.20 shows that none of the variables included in the owner motivations group are included in any of the three equations. However, the inclusion of the *unemployed* variable in Table 7.20 indicates that individuals who were unemployed immediately prior to starting their business were less likely to form a firm which subsequently became large, than is the case for employed founders. In some senses therefore it might suggest that motivations for the establishment of a business do influence its growth, even though our method of classifying motivations failed to identify any impact. Interestingly, however, the *unemployed* variable does not appear in the separate equations for USM and match firms.

One other variable in the entrepreneurial characteristics group also appears in section (a) of Table 7.20. This is the *bus ints* variable, indicating that founders currently with multiple business interests are likely to be owners of larger firms. This variable is particularly influenced by the USM group, where the variable appears in section (b) of Table 7.20.

The third group of variables relate to management expertise. Section (a) of Table 7.20 shows that current *size* is positively related to two variables – these are *change personnel* and *start-up (SU) gen man*. It is negatively related to *SU finance*. The two positive relationships are easy to explain.

For *SU gen man* it suggests that where the start-up team had relatively strong skills in general management they were able to develop a fast growing firm. The *change personnel* variable is also to be expected since it reflects, rather than causes, the growth of the firm. As we noted in the text earlier it often involves the establishment, for the first time, of a personnel department. Furthermore this variable is significantly positive in sections (b) and (c), covering USM and match firms.

The inclusion of a significantly negative sign on *SU finance* suggests that currently large firms were rarely started by individuals with much financial expertise. It may also be true that, looking back, those individuals are most clearly aware of their lack of knowledge in this area.

Turning now to an examination of the management expertise variables for the USM and match firms separately shows that, for match firms, current expertise in finance and production are associated with larger *size*. The somewhat curious result is that for both match and USM firms, *size* is significantly explained by the negative inclusion of the *change gen man* variable, although this is not included in section (a) of Table 7.20.

The fourth group of variables included in the tables are those categorized as relating to increasing expertise. In section (a) of Table 7.20 four variables are included, three of which, *outsiders finance*, *outsiders marketing* and *outsiders R&D*, have positive signs. These indicate that currently larger firms were likely to place greater emphasis in the recruitment of external managers in these functional areas. However, the larger firms would appear to be less likely to recruit production managers externally. An examination of sections (b) and (c) indicate that while the external recruitment of these functional specialists is not significantly associated with size, the external recruitment of general managers is included positively in both equations.

Two other variables in the increasing expertise group are included in section (a) of Table 7.20. These suggest that current *size* is negatively associated with firms which increased their marketing expertise through internal staff pro- motion, and where the start-up team provided the main source of increased expertise in general management.

From this we infer that it is the recruitment of outsiders which is positively associated with greater *size* and that other methods of increasing expertise are associated with generally smaller *size* firms. This general finding also appears to apply to the USM and match firms separately.

The fifth group of variables relate to management recruitment, covered earlier in this chapter. Section (a) of Table 7.20 shows that there are two variables positively related to current *size – perapp 2* and *advert 1*. It also shows there are three variables negatively associated with *size – remun 1, attjob 2* and *career 2*. Relating this to the first two managers appointed suggests that currently larger firms are more likely to have advertised for these appointments and the appointee was less influenced by remuneration considerations. Expressing these findings more positively it suggests that larger firms were, early in their life, more likely to use formal rather than informal methods of recruitment, and it supports our earlier findings that they were more likely to seek managers from outside their own organization.

Examining the last two managerial appointments suggests that larger firms were more likely to favour the personal approach and continued to be less likely to recruit managers who viewed the job as a career step.

An examination of Table 7.20 sections (b) and (c) indicates that management recruitment variables were much more likely to be included in explaining the size of USM companies – section (b), than in explaining match firm size. There are six management recruitment variables included in section (b) of Table 7.20. The pattern which emerges from the inclusion of these variables is that USM companies are smaller where more recent managerial appoint- ments have been internal and where non-work factors are important influences. Positive influences include company reorganization – often associated with growth, and where the first two managers were viewed as joining the company so as to provide a key career step for them. It also shows that the currently large companies continue to favour the personal approach to the appointment of managers.

The sixth group of variables relate to management qualities. Table 7.20 shows that current size is positively related to those firms who sought experience and knowledge from their first managerial appointments. It will be recalled that this related to managers having prior experience of the industry/market in which the firm operated. Interestingly this variable also appears with a positive sign in the separate equations for the USM and match firms. More surprisingly however section (b) of Table 7.20 shows that for USM firms current *size* is negatively related to the emphasis placed on personal skills (*peskill1*) in the first two managerial appointments.

No variables in the management training group are included in the equations, suggesting that this activity is unrelated to current firm *size*. Finally the two firm characteristics variables which are included indicate that USM firms are (not surprisingly) larger than match firms, and that among USM firms it is the younger firms which are larger than the older firms.

CONCLUSIONS

This chapter assessed the role of firm owners in influencing the labour market for managers, and the impact which this, in turn, has upon the performance of the firms in our sample. Two measures of firm performance are used. The first is whether or not the firm has its shares quoted on the Unlisted Securities Market (USM) and the second is the absolute size of the firm in terms of number of employees.

To assess this relationship seven types of influence upon firm performance are assessed: owner motivations, entrepreneurial characteristics, managerial expertise, methods of increasing managerial expertise, management recruitment, management qualities and management training. All of these are deemed to be influenced by the owner of the business at both start up and currently. Each of these groups of influences, however, have up to fifteen separate elements, each of which has been individually related to measures of firm performance. We recognize that it is difficult for the reader to assimilate this volume of information and so this section will attempt to synthesize results, so as to provide a coherent picture of the influence which owners exert on the managerial labour market in small firms and the impact of this upon firm performance.

The synthesis is presented in Table 7.21. For each of the seven managerial groupings, it presents two sets of information for the three types of firms. The three columns refer firstly to all 104 firms in the survey (*All*) and then to separate sub-samples of USM and match firms. The first type of information shown indicates, *when all variables were included simultaneously*, those variables which were individually statistically significantly relevant to performance. Where the variable was significantly positively related to performance this is shown as POS and where it is negatively related to performance this is shown as NEG.

The second type of information shown in Table 7.21 indicates that, *when only all variables in the group are included*, those variables which are statistically significant related to firm performance. The variables which are related to high performance are shown as (+) and those which are significantly related to poor performance are shown as (–).

Table 7.21 makes a number of clear points. First, it reaffirms that, in so far as we have chosen to measure them, owner motivations at start up appear unrelated to firm performance. Yet this is somewhat at variance with the first finding in the entrepreneurial characteristics group that those individuals who are unemployed (and so who are assumed to be starting a business for 'negative' reasons) prior to starting their business, ultimately have smaller firms than individuals who were employed. This latter finding is robust in the sense that it appears in both the 'group' model as (+) and the 'overall' model as POS. A similarly robust, though more predictable finding, is that founders currently with multiple business interests are likely to have larger firms.

It is, however, the findings from the next two groupings, management expertise and methods of increasing management expertise, which are central to this chapter. Examining the results for the management expertise

Table 7.21 Synthesis

Variable coding	All	USM	Match
Owner motivations			
1. Positive			
2. Negative			
3. Neutral			
Entrepreneurial characteristics			
1. Unemployed	POS (+)		
2. Business interests	POS (+)	POS (+)	(+)
3. Part-time	(−)		
Management expertise			
1. Start up marketing	(+)	(+)	
2. Start up finance	NEG		
3. Start up gen man	POS		
4. Change personnel	POS (+)	POS (+)	POS
5. Change gen man		NEG	NEG
6. Current finance			POS (+)
7. Current production	(+)		POS (+)
Methods of increasing expertise			
1. Outside marketing	POS (+)	(+)	
2. Outside R&D	POS (+)		
3. Outsiders gen man		POS	POS (+)
4. Outsiders finance	POS		
5. Promoted marketing	NEG	(−)	
6. Promoted R&D			(+)
7. Start up gen man	NEG	NEG	
8. Start up prod			POS
9. Start up finance			NEG
Management recruitment			
1. Perapp2	POS	POS	
2. Intern2		NEG	
3. Advert1	POS		
4. Recruit		NEG	
5. Reorg2		POS	
6. Attjob1			NEG
7. Attjob2	NEG		
8. Remun1	NEG (−)		
9. Career1		POS	
10. Career2	NEG		
11. Nonwork2		NEG	
12. Attco2	(+)	(+)	
13. Attpeop1			(+)

Table 7.21 Continued

Variable coding	All	USM	Match
Management qualities			
1. Expkn1	POS (+)	POS	POS (+)
2. Peskill1		NEG	
3. Peskill2			(+)
Management training			
1. Notrain			
2. External			
3. In-house			
Firm characteristics			
1. USM	POS (+)		
2. Firm age		NEG (–)	

Key: POS, NEG = Significant coefficient in 'all' variable equation.
(+) (–) = Significant coefficient in equation including only variables from their group.

group there are three significant variables which indicate managerial expertise at start up. The findings are that firms which viewed their managerial
expertise in marketing and general management as high at start-up subsequently became larger firms. It also indicates that those who regarded their
expertise in finance as relatively weak also became larger firms.

These are important findings. They suggest that it is the strength of
marketing/general management background of the owner which is
important in influencing subsequent growth of the firm. The marketing
finding serves to support our earlier results in this matter (Storey *et al.*
1989). It also shows that financial expertise does not have to be 'on board'
when the enterprise begins for it to be successful.

A second group of variables within the management expertise group
relates to changes in expertise in the functional areas. Here the robust result
is that firms which have performed well are those where expertise in
personnel has increased strikingly since start-up. In part this reflects the
generally low levels of managerial expertise among founders of all firms at
start-up, but it also reflects the fact that the relatively large firms currently
have now found it necessary to establish a new department dealing with
personnel. This also means that an individual is given specific responsibility for the direction of that department and hence owners now feel that
managerial expertise is in place.

Negative signs on the relationship between changes in general management and firm size are observed. This suggests that both USM and match

firms which have grown largest are those where general management expertise has grown least. This is not surprising given that expertise in general management at start-up was shown to be characteristic of subsequently larger firms.

Interestingly, however, none of the variables relating to current managerial expertise in any of the functional areas is robustly related to performance for all firms, although current finance and production expertise is related to larger size for match (but not USM) firms.

Overall, the management expertise group tells a consistent story. First, it reassures us that the larger firms are those which had more expertise both at start-up and at present – reflected in the predominance of positive relationships. They suggest that firms which will subsequently grow larger are established by owners with a background in general management and in marketing, but not in finance. They suggest that the major change since start-up among the larger firms has been that personnel expertise has increased most and general management expertise has increased least. Currently larger firms have high expertise in production and, among match firms in finance.

Turning now to the methods of increasing expertise group, the most persistent pattern to emerge here is that the recruitment of outsiders is generally associated with larger size. This is shown to be the case in four of the major functional areas of finance, marketing, R&D and general management. It must be considered as a robust result. Conversely those firms which appeared to emphasize the promotion of staff from within the firm into managerial positions for the first time, most notably in the area of marketing, were smaller. Finally the firms where the owner indicated that he or she continued to exercise a major responsibility for the functional area were smaller. Overall, then the message here is clear. The larger (faster growing) firms are those where the emphasis by the owner is in the recruitment of outside managers, almost irrespective of functional area. Where owners place an emphasis upon either taking over functional areas themselves or place individuals in managerial positions for the first time the growth rate of the firm is slowed.

Owners were asked identical questions about the first two managers appointed and the last two managers appointed. The responses to these questions are reported in the management recruitment group of variables. The answers about the first two managers have the suffix 1 and the variables relating to the last two managerial appointments have the suffix 2.

An examination of the first managerial appointment indicates that only one variable *remun1* appears significant in both respects for all firms model. Its negative sign suggests that those firms in which the owner felt the first two managers placed a high priority upon the remuneration package were likely to be smaller firms. The slightly weaker results relating to the first two managerial appointments suggest that, at least for USM firms, the first two managers were viewed, by the owners as joining the firm to develop a career – in contrast to the desire for remuneration. The indication that these individuals, in the subsequently larger firms, were recruited primarily through advertising, confirms our earlier findings that the larger firms were more likely to recruit externally – where presumably advertising was more likely to be required.

An examination of management qualities generates one robust result. It clearly shows that those firms which placed an emphasis on the qualities of experience and knowledge in the first two managerial appointments (*expkn1*) were likely to be very much larger than those who placed an emphasis upon other qualities. The strength of this finding is that it is significant both for USM and for match firms, and for all firms, whether in group equations or in the all variables equation. It will be recalled that this variable reflects the response of owners who indicated that they sought managers who had experience and knowledge, most notably in the industry or sector in which the firm operated.

Finally the absence of any relationship between firm performance and whether or not the first or last two managers received training while with the firm requires some comment. Though it appears to paint a fairly grim picture of the importance of management training in influencing firm performance, this may simply reflect the fact that USM firms tend to recruit trained professionals from other firms and/or most training is of a more informal on-the-job nature.

NOTES

1 t-statistic of 1.79, significant at 0.1 levels of confidence.
2 t-statistic of 1.74, significant at 0.1 levels of confidence.
3 t-statistic of 2.31, significant at 0.05 levels of confidence.
4 t-statistic of 2.08, significant at 0.05 levels of confidence.
5 t-statistic of 2.08, significant at 0.05 levels of confidence.
6 t-statistic of 1.83, significant at 0.1 levels of confidence.
7 t-statistic of 2.92, significant at 0.01 levels of confidence.
8 t-statistic of 1.66, significant at 0.1 levels of confidence.
9 t-statistic of 1.81, significant at 0.1 levels of confidence.

Appendix 7.1: Entrepreneurial characteristics

Motivations	Coded 1 if positive motivation score, 0 if different motivation score, −1 if negative motivation score.
Gender	Dummy variable coded 1 if male, 0 if female
Qualification	Dummy variable coded 1 if degree or above, 0 otherwise.
Bus ints	Dummy variable coded 1 if owner has other business interests, 0 otherwise.
Unemployed	Dummy variable coded 1 if owner was employed prior to start-up, 0 if unemployed.
Part-time	Dummy variable coded 1 if the firm was operated as a part-time concern at any time, 0 otherwise.
Owner age	The age of the owner in years at start-up of the firm.

FIRM CHARACTERISTICS

Location	Dummy variable coded 1 if the firm is located in London or the south-east, 0 otherwise.
Industry	Dummy variable coded 1 if the firm is in an industrial sector, 0 otherwise.
Firm age	Age of the firm in 1988 in years.

EXPERTISE WITHIN BUSINESS AT START-UP AND CURRENT (AT TIME OF INTERVIEW)

Production	Coded 1 if none, 2 if some, 3 if moderate, 4 if good and 5 if considerable.
Finance	Coded 1 if none, 2 if some, 3 if moderate, 4 if good and 5 if considerable.
Marketing	Coded 1 if none, 2 if some, 3 if moderate, 4 if good and 5 if considerable.

Personnel	Coded 1 if none, 2 if some, 3 if moderate, 4 if good and 5 if considerable.
R&D	Coded 1 if none, 2 if some, 3 if moderate, 4 if good and 5 if considerable.
General management	Coded 1 if none, 2 if some, 3 if moderate, 4 if good and 5 if considerable.

CHANGES IN EXPERTISE FROM START-UP TO CURRENT

Production	Calculated as the difference between the level of expertise in production at start-up and the level of expertise in production at the time of the interview.
Finance	Calculated as the difference between the level of expertise in finance at start-up and the level of expertise in finance at the time of the interview.
Marketing	Calculated as the difference between the level of expertise in marketing at start-up and the level of expertise in marketing at the time of the interview.
Personnel	Calculated as the difference between the level of expertise in personnel at start-up and the level of expertise in personnel at the time of the interview.
R&D	Calculated as the difference between the level of expertise in R&D at start-up and the level of expertise in R&D at the time of the interview.
General management	Calculated as the difference between the level of expertise in general management at start-up and the level of expertise in general management at the time of the interview.

METHODS OF INCREASING EXPERTISE

Production su team	Dummy variable coded 1 if expertise in production has been increased due to development by the start-up team, 0 otherwise.
Production outsiders	Dummy variable coded 1 if expertise in production has been increased via the recruitment of outsiders, 0 otherwise.
Production promoted	Dummy variable coded 1 if expertise in production has been increased via the promotion of the firm's personnel, 0 otherwise.

Similar variables were created for the functional areas of finance, marketing, personnel, R&D and general management.

QUALITIES AND SKILLS REQUIRED IN MANAGERIAL APPOINTMENTS

First managers

Peskill　　　dummy variable coded 1 if personnel skills were required in the first managerial appointments, 0 otherwise.

Expkn　　　Dummy variable coded 1 if experience and knowledge were required in the first managerial appointments, 0 otherwise.

Qualexp　　Dummy variable coded 1 if qualifications and expertise were required in first managerial appointments, 0 otherwise.

Perqual　　Dummy variable coded 1 if personal qualities were required in first appointments, 0 otherwise.

Similar variables were created for the last managerial appointments.

METHOD OF RECRUITING FIRST AND LAST MANAGERIAL APPOINTMENTS

Managers

Perapp　　Dummy variable coded 1 if personal approach, 0 otherwise.

Intern　　　Dummy variable coded 1 if internal appointments, 0 otherwise.

Advert　　　Dummy variable coded 1 if advertised post, 0 otherwise.

Recruit　　Dummy variable coded 1 if an external recruitment agency was used, 0 otherwise.

Reorg　　　Dummy variable coded 1 if recruited via the reorganiz-ation of the firm, 0 otherwise.

Similar variables were created for the last managerial appointments.

REASONS MANAGERS JOINED THE FIRM

Managers

Attc　　　　Dummy variable coded 1# if first managers joined com-pany due to the attractions of the company, 0 otherwise.

Attpeop　　Dummy variable coded 1 if first managers joined company due to the attractions of the people in the company, 0 otherwise.

Attjob	Dummy variable coded if first managers joined company due to the attractions of the job, 0 otherwise.
Remun	Dummy variable coded 1 if first managers joined the company due to the remuneration package offered, 0 otherwise.
Disenchant	Dummy variable coded 1 if first managers joined the company due to disenchantment with previous situation, 0 otherwise.
Career	Dummy variable coded 1 if first managers joined the company due to its career prospects, 0 otherwise.
Non-work	Dummy variable coded 1 if first managers joined the company due to non-work factors, 0 otherwise.

Similar variables were created for the last managerial appointments.

PROVISION OF TRAINING

No training	Dummy variable coded 1 if no training was provided to the first and last managerial appointments, 0 otherwise.
In-house	Dummy variable coded 1 if in-house training was provided to the first and last managerial appointments, 0 otherwise.
External	Dummy variable coded 1 if external training was provided to the first and last managerial appointments, 0 otherwise.

ORGANIZATIONAL CHARACTERISTICS

Rapport	Variable denoting the level of rapport required by the work role of the owner of the company. Coded 1 if none, 2 if some and 3 if a lot.
People	Variable denoting the level to which the owner perceived the organization to be people-orientated. Coded 1 if very much like this, 2 if quite like this, 3 if not sure, 4 if not really like this, 5 if not at all like this.
Leader	Variable denoting the level to which the owner perceived the organization to be leader-orientated. Coded 1 if very much like this, 2 if quite like this, 3 if not sure, 4 if not really like this, 5 if not at all like this.
Strucman	Variable denoting the extent to which potential growth is perceived to be inhibited by the need to introduce structured management. Coded 1 if critical, 2 if very important, 3 if of some importance, 4 if of minor importance, 5 if irrelevant.

Trade unions   Variable denoting the extent to which potential growth is perceived to be inhibited by trade union practices. Coded 1 if critical, 2 if very important, 3 if of some importance, 4 if of minor importance, 5 if irrelevant.

Inforcom   Dummy variable coded 1 if informal methods of communication are used in the company, 0 otherwise.

8 Ownership, organization and the financial performance of firms

INTRODUCTION

This chapter empirically examines the relationships between the ownership structures and organizational and management characteristics of our sample of USM and match firms and their reported profitability over the four-year period immediately prior to their being interviewed. It combines both interview data and the reported financial accounting information required by company law to be lodged with the Registrar of Companies. Although profitability is not the only financial performance measure, or even the most relevant in the case of many small-firm owners, it is a widely used index of firm performance and both private capital suppliers and public policy makers frequently use it for evaluating loan proposals and for making inter-firm and/or inter-temporal comparisons. Moreover, while the actual reported annual profits of a small firm may often be open to manipulation by its director-managers, legal and other regulatory constraints place limits on this form of behaviour. Also, it still remains the case that enterprises that are unable to cover their costs (which includes an 'adequate' return on the owners' human and financial capital) in the medium to long term will not survive. Hence, though the reported profits of firms may not be perfect indicators of the 'true' figures, we believe that a four-year average computed using the reported numbers is probably as close as it is practically possible to achieve.

Some of the literature on managerial and agency theories of the firm which has examined both the empirical and theoretical effects of different ownership and control structures on firm performance was reviewed in Chapter 2. In contrast to prior studies which have almost exclusively focused their analysis on large mature firms the primary purpose of this chapter is to examine

1 the effect of directors' shareholdings on firm performance; and
2 the hypothesis first put forward by Williamson (1975), and subsequently

tested on large UK firms by Steer and Cable (1978), that the internal organization of firms may affect their efficiency and hence their profitability.

While there has been extensive empirical testing of the relationship between the internal organization of the firm and performance based on Williamson's M-form hypothesis, little work has been conducted which examines the impact of internal organization on the performance of small and medium-sized enterprises (SMEs) (an exception is Covin and Slevin 1989).

The chapter is organized as follows. The following section draws upon the review in Chapter 2 by briefly reviewing the effect of ownership and control structures on firm performance. It also considers how the internal organization of the firm might impact on performance and how internal organization might be empirically captured for SMEs. We then discuss the model and variables utilized in examining the impact of both ownership and internal organization on firm performance. The results of the analysis are presented in the fourth section. The final section presents a discussion of the main findings and provides some concluding remarks.

THE ISSUES

Since Berle and Means' (1932) observation that the modern corporation is characterized by the separation of ownership and control, there has been a substantial body of literature which has examined the effect of the ownership-control structure of the firm on its performance.

Various managerial theories (Baumol 1959, 1962, Marris 1964) have argued that the separation of ownership from control allows managers to pursue their own objectives at the expense of the maximization of shareholder wealth. Opponents of this view suggest managers are effectively constrained from taking actions that are not in the best interests of shareholders, via several disciplining mechanisms. Fama (1980), for example, argues that competition in the managerial labour markets will limit management discretion. On the other hand Demsetz and Lehn (1985) argue that the type of ownership-control structure has no effect on performance because, in an efficient market, the structure of corporate ownership will vary systematically in ways that are consistent with value maximization.

The empirical studies on this topic have used the terms 'owner-managers', 'managers', 'directors' and 'insiders' to refer to individuals who control the firm. The empirical tests, however, have generally been based on the equity holdings of the board of directors, as this information is available from published accounting records. This information source does not, however, provide any details of the ownership stakes of non-director managers.

The empirical evidence on the effect of ownership-control structures on performance is inconclusive, with some studies showing that management controlled firms are less profitable than owner-controlled firms because of the non-profit maximizing behaviour of non-owner managers (see, for example, Monsen *et al.* 1968, Larner 1970, Radice 1971, McEachern 1975, 1976, Levin and Levin 1982). Other studies report either inconclusive or inconsistent findings (see, for example, Kamerschen 1968, Elliott 1972, Sorenson 1974, Demsetz and Lehn 1985 and Murali and Welch 1989, and, for an extensive review, Hunt 1986).

The majority of empirical studies which test for some relationship between firm performance and director ownership assume that this relationship is linear. However, Morck *et al.* (1988) suggested that the relationship may be nonlinear as a result of the combination of Jensen and Meckling's (1976) 'convergence of interest' hypothesis and Fama and Jensen's (1983a and b) 'entrenchment' hypothesis.

Subsequent work by McConnell and Servaes (1990) suggest the relationship between performance and director ownership is indeed nonlinear. Furthermore the assumption that firm performance increases as director ownership increases up to 100 per cent of equity is particularly unlikely to hold for small and medium-sized firms. The Demsetz and Lehn (1985) view that the structure of ownership varies systematically in ways that are consistent with value maximization assumes an efficient capital market in which firms are able to costlessly adjust their ownership structures to be consistent with value maximization. This is extremely unlikely to happen for small and medium-sized firms that are not listed on a stock exchange, where directors hold large proportions of their firms equity due to their inability to sell to outside parties or because of their desire to maintain control over the firm. Hence, while the firm may operate more efficiently and be more profitable at lower levels of director ownership, there may be reasons other than the pursuit of profit why directors hold more than the profit maximizing level of equity. Consequently, it may be hypothesized that in SMEs, firm performance does not increase monotonically with increased levels of director ownership.

The attitudes of directors towards risk may also influence firm performance. Baumol (1959) argues that directors are more risk averse than shareholders. Shareholders are assumed to have more diversified portfolios than directors who have firm-specific investments in the form of human capital and are hence more concerned about the possibility of bankruptcy. However, it may be hypothesized that the relative risk aversion of a director will depend on his/her portfolio of investments. For example, the risk aversion of a director may differ if the individual also holds directorships in other firms, or indeed, has only a small fraction of his/her personal wealth invested in the firm.

Empirically, the attitudes to risk of directors can include variables which measure the diversity of the director's portfolio. The clearest would be to use the number of other directorships as a proxy for portfolio diversity. Firms where the directors hold directorships in other firms would be expected to be less risk averse and should yield higher profitability measures than firms in which the directors have no other business interests.

Steer and Cable (1978) argue that the internal organization of firms is likely to affect their efficiency and hence their profitability. Moreover, they argue that the degree of owner or director control is likely to be correlated with the type of internal control apparatus employed and its effectiveness. Steer and Cable tested the extent to which large M-form firms exhibited favourable differential performance compared with other organizational forms. However, given the lack of data with which to classify SMEs into unambiguous organizational form categories and the lack of relevance of the M-form distinction to SMEs, an alternative approach is tested in this chapter.

The approach adopted in this chapter focuses on organizational characteristics which may affect the ability of directors to effectively control the firm. It is often argued (see for example, Bosworth and Jacobs 1989) that small and medium sized firm growth and performance is hampered by the desire of the original owner(s) to retain control over a large proportion of the firm's operations. Beyond a certain size and complexity of operations, the unwillingness to delegate decisions to management personnel is likely to result in the firm being operated less efficiently, due to the limits of the owner's specialist knowledge and time. Jensen and Meckling (1976) suggest a positive relationship between director ownership and firm performance. However, in reality, the ability to operate efficiently will depend upon the presence of efficient employee incentives and management control systems. It may be that firms in which the directors own substantially less than 100 per cent of the share capital but which have efficient management systems in place may perform better than 100 per cent director-managed firms which lack those systems. Hence, empirical analysis needs to control for internal organization as a constraint upon firm performance. This is particularly important in analysing young and/or rapidly growing firms where management control systems are being introduced for the first time or being adapted to reflect the rapidly changing scale of operations.

In summary, the above discussion suggests that a number of factors need to be taken into consideration when empirically analysing the effects of directors' ownership on firm performance. Firstly, the results presented by

Morck *et al.* (1988) and McConnell and Servaes (1990) highlight the possible shortcomings of any analysis which simply assumes that, if any relationship between ownership and performance does exist, the relationship is linear. There is a clear need to investigate the form of any possible relationship between ownership and firm performance. Secondly, an examination of the impact of director ownership on firm performance should control for the relative diversity of the directors' portfolios as this is hypothesized to affect the incentives facing directors. Thirdly, the possible effects of a firm's internal organization on firm performance need to be considered. Finally, some allowance needs to be made for the impact of directors' remuneration on firm performance.

SAMPLE, VARIABLES AND EMPIRICAL METHOD

Sample

To ensure that full data of the appropriate type was available, the sample used in this chapter consists of the seventy-two firms (out of the original total of 104) for which we had full financial and interview data. The financial data used in this paper spans the period 1986 to 1988 and were extracted from each firm's annual accounts on microfiche obtained from Companies House. The final reduced sample of seventy-two firms was primarily due to missing accounts or to the filing of modified accounts in which there is no requirement to state the profit for the year. Thus, although the sample may initially be considered to be small, the final sample size reflects the costs and difficulties of collecting data appropriate to testing the issues discussed above.

Variables

Dependent variable

The definition of performance used in the empirical analysis is the rate of return on capital employed. The return on capital employed may be defined as the return on shareholders' equity, on shareholders' equity plus long-term debt or on total assets (Steer and Cable 1978). However, given that this chapter focuses on the performance of SMEs, the definition of capital employed warrants some discussion. Empirical studies suggest SMEs rely heavily upon short-term debt to finance investment. Fazzari *et al.* (1988) show that firms in the smaller size classes accounted for the majority of net new short-term debt. Keasey and McGuinness (1990) show that banks are often unwilling to lend beyond the short-to-medium-term to small firms. The appropriate measure of capital employed for smaller firms should therefore include short-term debt, otherwise the return will be overstated. The return on total assets is therefore used as the dependent variable (*RTA*). In the numerator of *RTA*, profit is defined as accounting profit before interest payments and tax plus directors' remuneration. Directors' remuneration is added back because it often forms a large percentage of pre-tax profit that does not necessarily capture the necessary return to the management/entrepreneur factors of production. As shown by Watson (1991) the remuneration paid to directors' reflects tax considerations and the potential costs of firm insolvency, rather than payments for entrepreneurial and managerial inputs.

Independent variables

Owner control variables

Several variables were constructed to measure the significance and nature of the relationship between firm performance and directors' ownership. The basic unit of measurement is the proportion of shares in the firm owned by directors (*DC*) in 1986, the beginning of the period under consideration. In order to test the hypothesis suggested by McConnell and Servaes (1990) that the relationship is curvilinear, a second form of the variable DC^2 (the square of the proportion of shares owned by directors) was derived. In line with the earlier studies of the effects of ownership on firm performance, dummy variables were also derived to classify firms into one of two groups, dependent on the proportion of equity owned by directors. However, to meet Lawriwsky's (1984) criticism that the majority of studies have not established the sensitivity of their results to alternative definitions of control, the present study uses a variety of percentage point definitions of ownership. The cut-off points used to create the ownership dummy variables were 10 per cent, 20 per cent, through to 90 per cent equity ownership by the directors, which created the dummy variables *dir10*, *dir20*, through to *dir90* respectively. The form of these variables is detailed in Figure 8.1. The separate use of these nine dummies is warranted due to the lack of consensus regarding the proportion of shareholdings necessary to constitute control.

In addition to variables representing the proportion of shares owned by directors, a variable *othdir* was created to represent the other directorships held by the directors of the sample firms. *Othdir* is a dummy variable coded 1 if one or more directorships in other firms are held by the directors and 0 if the sample firm is the only directorship held. This is included as a proxy of the diversification of the portfolios of the directors and, for the reasons outlined earlier, is expected to be positively related to firm performance.

Dependent variable	Description	Expected sign
RTA	Return on total assets defined as accounting profit before interest and tax and directors' remuneration divided by total assets.	

Ownership variables

DC	Proportion of shares owned by directors.	+
DC2	Square of the proportion of shares owned by directors.	−
Dirx	Dummy variable coded 1 if the directors' share-holdings amount to *x* per cent or more of total shares, 0 otherwise (where *x* is 10 per cent, 20 per cent . . ., 90 per cent respectively).	+
Othdir	Dummy variables coded 1 if one or more directorships in other firms are held by the directors and 0 if the sample firm is the only directorship held.	

Organizational variables

Stucman	Dummy variable coded 1 if the owner felt that potential growth was constrained by the need to introduce structured management, 0 otherwise.	−
Leader	Dummy variable coded 1 if the owner felt that the firm was leader orientated, 0 otherwise.	?
People	Dummy variable coded 1 if the owner felt that the firm was people orientated, 0 otherwise.	?
Dirrem	Directors' remuneration divided by total assets.	+

Control variables

Size	Total assets averaged over the period 1986 to 1988.	+
Debt	Ratio of short and long-term debt and short term creditors to total assets averaged over the period 1986 to 1988.	+
Secure	Dummy variable coded 1 if the firm has a secured loan, 0 otherwise.	+
Growth	Growth in total assets measured over the period 1986 to 1988	+
Ind	Industry classification dummy coded 1 if the firm belongs to the electricals, engineering, textiles, oil, gas or miscellaneous industrials classifications, and 0 otherwise.	+
Age	Firm's age in 1986 in years.	+

Figure 8.1 Description of variables

Organizational characteristics and directors' remuneration variables

As noted earlier, it is hypothesized that a firm's internal organization may affect the performance of the firm through its impact on the ability of directors to pursue their own objectives. Therefore, a number of organizational variables (*strucman, leader* and *people*) were derived to proxy for the internal organization of the firm. These variables are detailed below and in Figure 8.1. As noted above, the data from which these variables are constructed were obtained from interviews with the firm owners.

It is hypothesized that SME growth and consequently performance is often constrained because the firm lacks the appropriate management control structures and procedures to successfully manage the growth in operations. This deficiency may sometimes be due to the owners' attempts to maintain control over all aspects of the firm's (much enlarged) operations. However, it may often be due to inertia or a lack of recognition of the need to change the way in which the firm is managed, due perhaps to the fact that the firm may still be highly profitable. If this is the case, then it is expected that the need for change will be most apparent to those firms whose profitability is relatively low.

It will be recalled from Chapter 7 that owners were asked to describe the degree to which they perceived that the need to introduce structured management was a critical factor inhibiting potential growth. This factor was described as being critical, very important, of some importance, of minor importance or irrelevant. A dummy variable *strucman* was coded 1 if owners perceived the need to introduce structured management as being a critical or important factor inhibiting growth and 0 otherwise. It is hypothesized that firms lacking structured management will be unable to operate efficiently and will be less profitable than other firms. Hence *strucman* is expected to be negatively related to firm performance.

Owners were also asked to describe the degree to which they felt their organizations were 'leader orientated', that is, dominated by their own personalities and characteristics. From the responses, based on a five-point scale similar to that noted for *strucman*, a dummy variable *leader* was coded 1 if the firm was perceived to be very or quite leader orientated, and 0 otherwise. This variable is included as a proxy of the control over the firm's operations exercised by the owners. This variable may be related to performance in a number of ways. Firms which are considered to be leader dominated may operate less efficiently if leader orientation is a signal of the unwillingness of the owners to delegate decision making or if it has a demotivating effect on subordinates. Alternatively, the domination of the firm by the owners may mean that their profit maximizing objectives are sought without hindrance from employees. The relationship between *leader* and firm performance is therefore unsigned.

People is a dummy variable coded 1 if the owner felt that their organization was 'people orientated', that is, dominated by its concern with
employees' welfare and team spirit, and 0 otherwise. The derivation of this
variable was similar to that of *leader*. This variable may be related to
performance in one of two ways. The concern shown for its employees may
allow the firm to pursue its profit maximization objectives without tacit
opposition from disgruntled employees. Alternatively, the emphasis on
employee relations may denote that the owners are pursuing objectives
other than profit maximization and are prepared to forgo profits in order to
maintain such relationships. Therefore, the relationship between *people* and
firm performance is unsigned.

In line with arguments presented in the first section of this chapter, the
final variable to be considered here is the variable *dirrem* used to capture
the relationship between firm performance and directors' remuneration.
This variable is defined as directors' remuneration scaled by total assets.
The scaling by total assets is to capture the relative impact of directors'
remuneration on firm performance defined as the return on total assets.
Following the theoretical literature on agency (see, for example,
Honkapohja 1989), firm performance is hypothesized to be positively
related to the directors' remuneration variable.

Control variables

Given the existing empirical literature on ownership and firm performance,
several independent variables are included in the analysis to control for
other factors which may be important determinants of the return on total
assets. The control variable *debt* is the ratio of total debt to total assets and
is included to capture the argument that higher levels of risk should be
accompanied by higher returns. Similarly, the secured loan variable
(*secure*) is included to reflect another dimension of risk; namely, that firms
with secured loans need to earn higher returns to ensure that they are able
to meet debt repayments. The variables firm age (*age*) and industry (*ind*)
are also included to capture the risk/return relationship. Younger firms are
argued to be more at risk because of their relative lack of business experience and relatively weak market position and *ind* is included to reflect the
possibility that some industries might be more risky than others. The
growth in total assets variable (*growth*) is included to reflect the possibility
that faster growing firms generate higher returns and firm size (*size*) is
included to control for any possible size effects. These variables are
described and signed in relation to the returns dependent variable (*rta*) in
Figure 8.1.

Empirical method

The empirical analysis consists of a series of OLS regressions of the dependent variable *rta* on the ownership, organizational characteristics and control variables. Due to the skewness of the distributions of the continuous variables *growth* and *age*, the natural log forms of these variables are used in the analysis. In view of the possibility of the existence of hetroskedasticity, the Halbert–White correction technique was employed. This technique calculates standard errors which are robust in the presence of unknown heteroskedasticity (White 1980). Furthermore, the correlation matrix in Appendix 8.1 indicates that multicollinearity does not appear to be a problem with the present data and variables.

As for most samples constructed to consider the performance of firms, it has to be accepted that the present sample may suffer from survivor bias: namely, those firms which report low profits may have been taken over or failed and disappeared from the sample. A survivor bias of this type is likely to be greatest for SMEs where poor performance brings with it the likelihood of eventual failure. For the present study, however, the presence of a survivor bias is likely to strengthen the testing of the hypothesis of interest – if performance is related to ownership and the poorly performing firms are not incorporated into the sample because of their demise, then the full strength of the relationship will not be captured in the data. Therefore, any relationship between performance and ownership found to be significant for the present sample is likely to be strengthened when tested on samples not suffering from survivor bias.

The analysis begins by first describing the distribution of the variables. This is followed by a number of stages of multivariate analysis. The first stage examines the relationship between directors' ownership and firm performance, testing the hypothesis that a positive (and implicitly linear) relationship exists between the two variables. Secondly, the hypothesis (supported by the results of McConnell and Servaes) that the relationship between directors' ownership and firm performance is curvilinear in form is investigated. The third and fourth stages of analysis further explore the potential nonlinearities between firm performance and directors' ownership, by respectively, piecewise fitting a regression function around a given break point and by the use of dummy variables to denote differing levels of director ownership.

Empirical results

Univariate statistics

To provide a background to the empirical results, Table 8.1 presents summary statistics for the variables shown in Figure 8.1. The statistics for the return on total assets (*RTA*) variable indicates that across the sample as a whole, firms earned approximately an 18 per cent return with the maximum and minimum of the range equalling 63 per cent and –27 per cent respectively. The mean of directors' remuneration scaled by total assets is 6 per cent, and this reduces the return on total assets after directors' remuneration to 12 per cent. The directors' ownership variable (*DC*) shows that the mean proportion of shares owned by directors for the firms in this sample is approximately 61 per cent. The maximum and minimum values of 100 per cent and 3.4 per cent for this variable indicates that the sample includes a wide range of ownership structures. In this respect the present sample is radically different from the samples employed by Morck *et al.* and McConnell and Servaes which had average directors' ownership of 10.6 per cent and 11.84 per cent respectively. Given the small size and unquoted

Table 8.1 Summary statistics

Continuous variables	*Mean*	*Standard deviation*	*Maximum*	*Minimum*
RTA	0.184	0.157	0.628	– 0.272
DC	0.609	0.327	1.000	0.034
Size *	6876.378	8281.212	47899.330	28.330
Dirrem	0.061	0.061	0.299	0.000
Growth	1.393	1.519	7.160	– 0.470
Debt	0.598	0.1765	1.180	0.120

Dummy variables	*Coded 0*	*Coded 1*
Secure	29	43
Othdir	9	63
Leader	24	48
People	14	58
Strucman	35	37
Ind	35	37

Note: * in £'000s

status of our sample, such a difference in average directors' ownership is be to expected because of the difficulties of attracting external shareholders.

The statistics for the variable *size* indicate that the mean of the total assets for the sample equals approximately £6.9 million which reflects the inclusion in the sample of our fast-growth USM firms. The other statistics reveal the large variation in the size of firms, ranging from a minimum asset size of £28,000 to a maximum size £48 million. The summary statistics also show that the sample as a whole experienced growth rates averaging 139 per cent over the period 1986–88. This average growth rate and the range of growth rates from –47 per cent to 716 per cent reflects the varied fortunes faced by the sample.

The statistics for the variable *growth* also reflect the age profile of the sample. Finally, in terms of the continuous variables, the statistics for the *debt* variable reveal that on average, loans and creditors fund 60 per cent of total assets. The variable *secure* indicates that the majority of the firms (approximately 60 per cent) obtain their debt through secured loans.

In terms of the other dichotomous variables, the statistics indicate that the large majority of firms (87.5 per cent) have directors who hold director- ships in other firms. Of the firms in the sample, 66.6 per cent of the owners thought their firms to be leader orientated, while 81 per cent thought their firms were greatly concerned with the welfare of their staff. Approximately half of the sample thought their growth potential (see the *strucman* variable) was hampered by the absence of structured management. The industry variable *ind* indicates that the sample is almost equally split between the two industrial categories.

Multivariate statistics

The first stage of the analysis examines the relationship between firm performance and directors' ownership by regressing *RTA* against *DC* and the other explanatory variables described in Figure 8.1. As shown by the results presented in Table 8.2, the overall regression explains approxi- mately 34 per cent of the variation in the dependent variable and it contains three variables which are significant at conventional levels of confidence. Of the three significant variables, there is evidence of a positive relation- ship between *RTA* and directors' ownership *DC* but the relationship is only significant at the 10 per cent level using a two tailed test (the general relationship between *RTA* and *DC* being unsigned). However, a weakness of this form of regression is the assumption that the hypothesized relation- ship between *RTA* and *DC* is linear, with performance increasing as directors' ownership increases up to the 100 per cent level. As noted earlier, however, a linear relationship may not hold for SMEs if the lack of a market

Table 8.2 OLS regression estimates – linear form dependent variable = *RTA*

Variable	Estimated coefficient	Standard error	t-statistic
DC	0.1326	0.0729	1.8180*
Othdir	0.1022	0.0500	2.0411**
Size	1.369E-6	2.090E-6	0.6550
Debt	– 0.0364	0.1162	– 0.3140
Secure	– 0.0204	0.0287	– 0.7123
LG(growth)	0.0720	0.0469	1.5358
Ind	– 0.0062	0.0400	– 0.1558
LG(age)	0.0027	0.0257	0.1084
Leader	– 0.0109	0.0313	– 0.3500
People	0.0287	0.0400	0.7180
Strucman	– 0.0497	0.0318	– 1.5607
Dirrem	1.1398	0.3491	3.2647**
Constant	– 0.0753	0.1229	– 0.6130

Notes: $\bar{R}^2 = 0.3436$ $F = 4.0972$
(Hetroskedasticity-consistent covariance matrix)
* Significant at 0.1 levels of confidence.
** Significant at 0.05 levels of confidence.

for their shares constrains their ability to choose profit maximizing levels of shareholdings. The other two variables significant in the regression results reported in Table 8.2 are *othdir* and *dirrem*. The positive coefficient on the *othdir* variables indicates that firms where directors hold directorships in other organizations have higher returns on total assets. The results also indicate that there is a significant positive relationship between firm performance and directors' remuneration (*dirrem*). Interestingly, none of the organization variables are found to be significant in this first stage of the analysis.

Given the results of the first stage, the second stage of the analysis involves testing McConnell and Servaes' findings that a curvilinear relationship exists between firm performance and directors' shareholdings. This is achieved by adding to the regression form of stage 1 of the variable DC^2. The regression results shown in Table 8.3 indicate that allowing for the possibility of a curvilinear relationship between performance and directors' ownership improves the general explanatory power (as measured by the adjusted R^2) of the equation. The results also present strong evidence of a curvilinear relationship between firm performance and directors' ownership, as the coefficient on the *DC* variable is positive and significant

Table 8.3 OLS regression estimates – curvilinear form dependent variable = *RTA*

Variable	Estimated coefficient	Standard error	t-statistic
DC	0.6417	0.2201	2.9148**
DC^2	– 0.4623	0.1807	– 2.5588**
Othdir	0.0942	0.0439	2.1439**
Size	1.283E-6	1.935E-6	0.6631
Debt	– 0.0225	0.1132	– 0.1989
Secure	– 0.0341	0.0276	– 1.2351
LG(growth)	0.0572	0.0451	1.2687
Ind	– 0.0007	0.0399	– 0.0194
LG(age)	– 0.0027	0.0250	– 0.1104
Leader	– 0.0116	0.0319	– 0.3630
People	0.0346	0.0398	0.8679
Strucman	– 0.0517	0.0291	– 1.7783*
Dirrem	1.3000	0.3396	3.8282**
Constant	– 0.1513	0.1344	– 1.1272

Notes: $\bar{R}^2 = 0.4017$ $F = 4.6675$
(Hetroskedasticity-consistent covariance matrix)
*   Significant at 0.1 levels of confidence.
** Significant at 0.05 levels of confidence.

at the 1 per cent level while the (smaller) coefficient on DC^2 is negative and significant at the 1 per cent level. These findings suggest that the return on total assets first increases and then decreases as directors' ownership increases – the estimated equation is graphed in Figure 8.2. At directors' ownership levels below 69.4 per cent, the positive effect of directors' ownership dominates any negative effects, but beyond ownership levels of 69.4 per cent, the negative effect dominates. Under this stage of analysis the *othdir* and *dirrem* variables remain significant and are joined at a 10 per cent level of significance by the *strucman* variable. The negative coefficient on this variable indicates that firms which perceive they lack structured management have on average a lower level of performance.

The third stage of the analysis further explores the nonlinearity of the relationship between firm performance and directors' ownership by the use of piecewise regression techniques, allowing the coefficient on the *DC* variable to change at 69.4 per cent of directors' ownership. To capture the potential nonlinearity an additional two variables were created based on the proportion of directors' ownership:

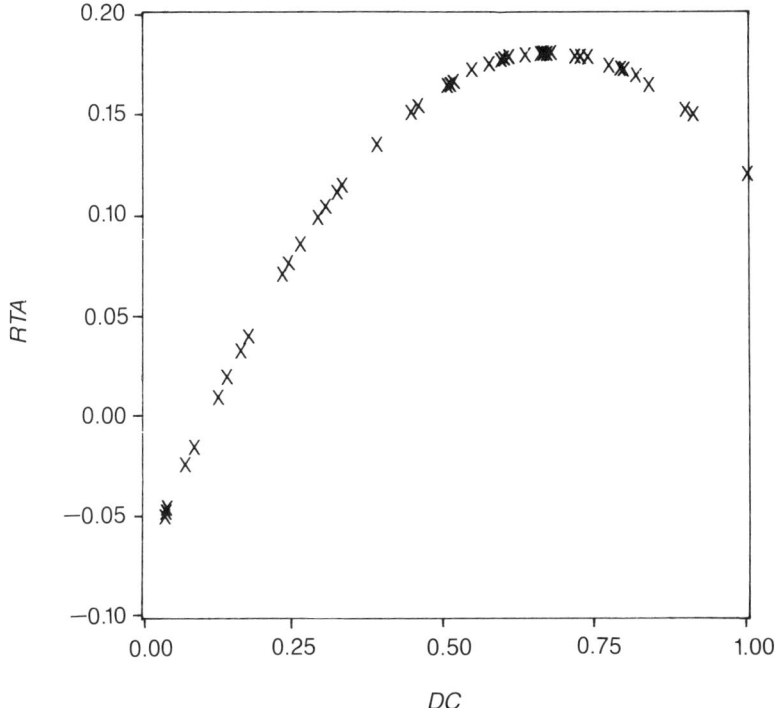

Figure 8.2 Relationship between performance and directors' ownership

$dir(0\text{–}69.4)$ = directors' ownership (DC) if $DC < 0.694$
                = 0.694 if $DC \geq 0.694$

$dir(69.4\text{–}100)$ = 0 if $DC < 0.694$
                = $DC - 0.694$ if $DC \geq 0.694$

For example, when directors' ownership is equal to 0.50, $dir(0\text{–}69.4)$ is equal to 0.50 and $dir(69.4\text{–}100)$ is equal to 0. When directors' ownership is equal to 0.75, $dir(0\text{–}69.4)$ is equal to 0.694 and $dir(69.4\text{–}100)$ is equal to 0.056. Therefore, taken together, the values of $dir(0\text{–}69.4)$ and $dir(69.4\text{–}100)$ sum to the proportion of shares owned by the directors. The results obtained when employing the piecewise variables in place of DC are presented in Table 8.4. The significance of the directors' ownership variables and the maintained R^2 reinforces the suggestion that the relationship between firm performance (RTA) and directors' ownership is indeed nonlinear.

As a final check on the results obtained above, the fourth stage of analysis follows the lead of the majority of previous studies by employing

Table 8.4 OLS regression estimates – piecewise form dependent variable = *RTA*

Variable	Estimated coefficient	Standard error	t-statistic
DIR(0–69.4)	0.3093	0.0966	3.2012**
DIR(69.4–100)	– 0.2750	0.1600	– 1.7189*
Othdir	0.1044	0.0439	2.3804**
Size	1.105E-6	1.870E-6	0.5910
Debt	– 0.0667	0.1143	– 0.2946
Secure	– 0.0372	0.0278	– 1.3372
LG(growth)	0.0543	0.0456	1.1896
Ind	– 0.0048	0.0387	– 0.1236
LG(age)	– 0.0070	0.0256	– 0.2730
Leader	– 0.0078	0.0324	– 0.2410
People	0.0266	0.0392	0.6786
Strucman	– 0.0505	0.0290	– 1.7403*
Dirrem	1.3452	0.3436	3.9146**
Constant	– 0.0970	0.1223	– 0.7928

Notes: $\overline{R}^2 = 0.4092$ F = 4.7828
  (hetroskedasticity-consistent covariance matrix)
  * significant at 0.1 levels of confidence.
  ** significant at 0.05 levels of confidence.

dummy variables to denote different ownership structures. The large number of regressions for this stage of the analysis, however, preclude the results being tabulated (these regressions are available on request from the authors). In terms of the analysis, nine dummy variables were created (*dir10*, *dir20*, etc., up to *dir90*). RTA was regressed against each of the ownership dummy variables. The coefficients on the variables *dir10* through to *dir60* were all positive and significant to at least the 10 per cent level (employing two-tailed tests of significance). The coefficients of *dir70* and *dir80* were positive but insignificant, while the coefficient of *dir90* was negative but insignificant. Thus, in general these results reinforce those obtained under stages two and three of the analysis. However, while the use of several dummy variables denoting differing levels of ownership provide some insight into the relationship between directors' ownership and firm performance, they provide a somewhat incomplete picture. Given that the majority of previous studies have based their analysis on the use of a single ownership dummy without theoretical guidance or sensitivity analysis (Lawriwsky 1984), the results of the analysis presented here suggest that any examination of the relationship between firm performance and ownership need to investigate the *form* of the relationship.

Overall, the results suggest that a significant curvilinear relationship exists between firm performance and directors' ownership for SMEs. In addition, the performance of SMEs is positively related to the presence of directors holding directorships in other firms and to directors achieving relatively higher levels of remuneration. Finally, there is some evidence to suggest that firms in which the owners perceive present management practices to be lacking in structure are found to have significantly lower performance.

CONCLUSIONS

This chapter has investigated the relationship between firm performance and ownership and organizational variables for our combined sample of USM and match firms. It suggests that the nature of the relationship between firm performance and directors' ownership is more complex than the linear form implicitly assumed in the majority of prior studies. In line with the work of McConnell and Servaes, the analysis has suggested that the relationship is curvilinear in nature, with the return on assets increasing as directors' ownership increases up to a level of ownership of 69.4 per cent and thereafter the return on assets decreases as directors' ownership increases up to 100 per cent.

Our work finds that maximum return on assets is at ownership levels of 69.4 per cent, whereas McConnell and Servaes found the maximum value to be less than 40 per cent. The McConnell and Servaes findings are also consistent with the model derived by Stulz (1988) which predicts a curvilinear relationship to exist between firm value and management ownership. In addition the Stulz model predicts that value of the firm will be maximized below the 50 per cent level of management ownership. However, such findings assume firms are able to adjust their ownership structures to be consistent with value maximization, which may not be the case for SMEs.

The finding that those firms which feel constrained by the need to introduce structured management systems are less profitable than others suggests that they are not profit maximizing. The inability or unwillingness to delegate decisions may constrain firms with high director ownership from operating to their full potential. In addition, the finding that firms whose directors hold directorships in other firms are more profitable suggests that the relative risk aversion of the directors may affect performance. Moreover, it may be argued that those directors without other business interests are more likely to operate their firm for reasons other than profit maximization, such as for family employment or other 'lifestyle' benefits.

Finally, the results suggest a positive relationship between firm perform-ance and directors' remuneration.

In spite of the strong empirical results, this study has focused on the shareholdings of directors, without considering the distribution of external shareholdings. As argued by Cubbin and Leech (1983), such an approach takes no account of the differences in shareholding dispersion between firms. Further work in this area would need to consider the impact of other large shareholders on firm performance. The significance of the variable proxying the diversification of directors' portfolios suggests that additional work into the attitudes to risk and their subsequent effect on performance of the different parties is warranted. In addition, the proxies used for internal organization are preliminary attempts to empirically capture internal organization and further work may profit from examining the use of alternative methods of empirically measuring internal organization in SMEs.

Appendix 8.1 Correlation matrix

	RTA	DC	DC²	Othdir	Size	Debt	Secure	LG(growth)	Ind	LG(age)	Leader	People	Strucman	Dirrem
RTA	1.000	0.373*	0.321*	0.200	-0.052	-0.026	-0.177	0.232	-0.225	0.035	-0.026	0.126	-0.123	0.476**
DC		1.000	0.973**	-0.084	-0.244	-0.101	-0.105	-0.043	-0.319*	-0.032	-0.072	0.183	0.224	0.414**
DC²			1.000	-0.104	-0.282	-0.086	-0.146	-0.093	-0.284	-0.031	-0.070	-0.157	0.206	0.458**
Othdir				1.000	0.174	0.067	-0.054	0.086	0.137	0.227	0.000	0.239	-0.200	-0.178
Size					1.000	-0.136	0.091	0.282	-0.189	0.003	0.004	-0.038	-0.076	-0.410**
Debt						1.000	0.190	0.340*	-0.085	-0.221	0.142	0.044	0.186	-0.020
Secure							1.000	0.076	0.051	-0.113	0.020	-0.046	0.108	-0.152
LG(growth)								1.000	-0.373*	-0.255	0.220	-0.015	0.071	-0.044
Ind									1.000	0.198	0.020	-0.127	-0.112	-0.107
LG(age)										1.000	-0.074	0.009	-0.059	0.058
Leader											1.000	0.248	0.196	0.099
People												1.000	-0.197	0.072
Strucman													1.000	0.088
Dirrem														1.000

Notes: * denotes significance at 0.01 using a two-tailed test.
       ** denotes significance at 0.001 using a two-tailed test.

9 Teams and teamworking

INTRODUCTION

This chapter examines managerial teams and teamworking from a different perspective to that of the earlier three empirical chapters. Here the intention is to provide qualitative insights into the operation of managerial teams in both fast-growth and match firms. The questionnaire administered both to owners and managers contained a number of qualitative or 'open-ended' questions and this chapter examines the responses to such questions.

The ability to develop and sustain an adequate managerial team is probably a major distinguishing feature of successful growing firms. This is because most small firms remain small throughout their entire existence and, therefore, have no need to recruit and develop a management team. For a rapidly growing small firm, however, it is likely to be the case that the largely informal management style of the typical owner-manager will need to be supplemented by the recruitment of new managers and the development of a more formal managerial structure in order for growth to be successfully achieved. Indeed, the managerial problems associated with the transition(s) to formal management control and communication systems and the development of teamworking will be unique to rapidly growing small firms.

To assess the impact of teamworking within respondent firms three groups of questions will be considered. The first set of questions determines whether owners feel that some individuals are more important than others to the managerial team. The implication is that where owners are prepared to stress either 'most important' or a 'least important' manager, then teamwork is regarded as being of less importance than the contribution of individuals. Conversely, where owners are reluctant to specify key managers and instead place a greater emphasis upon all participants in the team, we infer that the business is characterized more by a collective contribution.

The prime emphasis of the chapter however is to address the question of teamworking in practice. The second set of questions determine how owners operationalize teamwork, and furthermore, what were the limitations and problems they faced in assembling appropriate teams.

At the heart of teamworking is the question of dissemination of managerial information and this forms the core of the third set of questions. Owners are therefore asked about the procedures which they implement to ensure that managerial information is disseminated to all managers in the business. A distinction is made between formal procedures for information dissemination and less formal procedures, and this is related both to the size of the firm and whether or not it is a USM or match firm.

THE IMPORTANCE OF MANAGERS TO THE SUCCESS OF THE BUSINESS

Most important managers

All business owners were asked whether they thought some managers were more significant than others to the success of the business. Of the USM respondents, 88 per cent indicated they thought some were more significant, compared with 78 per cent of match respondents.

Respondents were then asked about those managers, and why they were viewed as particularly significant. Their responses are shown in Table 9.1.

The table suggests there are some differences between the two groups of firms. The first is that, as already observed, USM respondents are more likely to identify a key manager, and from Table 9.1 they appear to be more likely to identify more than a single individual. It shows that the total number of responses per individual for USM firms was in excess of 1.5, compared with 1.3 individuals identified by match firm owners. This, of course, is not surprising given the larger size of the USM firms.

The main area of interest, however, is in the different types of responses of both groups of firms. Broadly we have identified four groups of responses. The first includes those owners who said that all managers were significant to the success of the business. The second group covers responses which made reference to the personality of the managers, rather than the work which they do. The third group of responses refer to the functions which those individuals undertake within the business, and fourthly, more general comments about significant managers are considered.

Owners may provide an answer which is included in more than one group. For example, one answered in the following way:

Table 9.1 Managers who are most significant to the success of the business

		USM		Match	
		No.	*%*	*No.*	*%*
1	All	6	9	8	16
2	Personality	6	9	3	6
3	Production	3	4	2	4
	Finance	8	12	5	10
	Marketing/sales	10	15	9	18
	R&D	4	6	–	
	Senior/top people	22	33	11	21
	Administration	–		1	2
4	General	8	12	12	23
	Total responses	67	100	51	100
	Total firms	44		39	
	Responses per firm	1.52		1.31	

'All the people in the company are significant because they were brought in because they have the skills to be effective in the sector they are operating in. The most important person in the company besides me, is without doubt Mr X. He has considerable management experience in the "Y" business. Much longer than me. He was with one of the biggest "Y" companies in the world for sixteen years before us. He has recruited and reformatted the whole of the sales force and is primarily responsible for our UK markets, but is an essential adviser on overseas sales as well.'

In the case of this respondent we have classified his answer as being included within the 'all' category but we have also included it within the 'general' category in the sense that he refers to a manager without referring to a particular job title or functional specialism. Finally it is also included in the 'top people' category since the respondent indicates that Mr X is the most important person in the company 'besides me'.

The second category in Table 9.1 includes those cases where respondents referred to the personality of an individual, rather than the function which she or he undertook. We have included within this category responses such as that of the following owner:

'There are key personnel in any company who are leaders and it is around that nucleus of personnel that others develop their skills that subsequently motivate and provide leadership to the whole team.'

The personality of the significant manager is referred to more frequently by USM than by match firm owners. Match firm owners are much more likely to indicate that all managers in the business are significant to its success.

The third group identified in Table 9.1 are those who replied that the significant managers are those having specific functional responsibilities. The single most frequent response is that the owners identify themselves as the most significant person in the success of the business. One-third of all responses, and one-half of all respondents among USM firms, said senior/top people were the most significant in the success of the business. This is very much higher than for match firms where only 21 per cent of responses, and less than 30 per cent of respondents, referred to themselves as being particularly significant to the success of the business.

An illustration of this is the respondent who, when asked who the managers were who were significant to the business, replied:

'Well there's me . . . . There are probably half a dozen people who if they left would be sorely missed, but in all modesty, the only person who could leave and put the whole place in danger of sinking would be me.'

Another response was by a founder who said:

'Look, there's only one reason why this company is still in business and that's because I work eighty hours a week . . . If I'm not here this company grinds to a halt. I know it sounds big-headed, but it's a fact.'

The finance and marketing/sales functions are identified most frequently as the functional areas most significant to the success of the business in both USM and match firms. Conversely production and administration are seen as being almost unimportant, as is personnel. No clear differences between the two groups of firms exist, except that four USM firms identify research and development personnel as being important. No match firms regard R&D managerial personnel as significant.

Clearly the sector in which the business operates is of considerable importance in answering this question. For example, for those businesses in the leisure sector, the role of the finance director as controller of cash is vital to the success of the business. One respondent in this sector replied to our question about crucial individuals in the following way:

'The Finance Director is critical as is the necessity for keeping very strong controls of our business. In our business you are dealing with cash, liquor and food, and all of them can be stolen. It's a business which, if you do not control it efficiently, you are going to get robbed all ways. We've always been strong in that department which I think is one of the reasons for our success.'

Table 9.1 shows that the most frequently mentioned functional area was marketing/sales. A fairly typical response of owners who identified marketing as the crucial component was the following:

> 'Because we are operating in a growing market with lots of competitors, the marketing function is particularly important. We've become the sole UK agents for several Swiss products and if we don't push the products then we may not retain the agency.'

The final group in Table 9.1 is headed general, and it shows that match firms were much more likely to identify non-specialists as being significant to the success of the business. In total 23 per cent of responses of match firms identified generalists, compared with only 12 per cent of responses for USM firms. This may be characteristic of match firms, partly because some individuals may not have a single function or job title, and are referred to within the firm as general managers or simply as managers.

The role of significant managers in the success of the business is further explored in Table 9.2. This reports the responses which owners gave to the question as to why particular managers were crucial to the success of their firms. We have chosen to group the responses into four categories. The first relates to the particular jobs which the managers do, the second to the technical ability of the individuals in doing those jobs, the third to the personal qualities of the individual and a final group includes all other responses.

Table 9.2 Reasons managers are crucial

		USM		Match	
		No.	*%*	*No.*	*%*
1	The jobs they do	27	52	17	39
2	Technical ability	12	21	13	29
3	Personal qualities	11	21	11	25
4	Others	3	6	3	7
	Total	53	100	44	100

The main difference between the two groups of firms is that USM respondents are more likely to regard managers as crucial because of the jobs which they do, rather than because of their technical ability or their personal qualities. From the table it can be seen that 52 per cent of USM respondents referred to jobs which managers did, compared with 39 per cent of match respondents.

A typical response which emphasized the nature of the jobs is the following:

'The managing director is the most crucial because he's in control of directing the business and this is our core activity, so if we don't produce it then we don't sell it. We don't have problems with markets, our main concern is with quality at the right price.'

In some instances it was not possible to distinguish the jobs which managers did and their technical ability in the conduct of these jobs. For example, we have chosen to regard the following quotation as reflecting primarily the job which a manager does, even though the respondent regards the individual as crucial, at least partly, because of his technical ability:

'The managing director is crucial because he is so good with clients – he can get the business. He's a totally charismatic person with vast inter-personal skills. Of course he needs the support of the remaining staff in conducting the work, but it is his skills which initially get the business.'

We noted in Table 9.1 that one of the characteristics of USM firms, which was not shared by the match firms, was that some regarded R&D managers as being particularly crucial to their business. One illustration of this is the following:

'The success of this company particularly in the early stages was de-pendent upon its ability to develop a new product.'

The third group in Table 9.2 are respondents who referred to the personal qualities of individual managers, rather than to the jobs which they under-took. One company, for example, referred to the finance director as being the key person, but it was his ability to understand the totality of the business, rather than his function as a finance director, which they regarded as crucial.

The table suggests USM firm owners are more likely to refer to crucial managers in terms of their functional expertise than match firms. This is not a surprising result given that managers in the match firms are more likely to be generalists.

Overall there are some differences between the two groups of firms. Differences occur between firms in different industrial sectors. For example in leisure businesses managing systems for dealing with cash is regarded as being important, whereas in the electronics sector the ability to introduce new innovative products is regarded as being absolutely crucial; in the consultancy sector the ability to liaise with clients and to build up personal reputations is regarded as being the key consideration. These differences probably appear to outweigh the differences between USM and match firms. In other words, the factors regarded as critical to key management achieving business success reflect the dimensions of activity that are seen as forming part of the core of the strategic environment.

Least important managers

To obtain a balanced picture of the managers crucial to the development of the business, owners were also asked about managers who were perceived to be least important to the success of the business. The responses to this question are provided in Table 9.3, which should be compared with Table 9.1. The comparison shows that there are both similarities and differences.

As for Table 9.1, Table 9.3 divides responses into four groups. Not surprisingly, fewer owners were prepared to identify managers who were least important to the success of the business. Thus the total number of responses among USM firms is 49 in Table 9.3, compared with 67 in Table 9.1. Even fewer match firms were prepared to identify managers who were least important.

The most striking finding in Table 9.3 is that 46 per cent of match firms owners indicated that all people were 'least important'. This is primarily because all managers were regarded as making an equal contribution, and so no individual was identified as 'least important'. The general response of match owners was that if managers did not make a major contribution to the development of the business, then they would not be employed in the organization.

Table 9.3 Managers who are least important to the success of the business

	USM		Match	
	No.	%	No.	%
1 All	6	12	12	46
2 Personality	1	2	1	4
3 Production	6	12	2	8
Finance/accounting	7	14	1	4
Marketing/sales	5	10	–	
R&D	–	–	1	4
Senior/top people	2	4	4	15
Administration	11	23	3	11
Personnel	1	2	1	4
4 General	10	21	1	4
Total responses	49	100	26	100

'I don't think I've got anybody I could put in that category, to be quite honest with you. We are very short on managers. There isn't really anybody in a high supervisory or management position who we could do without. It gets down to the top four people and you couldn't cut any of them. It's like "which arm would you like to lose, your right or your left one?". I can't see anywhere in the organization where you could dispense with anyone. You would immediately have to replace them. We sometimes get problems in levels of staff – you may find you have too many test engineers for the amount of test work. This is usually only a phase. It's probably a trough. If you start laying people off and losing them, you can guarantee that round the corner is a peak. We don't have anybody in such positions, we have got rid of them all; if they are not needed, they're not here.'

Table 9.3 shows that, in identifying the least important managers, USM owners generally referred to the functional area in which such individuals operated. Virtually one-quarter of responses from USM owners referred to managers conducting an administrative function. Their view was that administrators were capable of being replaced. Perhaps surprisingly, given the emphasis placed upon finance and accounting skills within USM companies, 14 per cent of all responses referred to the finance and accounting function. Again the main reason given was that these skills were, in principle, replaceable within the market place.

'It is confidential but I would imagine it's the financial side. It's less crucial, not because it's not important, but because we could replace it without too much problem. In terms of the production side it's going to be very difficult to replace, as these guys are premium, and they know their business. On the administrative side, that is a function that could be duplicated by other people, so I suppose it's the administrative and the financial side that are most easily replaced.'

Clearly, some owners perceived that the administrative and finance functions did not require the development of highly firm-specific skills which would be costly to replace and that therefore the recruitment of suitably qualified outsiders would not present any major problems.

In some cases owners expressed strongly an objection to certain functional specialisms, of which the following directed towards personnel officers was fairly typical:

'Good managers should be able to do what the personnel function does. Personnel is to some extent a luxury, but we now have a personnel function because we have a very delegated notion of responsibilities. The trouble is that Personnel divorces people from each other, and managers don't know clearly what's in the mind of the workforce. They know what the personnel staff *tells* them is in the mind of the workforce. Employees are people, with their own problems and difficulties, opportunities, career motivations, etc. You have to get to know them or else you can't hold the business together. The Personnel function takes away from management one of its most important aspects, relationships with the people it works with. The Personnel Manager always wants to extend his role, help with evaluations, take on more of the manager's role. But the managers must deal with people who are a problem, not pass it on.'

Perhaps not surprisingly the senior and top people appear infrequently among those who are thought to be least important to the success of the business, constituting a major contrast with Table 9.1. Thus only 4 per cent of USM owners refer to this group and 16 per cent of owners of match firms. Again this appears to reflect the greater informality in match firms, and the rather more hierarchical organization of the USM firms.

These differences are also identified in Table 9.4 which categorizes the responses as to why managers are regarded as being least crucial to the organization. It shows some striking differences between USM and match firms. The most frequent response by match firms is that nobody is 'least crucial' since everyone within the organization is important. This was given by 56 per cent of match firm respondents. Only 22 per cent of USM firms responded in this way; instead they were much more likely to emphasize the availability of replacements as the reasons why people could be deemed to be less crucial. Of the USM responses, 41 per cent were in this category, compared with 26 per cent of match responses. A third difference is that the USM firms were more likely to emphasize the jobs which managers do as factors which make them less crucial. While 32 per cent of USM firm owners mentioned a particular functional area, only 7 per cent of match firm owners identified the functional responsibilities of managers. The

Table 9.4 Reasons why managers are least crucial

	USM		Match	
	No.	*%*	*No.*	*%*
1 Everyone important	8	22	15	56
2 Jobs they do	12	32	2	7
3 Technical ability	2	5	2	7
4 Personal qualities	–	–	1	4
5 Availability of replacements	15	41	7	26
Total	37	100	27	100

functional areas most frequently identified were administration, accounting and finance. Here respondents were likely to refer to these managers as least crucial 'because they perform a support function only', 'they do not finalise sales deals', 'we can manage without them in times of a crisis', or 'their jobs are more tactical than strategic'.

Overall there appear to be differences in the way in which owners of USM and match firms respond to these questions. Match owners are more likely to regard everybody as equally important to the success of the organization, and so less likely to highlight any manager as being less crucial. USM owners, on the other hand, are more likely to identify such managers and, where they do, to refer to the availability of replacements as the reason why these managers are deemed least crucial. USM owners are also more likely than match firms to identify less crucial managers according to their functional responsibilities. Clearly these two issues may be strongly linked. It raises therefore the question of teamwork and the extent to which managers work independently or collectively within the organization and it is to this question that we now turn.

TEAMWORK

The literature reviewed in Chapters 2 and 3, indicated that, because of the many and varied interests of organizational participants, conflicts over goals and methods of working would be inevitable. Hence, organizations would need to devise strategies, such as the creation of a relational team (Williamson 1984), clan structure (Ouchi 1980) or dominant coalition (Cyert and March 1963), in order to contain such conflicts and provide a measure of cohesion and direction to the organization. In this section we examine how the firms in our sample attempt to achieve this.

All firms were asked about the extent to which senior personnel worked together as a team. There is almost no difference in the responses of USM and match firms on the extent to which managers work together as a team, with two-thirds of both groups of firms saying this happened to a considerable extent. The bulk of the remainder reported that teamwork was of some importance to the business, and only a handful indicated that teamworking was either limited or did not exist at all.

However, the nature of the teamworking does seem to differ between USM and match firms. In match firms, owners were more likely to stress the inevitability of teamwork because of the small size of the firm. On the other hand, teamwork is more consciously encouraged in USM firms where it is perceived to be necessary for the efficient control of the organization. One firm making the transition towards larger size illustrate these two characteristics.

'Because of the way the company has developed the production and sales people have begun to work much more as a team than as individuals. Prior to that we weren't structured at all but it's now become necessary as the firm has grown.'

In some instances the development of teams and teamworking evolved naturally, as described by one owner:

'We tend to look for niche business areas and the marketeers will meet with the engineers and identify an opportunity for this particular radio, or that particular component, or even a particular system. Then the engineers will say we have the expertise to do it and if two or three of them get together as a team they will produce some form of microwave link. It's no good the marketeers selling something which the engineers can't engineer in the first place and we haven't got the production capability to make later. It seems to me that is the essence of teamworking, even though each individual brings a particular expertise to the team.'

Most of the respondents, however, indicated that teamworking did not occur automatically. With firm growth owners emphasized it was necessary to encourage teamworking without being seen to impose on it on managers. An illustration of this is the following firm:

'This is a company of primadonnas. You can't run a company like this on a tight Victorian basis. Equally you can't expect a smooth-running well-oiled machine. Most of our work is bound up with argument, friction and the expression of powerfully felt views in the face of brilliantly expressed criticism. The thing doesn't work together very well, but in many ways it's out of the frictions, combined with a generally understood sense of direction, that we get by. We've got the knack of being able to pull into a team and I think enable people to operate who come from a very diverse range of backgrounds . . . . I'm not very interested in people but I'm interested in operators in the field of intellectual activity. That's a terrible thing to admit, and I feel it's a criticism of me that I actually forget people's names, because I believe it's a reflection of not actually being interested in them as people, as individuals, so much as in the formation of the ideas. That's the nature of the business.'

Another firm illustrated problems of teamwork in the following way, showing that implementing teamworking has presented its problems.

'It's been very difficult. Getting personnel to work together as a team has been one of the difficulties. You look at the business, and most of the managers have been growing with the company, which has been a mistake. Our original strategy was that we didn't have managers at all, we only had team leaders. The team leaders took responsibility for specific projects. We got to the point where we only had so many team leaders and could only handle the amount of work they could do. So we decided to change the strategy and have divisions and departments and converted the team leaders into managers. That was the beginning of the problems, because they were not experienced managers. A team leader leads one project, whereas a manager would be expected to oversee five or six projects. There is a vast difference between a person who can manage a project and a person who can manage people. I think one of the most important things, when we changed from our team leader approach to our management approach, was that we did tend to build up barriers between them. It was very much "I've done my part, you make a mistake and I'm not going to tell you about it". Maybe we didn't develop the management team properly – the team spirit disappeared.'

Given the changes in activity that they are likely to have undergone, USM companies were more likely to recall the changes in emphasis on team-working. One owner responded somewhat wistfully:

'In the old days we were so small that we could just shout and everyone would hear. Nowadays we have much more formal mechanisms but we still talk to each other a lot. For example we have a company newsletter which comes out weekly and tells people about the business, and also about the social events that are happening.'

Some interesting differences occur between responses of USM firms and match firms to this question of team building. The following match firm, when asked about the extent to which senior personnel worked together as a team, said:

'Not enough to be honest. You can see what it's like. We're always too busy. This is my office, but in fact it's Christine's office, the staff common room and everything else as well. It's impossible sometimes. I then say "come on, let's go down to the local" it's the only place we can talk without being interrupted all the time.'

This might be contrasted with a USM owner who responded that:

'Senior personnel work together a great deal as a team. We specialize in having training weekends. Last weekend we were at our local Airport and the sales team also came together. I regularly have eight or ten people on my boat. I get them up at 7 o'clock in the morning for a bit of gymnastics and a run. This is all mandatory training and encourages the individuals to work together as a team over the whole of the weekend on a variety of different activities.'

Although there is an emphasis upon teamworking it is clear from the above quotation that a number of respondents were aware that they were certainly the first among equals. A particularly personalized account is the following:

'I am personally a walkabout manager with a very good nose, and I enjoy being with the people who work with me. I emphasize that they're not people who work for me, they are very much part of the team. There's a good buzz about the place. You've got to have competition and interactive debate, but if people become political or cutting – I'm not interested in that. We kill it stone dead.'

For the bulk of both USM and match firms, teamwork is thought to be a key ingredient for their success. It is, however, noticeable that some of the match firms suggest teamwork was greater in their early days than currently. One firm said:

'I think we do work together as a team to a high degree, but this has become strained through growth. The team worked better in the early days.'

Another match firm also indicated that there had been a decline in the extent to which teamworking occurred said:

'Senior personnel worked together very much in the early days. But as the business became developed it became far more structured and therefore now these people tend to stick to their responsibility.'

A third match firm specifically moved away from the concept of teamworking:

'We do not work together as a team now. Indeed we have gone the other way. We have made the three sections of the firm into independent profit centres and now break out all our costs and internal P & L by these divisions.'

Clearly, for some firms, particularly where interdependency between different parts of the business were limited, alternative organizational arrangements such as the creation of separate divisions or profit centres may reduce the need for explicit teamworking.

The nature of teamworking in match firms also appears to be somewhat different from that in the USM firms. In several of the match firms there is clear evidence that the owner is still able to involve him or herself in the detailed operations of these teams. Fairly typical among the responses is:

'Senior personnel work together a great deal as a team, though I must admit I still tend to stick my nose into most things.'

On the other hand the large USM firm owners see their role as that of controlling the divisions of the company and being somewhat divorced from the day-to-day routine decisions.

Perhaps surprisingly there is not a major difference between responses of USM and match owners to the question of teamworking. It is possible to broadly categorize responses to this question into three groups. The first are those who indicate that teamworking is very important or who say it is at the heart of their activity. This constitutes about two-thirds of responses in both the USM and match firm categories. Approximately one-sixth of both USM and match firms qualify the extent of their teamworking to some degree and a further one-sixth indicate that relatively little teamworking takes place.

The reasons for indicating that teamworking either does not take place or takes place on only a modest scale does differ between USM and match firms. Match firm owners are particularly likely to refer to their unwillingness to implement teamworking, either because they perceive themselves to be too busy or are reluctant to share the responsibilities of management with others. In the case of USM firms the reasons are rather different and normally relate to the independence of particular sections of the business.

For example one firm pointed out that:

'Team-work here is limited. We have twenty-nine centres which are all pretty well independent and they stand or fall by their own efforts. We do have three-monthly meetings at which we discuss prices, products and suggestions for improvements, but this is the only time when we collectively come together.'

It therefore appears that those USM firms which do not regard themselves as emphasizing teamwork, have made a conscious decision to create independent divisions. This contrasts with the match firms in which less clear decision taking has occurred.

With probably only one exception in the survey most firms indicated that the creation of teams had presented some problems. Given the often 'strong' personality of the owner and his desire to remain firmly in control of 'the team', it should not be too surprising to find that teamworking has often proved difficult to implement effectively and that it is frequently not the panacea Williamson and others naively suggest it to be. Only one firm indicated that teamworking had 'clicked naturally'. A far more typical response, particularly from the USM firms which had experienced rapid growth, was the following:

'We have steering groups on special projects which we draw from all parts of the business. We choose individuals to be part of industry boards and consortia: we have a special projects director which is leading to much better communication. This in fact is the biggest problem as the company grows. I used to know everybody by name but I don't know them now. It's impossible to get all our staff together – we provide a twenty-four-hour service so there is always somebody missing. The joint Managing Directors get round to all the branches and meetings that they possibly can but even so communication is imperfect.'

This role of teams providing information within the company is clearly related to the circulation of information within firms. It is this aspect of information which we now discuss in the next section.

ENSURING MANAGERS HAVE ENOUGH INFORMATION

To obtain a better understanding of how information circulated within firms, owners were asked about the formal and informal channels which they used to communicate with other managerial staff. It was assumed that as firms grew larger that they would become increasingly formal in their information dissemination. It was also assumed that evidence of good practice in the distribution of information could be identified from the responses of owners.

Formally owners were asked 'how do you ensure that managers have enough information to do their job properly?' We have chosen to categorize the answers into four levels of formality, as shown in Table 9.5. The four categories are defined as formal, some formality, informal and not developed.

The table distinguishes between the responses of owners of USM firms and those of match firms. Somewhat surprisingly it suggests there is no difference in the levels of formality of information dissemination in the two groups of firms. This result requires further examination and so illustrations of the verbatim responses of owners to this question, which are subsequently classified into the groups, are now given. We have identified formal information provision systems where the respondent clearly indicates that regular meetings take place. These may either be on a weekly or monthly basis and at these meetings matters are conducted formally in the sense of minutes being taken, targets being set, and appraisals undertaken. In other instances formality will refer to the existence of computerized management information systems, they will refer to the existence of company newspapers, newsletters and other formal information systems. In other instances a department of information may exist within the company.

Reference may also be made to memo's being a conventional mode of communication. Of course this does not mean that informal information networks do not either exist, or are not even encouraged, by existing management. Also the fact that formal systems exist does not preclude the existence of parallel informal systems to which respondents also refer.

Thus where respondents indicate the existence of both formal and informal information networks they are classified into the formal category where it is clear that the prime emphasis is upon formality.

In particular we have chosen to regard those answers by owners which replied primarily in terms of regular formal meetings and written memos as formal, even where they subsequently mentioned the presence of informal processes.

The following is an illustration of a firm which has a comprehensive strategy to ensure that managers do have enough information to do their jobs:

> 'Most information in this company is public. We clearly match our own performance against those of others in the markets. So far as meetings are concerned we have regular breakfasts at which all business matters are discussed, we have a company mission statement, performance reviews, job descriptions and evaluations and reward systems which reflect those evaluations.'

The majority of owners refer most frequently to the existence of regular meetings on a weekly or monthly basis. They indicate that these are the most important sources by which information for managers becomes available to them. It is, however, the firms which indicate that formality is not central to their dissemination activities which are the most interesting. We observe from Table 9.5 that approximately 60 per cent of both USM and match firms use 'formal' procedures for disseminating managerial information. Our interest, is upon those firms which clearly indicate that informal procedures are of greater importance than formal procedures. In category two defined as 'some informality' we would include firms which,

Table 9.5 Formality of managerial information provision

	Formal	Some informality	Informal	Not developed	Total
USM No.	24	7	5	4	40
%	(60)	(18)	(12)	(10)	(100)
Match No.	29	6	5	6	46
%	(63)	(13)	(11)	(13)	(100)

although having formal meetings, very clearly indicated that the prime mechanism for communication of managerial information was through informal channels. The following is illustrative:

'We have regular board meetings. The majority of senior managers here are board members and being a relatively small company, you don't need the different layers of management as you do in a very large company so things are done very differently. We have regular formal board meetings, but we try to ensure that all communications are face to face and direct. We don't have any emphasis at all on internal memos. We believe that in a company of this size if you can't speak face to face and let people know what you want, then there is something wrong with the company. So it's basically face to face as often as possible.'

A match firm which illustrates a reasonably high level of formality, but indicating informal elements, and so is included in the 'some informality' group said:

'We have written procedures for the way all things should be done, procedures for the transfer of information. In addition to that I think we just talk to people all the time. It still falls down though. We have regular meetings once every couple of months and we haven't had them of late because of other pressures but, yes, generally we do. Sometimes they go down to the whole management team so it goes down to the supervisors.'

The third group in Table 9.5 identifies firms whose information dissemination system could be judged to be informal. It includes firms who refer primarily to informal meetings, who refer to meetings being scheduled on an *ad hoc* rather than a regular basis, or who refer to talking to each other and sharing experiences. Most respondents in this category recognize that these informal procedures were unusual, but most indicated that they felt they were effective. One company said that it almost never had formal meetings but the managing director was confident that any crucial pieces of information were known by all managers within the company within twenty-four hours of it being known by anyone. The following firm also illustrates that an informal mechanism for transferring information did not, in their view, impair the efficiency of the business.

'The transfer of information is done very much on a day to day basis. We tend not to have too much training anyway. We have a training programme which is mainly for lower level staff and senior members. Management is by communication. We encourage people to talk to each other and information to get down in that way and we share experiences. I think it is our way of running the company.'

The final group of owners responses in Table 9.5 are those which we have categorized as not having a developed system for managerial information provision. In some instances this reflects the relative unimportance given to this subject, and in other cases it reflects the unwillingness of the owner to share information with his or her colleagues. Again from the table it is evident that there is no clear difference between the match and USM firms, with approximately 10 per cent of firms being placed in this category. One USM firm replied in the following way:

> 'Managers have reports as necessarily applicable to their particular function. The marketeers need to have statistics with the order intake and sales output and so forth but they don't need to know the number of widgets in stock. They have the information necessary for them to make conclusions, take actions in their particular functions. In a company of this size, and the way it is structured in smaller product groups and subsidiaries, I think the formality of passing information down in a structured way doesn't happen; it's more likely that I or John X will wander down the corridor and have a chat with someone and together they will formulate the plan of action for attacking a customer or agreeing prices or that sort of thing. I think it's the difference between the large company where there has to be a structure, and lets face it large companies tend to cover their backsides, and so therefore like to get together in meetings and minutes are taken at these meetings. It's much less formal here.'

In the case of some firms there is a clear restriction on the dissemination of information possibly on the grounds that information dissemination leads to a loss of 'control'. One firm owner when asked how he ensured that managers have enough information to do their jobs properly, replied:

> 'Because I feed it to them!'

Another replied:

> 'They are generally self sufficient in respect of information. Their goals should be well understood and they should be able to achieve them. Obviously they can turn to me if they need extra information but generally they will be able to obtain that themselves.'

Another said:

> 'There is something very self-governing about this company. Each manager has his own area of responsibility, and there aren't many of them. I don't think our company is big enough yet to need some kind of mobile management structure. If we do grow that will become essential.

We have no formal meetings and in fact we just have running conversations. There is a lot of informal contact.'

Overall the responses to the question of ensuring that managers have enough information to do their jobs properly does not clearly relate to either the size of the business or whether or not it is a USM company. Even among the USM and match groups there did not appear a clear pattern of information dissemination procedures being clearly related to either size or age of firm. Further analysis, particularly of the firms which indicated that they relied primarily upon informal systems, suggested they were more likely to be found in the service sector than in manufacturing. Again here sectoral considerations seem to transcend size or age differences.

Interestingly relatively few of the firms which currently have formal information systems made reference to having implemented these as the company grew. Much more frequently they suggest that these information structures have always been present, but have become increasingly structured. The implication appears to be that dissemination of information remains a company characteristic, almost irrespective of size. Thus some quite substantial firms, even in the match category, with more than 3–400 employees and several sites, would still have their managing director saying:

'I talk to my managers a lot, I would say that 80 per cent of my time if not more is spent talking to people, finding out what's going on, telling them what I would like to happen imparting ideas or whatever. I'm still trying to develop my communications skills. I'm told that I overwhelm people and that I tend to be a bit aggressive and overbearing, I'm told by lots of people that I'm a powerful personality. I do not like memos much. Before we do something really important like change the bonus system for example, I wrote to everyone at home. I believe in writing to people at home so most of my communication is verbal with some written.'

CONCLUSIONS

This chapter has presented some qualitative evidence of the extent to which firm owners indicate that teamworking is the core of their business activity. It also examines their strategies for ensuring that such teamworking is effective. In principle we had expected to find that teamworking became increasingly important with the greater size and complexity of the organization. Firms were expected to make an ordered transition from a relatively simple organization form, into a more complex and team-orientated form.

These hypotheses are only partly supported by the evidence in the chapter. Broadly it appears to be the case that there are *not* major differences between USM and match firms according to many dimensions of teamworking. The main exception is that owners of match firms are more reluctant to identify managers who are crucial to the success of the firm, than is the case for USM owners. Managers of match firms are more likely to indicate that the success of the firm is based upon a team effort in which the contribution of no single individual can satisfactorily be singled out as the key contributor. On the other hand USM owners are much more likely to point to a key individual with, in most cases that key individual being themselves. It was also noticeable that when discussing the contributions of key individuals the USM owners were more likely to point to managers with particular functional skills, whereas match firm owners were more likely to point to managers with more general responsibilities. In short it appears that USM respondents were more likely to regard managers as crucial because of the jobs which they did, rather than because of either their technical abilities or their personal qualities.

Probably the central finding of this chapter is that there is no clear difference in the responses of USM and match firm owners on the extent to which managers work together as a team. Even so the reasons for teamwork appear to be somewhat different in the two groups of firms. In the case of the USM firms, teamworking is regarded as the inevitable consequence of operating a larger organization and ensuring that it is adequately managed and controlled. In the case of the much smaller match firm, owners are likely to stress the inevitability of teamworking because of the small size of the firm. In some cases, as the firm has grown, owners emphasize that teamworking is encouraged, but the relatively unchanging character of the organization, despite increases in scale, is quite striking. Several firms indicated that teamworking was not encouraged within their organization, even though the firm itself could be of some considerable size. This was often because alternative organizational arrangements such as the creation of independent profit centres or divisions, reduced the necessity of teamwork – particularly when interdependencies were relatively small.

The extent to which these firms operate upon both formal and informal lines can be considered to be the mirror image of teamworking. Thus it would be difficult to argue that the organization operates on a team basis where there is restricted access to key items of information. It would be expected that, as the firm grows, more formal systems of information dissemination would be implemented, but again the evidence for this appears somewhat ambiguous. Less than two-thirds of firms use formal methods to disseminate information to their managers. The rest appear to emphasize the importance of elements of informality, and a significant proportion have no developed system for providing managers with information. Although the pattern is unclear, there is no evidence that firms begin in their early days with informal information procedures and move with increasing scale to greater formality. Instead it appears more likely that certain businesses have characteristics which they manifest early in life. Thus firms which begin by using fairly informal methods and placing great emphasis upon teamworking appear to retain these characteristics even though they grow to some considerable size. As we have seen often this is largely due to the owner's personality and wish to maintain control over 'his business'. On the other hand some medium-size firms appear to have implemented formal information procedures at an early stage in their life. Clearly there are instances of firms making a transition from informal to formal procedures, but it is the similarity over a considerable period of time which is the more striking. If this may be considered an aspect of company 'culture', then it appears that this culture may, for many firms, be established in the early stage of a firm's life.

10 Conclusions

INTRODUCTION

In our 1987 text *The Performance of Small Firms* we were aware of two distinct groups of potential readers. The first were our academic colleagues who were primarily interested in relating our findings to the existing theoretical and empirical literature. The second were a group whom we will refer to as policy makers, who had relatively little interest in theoretical issues. They were interested in obtaining insights into the performance of small firms that had immediate and practical applications. Included in this group were public policy makers interested in promoting the development of the small-firms sector, financiers involved in providing loan and equity to small firms, and small business owners themselves. In the 1987 volume we did not explicitly distinguish in our conclusions, those which were relevant to the two groups. In that sense we were probably less effective in communicating our main findings and their policy relevance than should have been the case.

For this reason this concluding chapter makes a clear distinction between those findings and issues which are most closely related to evaluating and extending the existing theoretical and empirical literatures, which we covered in the first four chapters, and those that are related to a discussion of the practical relevance of the empirical findings presented in Chapters 6 to 9.

In making this distinction we do not, of course, suggest that our academic colleagues are not interested in policy nor do we suggest that policy makers are wholly disinterested in prior empirical work on this subject. The purpose in making the distinction is merely to present the findings in a more acceptable and efficient form from the point of view of the two groups of readers.

Both groups, however, need the context for this study. Our overall objective is to identify the managerial factors most closely associated with successful small firms. To do this we identify certain key words within that objective: these key words are 'small', 'successful', and 'managerial'. Each of these key words will now be discussed.

It has been a consistent theme, both of this book and of our 1987 volume, that the small firm cannot be considered as simply a 'scaled down version of a large firm'. We have pointed to the fact that there is an endemic uncertainty associated with the operations of the small firm which is not characteristic of the large firm. This is reflected in differences in very much higher failure rates of small businesses, in their inability to influence market conditions, in their dependence upon often single customers or key suppliers or upon finance being provided by institutions. In this volume we have also addressed more closely the question of change within the smaller firm. We have pointed to the fact that a small but very important section of the small-firm population is growing extremely quickly. These firms are likely to undergo major transformations and experience growth rates which very few large firms experience. In principle therefore the character of these fast-growing small businesses could change considerably in a way which is much less likely in the case of large firms.

In this sense the current study is not only about small firms but about successful firms. To conduct research on this matter some definition has to be employed of 'successful'. We have chosen to regard a successful firm as one which begins as an independent start up but which reaches the Unlisted Securities Market within approximately ten years. We do not suggest that this is the only definition of 'successful' but it is valuable from our point of view in the sense that clearly all firms which reach the USM according to this criteria are highly successful. It certainly does not suggest that all firms which do not meet this criteria are not successful.

The third key word is 'managerial'. We are interested in the managerial factors which influence the success of a small firm. The definition of 'managerial factors' includes:

1 the motivations, personal characteristics and current managerial styles of the original founders of the enterprise;
2 How they set about organizing the growth process, in particular, the recruitment, motivation, rewarding and control of their subsequent managerial personnel; and
3 the organizational structures, information flows and methods of teamworking adopted to produce their desired outcomes.

To empirically examine these issues we have taken our successful small firms and matched them against less successful firms. To do this we identify four criteria for matching purposes: location, sector, age, and ownership. The logic of this is that our prime interest is in the 'unique' internal or organizational aspects of fast-growing small firms. It is therefore important to hold constant other factors which we know from previous work influence the performance of small firms.

In essence we need to ensure that a manufacturer of printed circuit boards, located in South-East England, which is currently nine years old and started as an independent and which has reached the Unlisted Securities Market, is compared with a similar firm on all these criteria but which has not obtained a USM listing. The logic is that once these four factors are held constant we are more likely to observe differences in the management or internal organization of the firm than if they are not explicitly held constant. We therefore have a group of firms which we call 'fast growers' and we have a group of small firms which we call 'match' firms. It is important to point out, however, that the match firms are *not* to be regarded as poor performers. The bulk of them have survived for ten years which makes them unusual and their median employment is twenty-four workers. It is for these reasons that the study may legitimately be considered as an examination of the managerial differences between the steady bedrock of the SME sector in Britain and the genuine 'high flyers'.

We now distinguish within the conclusions between our two groups of readers. Policy makers who are less interested in conceptual issues may wish to omit the next section.

CONCEPTUAL ISSUES

We begin by repeating the view of Edith Penrose (1959) in which she says that the capabilities of the existing managerial personnel of the firm necessarily impose a limit to the expansion of that firm. This point seems in subsequent years to have been lost upon those interested in smaller firms. In particular the Bolton Committee (Bolton 1971) identified the small firm as one in which owners and managers were the same person. The implication of this has been that there have been almost no studies of the individuals within a small firm who exercise managerial functions but who are not owners of businesses.

It is probably only with the work of Casson (1982) that theorists at last began to examine the Penrose question. Casson made a distinction between the internal and external labour market and theorized that because of the uncertainties of recruitment and the potential adverse selection and possible subsequent moral hazard problems that small firms would rationally choose to use, at least initially, the internal labour market, rather than the external one. In this he appears to suggest an economic rationale for the small firm's extensive use of family members in managerial positions. Clearly, the presence of many family firms, and particularly the use of family workers in ethnic businesses, suggests that monitoring and other agency costs can be considerably reduced in this way. Casson also suggests that the use of family members will soon be exhausted if the firm grows quickly and that it will have to seek external managers. He does not, however, develop the theoretical framework for the factors which will influence this choice.

A second major theoretical issue which this book has addressed relates to the existence of 'internal labour markets'. Here the literature defines the internal labour market rather more widely than that used by Casson above. In the literature to date, ILMs have been thought to be applicable only to large firms who use it to overcome the problem that managerial services are non-standard, difficult to monitor and where there are clearly information asymmetry problems between the employer and the employee. In this situation there are clear moral hazard problems and therefore ILM theory should be capable of offering some insights into the recruitment and control of managers.

In principle this theory suggests it is in the interests of firms to provide an ILM which screens out low-quality managers and which provides a career hierarchy for those perceived to be of high quality. It is therefore in the interests of firms to recruit only junior staff from the external labour market, and to draw on its existing managerial pool for more senior appointments. In this sense the large firm is able to obtain more information about these individuals than it would if they been employed by other firms. An interesting issue is whether any part of the small-firm sector is capable of operating an internal labour market.

The literature has generally assumed that an internal labour market could only be operated by large firms. This is not, prima facie, an unreasonable assumption since only large firms can afford to pay the high salaries associated with the employment of highly trained and educated managerial talent. Moreover, the high failure rates of small firms can hardly be said to be conducive to the provision of long-term employment contracts which are meant to provide a credible and progressive career structure and a sufficient variety of jobs to retain managers within the company.

Our findings provide insights into these theories. The first is that it is inappropriate to regard the managerial structure of the whole of the small-firm sector as consisting solely of owner-managers. The evidence presented here suggests that only the very tiniest of firms – those perhaps with ten workers or less, can be considered exclusively as owned and managed by the same individuals. Once the firm reaches say twenty workers there is no doubt that individuals have to be employed to manage and supervise the work of others and therefore to be involved in making decisions, but who are often not significant owners of the business. The second point which is recognized by those favouring a case study method of analysis (Grieve-Smith and Fleck 1987) is that these managerial appointments are central to the growth of the small firm. In this sense it supports the work by Casson which addressed the development of managers but from a purely theoretical and entrepreneurship perspective.

Our observations on the possible existence of internal labour markets within the small-firm sector are derived from two perspectives. The first consists of asking a sample of managers currently employed in both USM and match firms about both their current jobs and their prior work history. The second is based upon asking owners about the first two and the last two managerial appointments within the firm. In some cases the managers whom the owners were discussing are the same individuals as those whom we interviewed, but in the bulk of the cases the individuals differ. Our findings support the idea that for fast-growing small firms there is almost no internal labour market. These firms, because of their rapid growth, are forced to seek managers from outside the firm to appoint to senior positions. Furthermore, we observe that the provision of firm-specific training, which is characteristic of large firms operating an internal labour market, is not found among the USM firms.

The interesting point is that it is among the match firms that there is evidence of the use of internal labour markets. Match firms are much more likely than the USM firms to appoint from inside the firm to managerial positions. The difference is that the match firms are likely to appoint individuals employed within the firm, but without managerial experience, into managerial positions. The USM firm on the other hand is more likely to appoint people who have managerial experience, often in large firms, but who were employed outside the firm.

This perhaps reflects differences in the concept of risk/adverse selection associated with these managerial appointments. The USM firm seeks to minimize its risk by seeking high quality 'signals' from its managerial appointments. In this sense it looks for individuals who already have managerial experience. It also is more likely to seek individuals with higher educational qualifications. Furthermore, in the early stages of its development, it seems to place more emphasis in its recruitment strategy in knowing the individual, and by the owner of the firm making a personal approach in the recruitment procedure. Conversely the match firm appears to choose to minimize its risk by taking individuals who are either already employed in the firm, or those whom the owner knows have a detailed knowledge of the particular sector.

A further topic which has been the subject of considerable interest by scholars of small-firm development and which we are able to empirically examine, is that of stage theory. This was discussed in Chapter 2 in which it was argued that growing firms go through several stages of development.

A total of five stages were identified. Associated with each of these five stages were differences in the role played by top management, its managerial style and the organization structure. Essentially it was argued that the organization moved from being unstructured at the earliest inception stage, to being decentralized in the highly mature stage. It was also argued that the managerial roles and styles moved from being directly supervisory and entrepreneurial in the early stages to decentralized, almost watch-dog managerial style, at the mature stage.

Our observations of both rapidly growing and match firms do not provide support for this type of clear transition. Putting aside the question that the bulk of small firms are likely to cease trading within ten years of starting up and therefore that 'death' is the most likely outcome, the notion of a triggered sequences of movements does not seem to accord with the experiences of our group of firms. For example in Chapter 9 we do not find that there are very striking differences in the managerial style and dissemination of information between the USM firms and the match firms.

In some ways this is surprising since, on average, the USM firms have ten times as many employees as the match firms. Yet in asking owners to describe the functions which they conduct and the way they go about organizing their business, the differences do not appear stark. Indeed one of the characteristics seems to be that the culture of the organization appears to be set at an early stage in the firm's life. Making a crude distinction between formal and informal organizations, formality appears to be as characteristic of organizations with only twenty employees as it is with organizations of 200 employees.

As the firm significantly expands its operations, new managerial talent has, of course, to be acquired. This, however, does not necessarily imply that major organizational changes, new working practices or a reduction in the control exercised by the owning group occurs. Strong owner control of operations is often retained via autocratic leadership of the management team or, in industries where interdependencies between functions and operations is relatively low, the owning group can avoid the need for close teamwork by creating independent profit centres and/or operating divisions. Thus, even in USM firms, the business can still be dominated by the personalities and personal objectives of their original founders.

Our second conceptual problem with stage models, which is recognized by a number of other authors, is that few of our firms appear to make any form of clear transition from one stage to another. Certainly none appear to begin at stage 1 and make the transition through the four stages to arrive at stage 5. They also do not appear to have been triggered in their movement from one stage to another by some crisis event. Perhaps the only exception to this are the firms which reach the USM and at that point are required to provide both additional information to the capital market and to make changes in their managerial team. At a more simplistic level, the owners of some fast-growth firms did lament the fact that they no longer knew the names of all of the workers in the business, and in that sense the character or culture of the firm had changed. Even so, even these individuals were reluctant to admit that their style of management had changed significantly since start-up.

The third major theoretical question which is indirectly addressed in this research relates to the view of the firm as outlined by economists on the one hand and by business strategists on the other. Chapters 2 and 3 showed that few economists hold the neoclassical economic view of the firm as competing in perfect markets on the basis of price alone. Instead they would be likely to recognize market imperfections, in the form of product differentiation and segmentation. Nevertheless the structure–conduct–performance paradigm continues to dominate empirical economics. The key assumption which distinguishes this from that of the business strategist is that, in the economics paradigm, the structure of the market is the dominant influence. On the other hand, business strategy analysts generally assume that it is conduct which is the central influencing factor. Their paradigm assumes that owners or managers of businesses will, by their own actions, influence the performance of the firm and it is the performance of the firms which ultimately influences the structure of the marketplace.

Again we are in a position from the material presented here to make some observations on these forms of relationship. It will be recalled that in making the distinction between USM and match firms we explicitly held the structure of the marketplace constant, in the sense that the USM and the comparable match firm were both competing in the same sector. Even so we were struck during the matching process by the limited extent to which, although firms were formally classified as being in the same sector or even in the same marketplace, they actually rarely if ever competed with one another. In particular we find ourselves re-emphasizing the point made in our study of fast-growth businesses in Northern England (Storey *et al.* 1989), that the faster-growing firms were much more likely to be occupying particular market niches or specialisms than was the case for the match firms. In this sense the faster-growing firms were often not competing against their match counterparts and so cannot be considered to be operating within the same marketplace.

Hence although we were, in principle, comparing groups of firms in the same marketplaces, they were rarely formally competitors. It may therefore be argued that to reach a conclusion which suggests that conduct is the dominant element in influencing performance, when strictly speaking the marketplaces are different, is unjustified. Nevertheless at the normal level of disaggregation of markets favoured by empirical economists the USM and the match firm were in the same sectors. Given that these firms were also of a similar age and located in the same regions, it is very striking that the substantial differences in firm performance actually occurred. It does suggest that there is considerable validity in the argument that it is conduct, rather than market structure, which is the dominant element influencing firm performance.

Recognizing that conduct is a major element, if not the major element, influencing firm performance does not imply that there is a clearly identifiable blueprint for success. Here we believe that much of the organizational theory literature is compatible with our findings in this study. In Chapter 3 we emphasized that the organizational structure had to fit appropriately with its environment, its technology, its firm size and its human resources. We also emphasized that there had to be cohesion and commonality of interest and a balance of complementary skills between members of the top management team. Our empirical work has underlined the importance of these issues as well as those of identifying the criteria by which firms are judged to be successful. In particular we again emphasize that match firms are not only successful by objective standards of survival and reaching some significant size, but they are also successful in terms of the non-financial and economic objectives which their owners set for themselves. As we saw in Chapter 8, a number of factors, such as the proportion of directors ownership, the unwillingness (or inability) to introduce structured management systems, the perception of uncertainty and exposure to risk, are all important determinants of firm performance.

For these reasons it is important to emphasize that there is no single best way of organizing for the success of the business. Chapter 9 showed that, although the ability of the owner(s) to motivate their management team was important to the achievement of desired objectives, there were many ways in which this was achieved. The notion of teamwork employed by owners ranged from the relatively democratic 'relational teams' or 'clan' forms to the highly autocratic leadership of the owner. There were instances in which organizational arrangements, such as the creation of profit centres and separate divisions, seemed to be primarily motivated by the desire of owners to retain control without the need for a team-based management structure.

Even so there do appear to be some lessons to be learned in the sense of fairly clear associations between dimensions of management among small firms and those small firms which appear to have grown most rapidly. We therefore offer the following summary plus comments on these key findings, changing style towards readers interested primarily in policy implications.

POLICY IMPLICATIONS

In this section we highlight the main findings and discuss their implications for policy makers, defined as those implementing public policies, financial analysts and small businesses themselves.

1 There are major differences in terms of the current size and profitability of firms which were of similar age which operated in the same sectors, the same regions and which started as independents. The results suggest there are factors which account for some of these differences in firm performance.

2 Fast-growing firms are more likely to have been founded by an individual who was employed rather than unemployed. The managerial experience of the key founder of the fast-growing firm was most likely to have been in marketing and general management.

3 The residual claimant status of the directors, the proportion of the firms' equity held, whether or not they have other business interests and whether or not they are prepared to introduce more structured management systems, have a significant impact upon the (reported) profitability of the enterprise.

4 Very few firms, irrespective of their subsequent growth, are founded by individuals with expertise in finance. For this reason managerial teams at start-up tend to be unbalanced, and the finance expertise only comes on board once the business is relatively well established.

5 The managerial appointments made during the early life of the firm are crucial. Where they are successful, these appointments tend to be made through informal contact by the owner of the business with an identified individual. The individual is perceived to wish to join the firm because of its potential for growth, rather than because of the remuneration package which is immediately on offer.

6 The USM firm is much more likely to recruit its managers from outside the firm, whereas the match firm is more likely to make managerial appointments from individuals within the firm, but who lack managerial experience.

7 USM managerial appointments tend to be of individuals with managerial experience in their previous jobs, who have worked in larger firms and/or possess high educational and professional qualifications. Managerial appointments in match firms, where these are made externally, are of individuals without managerial experience, who have previously worked in a small firm, probably in the same sector as the match firm.

8 Managers currently employed in USM firms express higher levels of satisfaction with their job than managers employed in match firms.

This may reflect the higher salaries which those individuals have, together with the additional fringe benefits. It may also reflect a more satisfying working environment which USM firms provide. The basis for this view is that, although USM managers have always been paid more than match managers throughout their careers, in their prior jobs USM managers were no more likely than match managers to express high levels of job satisfaction.

9   Job satisfaction is also related to differences between USM and match managers in how they perceive their boss. In both groups of firms the boss is likely to be the owner of the firm, and in the case of USM managers, they have a generally higher regard for their boss than is the case for match managers. In particular, this regard is related to the professionalism which the boss exhibits in his or her job. It is interesting to observe that the only characteristic in which the USM owner appears to score less well than his/her match counterpart is related to personal characteristics such as approachability and qualities which one might place under the heading of 'niceness'.

10   There is a high proportion of managers in match firms who indicated no intention of leaving the firm within the next two years, but who were dissatisfied in their work. This suggests the somewhat turbulent environment which a USM firm provides, or even creates, is one in which managers derive considerable job satisfaction primarily because of a combination of relatively high salaries, and superiors for whom they have considerable professional respect. There is little evidence, however, that the more autocratic management styles of some owners either produced more dissatisfied managers or that it had a deleterious effect upon the performance of the enterprise, particularly where alternative organizational arrangements, such as the creation of independent profit centres or operating divisions rendered close teamwork less necessary.

Bibliography

Alchian, A. and Demsetz, H. (1972) 'Production, Information Costs and Economic Organisation', *American Economic Review*, 62: 777–95.

Argyris, C. (1972) *The Applicability of Organisational Sociology*, Cambridge: Cambridge University Press.

Bain, J.S. (1959) *Industrial Organisation*, New York: Wiley.

Baker, G.P., Jensen, M.C. and Murphy, K.J. (1988) 'Compensation and Incentives: Practice vs Theory', *Journal of Finance*, 43(3): 593–616.

Bannock, G. and Doran, A. (1987) *Going Public: The Markets for Unlisted Securities*, London: Harper and Row

Bantel, K.A. and Jackson, S.E. (1989) 'Top Management and Innovation in Banking: Does the Composition of the Top Team Make a Difference?', *Strategic Management Journal*, 10, Special Issue, Summer: 107–24.

Bates, T. (1990) 'Entrepreneurial Human Capital Inputs and Small Business Longevity', *Review of Economics and Statistics*, 72(4): 551–9.

—— (1991) 'Financing Capital Structure and Small Business Viability', in R Yazdipour (ed.) *Advances in Small Business Finance*, Dordrecht: Kluwer Academic Publishers.

Baumol, W.J. (1959) *Business Behaviour, Value & Growth*, New York: Macmillan.

—— (1962) 'On the Theory of Expansion of the Firm', *American Economic Review*, 52: 1078–87.

—— (1967) *Business Behaviour, Value and Growth*, revised edition, New York: Harcourt Brace.

—— (1968) 'Entrepreneurship in Economic Theory', *American Economic Review*, 58: 64–71.

Bendix, R. (1966) *Max Weber: An Intellectual Portrait*, London: Methuen.

Berle, A. and Means, G. (1932) *The Modern Corporation and Private Property*, New York: MacMillan.

Binks, M. and Vale, P. (1990) *Entrepreneurship and Economic Change*, London: McGraw-Hill.

Birley, S. (1982) 'Corporate Strategy and the Small Firm', *Journal of General Management*, 8(2): 82–6.

Blanchflower, D.G. and Oswald, A.J. (1992) *Entrepreneurship and Supernormal Returns: Evidence from Britain and the US*, paper presented at the International Conference on Birth and Start up of Small Firms, Milan, June 18–19.

Bolnick, B. (1975) *Toward a Behavioural Theory of Philanthropic Activity*, in E.S. Phelps (ed) *Altruism, Morality and Economic Theory*, New York: Russell Sage Foundation.

Bolton, J.E. (1971) *Small Firms: Report of the Commission of Inquiry on Small Firms*, Cmnd.4811, London: HMSO.

Borjas, G. (1979) 'Job Satisfaction, Wages and Unions', *Journal of Human Resources*, 14: 21–40.

Boswell, J. (1973) *The Rise and Decline of Small Firms*, London: Allen and Unwin.

Bosworth, D. and Jacobs, C. (1989) 'Management Attitudes, Behaviour and Abilities as Barriers to Growth', in J. Barber, J.S. Metcalfe and M. Porteous (eds) *Barriers to Growth in Small Firms*, London: Routledge.

Bradburd, R.M. and Ross, D.R. (1989) 'Can Small Firms Find and Defend Strategic Niches? A Test of the Porter Hypothesis', *Review of Economics and Statistics*, LXXI, (2): 258–62.

Bragard. L., Donckles, R. and Michel, P. (1985) *New Entrepreneurship*, Belgium: Universite de Liege.

Brusco, S. (1986) 'Small Firms and Industrial Districts: The Experience of Italy', in D. Keeble and E. Wever (eds) *New Firms and Regional Development in Europe*, London: Croom Helm.

Buchanan, D.A. and Huczynski, A.A. (1985) *Organisational Behaviour*, London: Prentice-Hall.

Buckland, R. and Davis, E.W. (1989) *The Unlisted Securities Market*, Oxford: Clarendon Press.

Burns, P. and Dewhurst, J. (eds) (1989) *Small Business and Entrepreneurship*, London: Macmillan.

Burns, T. and Stalker, G.M. (1961) *The Management of Innovation*, London: Tavistock Publications.

Cannings, K. (1991) 'An Interdisciplinary Approach to Analysing the Managerial Gender Gap', *Human Relations*, 44(7): 678–95.

—— and Montmarquette, C. (1991) 'Managerial Momentum: A Simultaneous Model of the Career Progress of Male and Female Managers', *Industrial and Labour Relations Review*, 44(2): 212–28.

Carter, S. and Cannon, T. (1989) *Female Entrepreneurs: A Study of Female Business Owners, their Motivations, Experiences and Strategies for Success*, Department of Employment, Research Paper No. 65.

Casson, M. (1982) *The Entrepreneur: An Economic Theory*, Oxford: Martin Robertson.

—— (1987) *Multinational Firms*, in R. Clarke and T. McGuinness (eds) *The Economics of the Firm*, Oxford: Basil Blackwell: 133–64.

—— (ed.) (1990) *Entrepreneurship*, Aldershot: Edward Elgar.

Caves, R.E. (1972) *American Industry: Structure, Conduct Performance*, 3rd edition, Englewood Cliffs, NJ: Prentice-Hall.

Chell, E. (1985) 'The Entrepreneurial Personality: A Few Ghosts Laid to Rest?', *International Small Business Journal*, 3(3): 43–54.

Child, J. (1972) 'Organisational Structure, Environment and Performance: The Role of Strategic Choice', *Sociology*, 6: 1–22.

Churchill, N.C. and Lewis, V.L. (1983) 'The Five Stages of Small Business Growth', *Harvard Business Review*, 61(3): 30–50.

Clark, J.M. (1961) *Competition as a Dynamic Process*, Washington DC: Brookings Institute.

Clarke R. and McGuinness, T. (eds) (1987) *The Economics of the Firm*, Oxford: Basil Blackwell.

Coase, R.M. (1937) 'The Nature of the Firm', *Economica*, 4: 386–405.

Cohen, M.D., March, J.G. and Olsen, J.P. (1972) 'A Garbage Can Model of Organisational Choice', *Administrative Science Quarterly*, 17: 1–25.

Collins, O. and Moore, D. (1970) *The Organisation Makers*, New York: Appleton-Century-Crofts.

Commons, J.R. (1934) *Institutional Economics: Its Place in Political Economy*, New York: University of Wisconsin Press.

Cosh, A. (1975) 'The Remuneration of Chief Executives in the United Kingdom', *Economic Journal*, 85(1): 75–94.

Covin, J.G. and Slevin, D.P. (1989) 'Strategic Management of Small Firms in Hostile and Benign Environments', *Strategic Management Journal*, 10: 75–87.

Creedy, J. and Whitfield, K. (1988) 'The Economic Analysis of Internal Labour Markets', *Bulletin of Economic Research*: 4, 4: 247–67.

Cubbin, J. and Leech, D. (1983) 'The Effect of Shareholding Dispersion on the Degree of Control in British Companies: Theory and Evidence', *Economic Journal*, 93: 351–69.

Cummings, L.L. and Staw, B.M. (1987) *Research in Organisational Behaviour*, Greenwich, CT: JAI Press.

Curran, J. (1986) *Bolton Fifteen Years On: A Review and Analysis of Small Business Research in Britain 1971–86*, London: Small Business Research Trust.

Cyert, R.M. and March, J.G. (1963) *A Behavioural Theory of the Firm*, London: Prentice-Hall.

Daly, M. (1991) 'VAT Registrations and Deregistrations in 1990', *Employment Gazette*, November: 579–88.

Davies, J.R. and Kelly, M. (1972) *Small Firms in the Manufacturing Sector*, Research Report No. 3, Report of the Committee of Enquiry on Small Firms, Cmnd 4811, London: HMSO.

Davies, S. (1987) *Vertical Integration*, in R. Clarke and T. McGuinness (eds) *The Economics of the Firm* Oxford: Basil Blackwell: 83–106.

Deeks, J. (1972) 'Educational and Occupational Histories of Owner Managers and Managers', *Journal of Management Studies*, 9: 123–49.

Demsetz, H. and Lehn, K. (1985) 'The Structure of Corporate Ownership: Causes and Consequences', *Journal of Political Economy*, 93: 1155–77.

Dolton, P.J. and Makepeace, N. (1990) 'Self Employment Amongst Graduates', *Bulletin of Economic Research*, 42, 1: 35–53.

Elliott, J.W. (1972) 'Control, Size, Growth and the Financial Performance of the Firm', *Journal of Financial and Quantitative Analysis*, 7: 1309–20.

Emery, F.E. and Trist, E.L. (1963) 'The Causal Texture of Organisational Environments', *Human Relations*, 18: 20–6.

Evans, D.S. and Leighton, L.S. (1989) 'The Determinants of Changes in U.S. Self Employment, 1968–1987', *Small Business Economics*, 1(2): 111–20.

Ezzamel, M. (1987a) *Organisation Design: An Overview*, in M. Ezzamel and H. Hart (eds) *Advanced Management Accounting: An Organisational Emphasis*, London: Cassell: 15–39.

—— (1987b) *Organisational Goals*, in M. Ezzamel and H. Hart (eds) *Advanced Management Accounting: An Organisational Emphasis*, London: Cassell: 40–62.

Fama, E.F. (1980) 'Agency Problems and the Theory of the Firm', *Journal of Political Economy*, 88: 288–307.

—— and Jensen, M.C. (1983a) 'Separation of Ownership and Control', *Journal of Law and Economics*, 16: 301–25.

—— and —— (1983b) 'Agency Problems and Residual Claims', *Journal of Law and Economics*, 16: 327–49.

Fazzari, S., Hubbard, R.G. and Peterson, B.C. (1988) 'Financing Constraints and Corporate Investment', *Brookings Papers on Economic Activity,* Journal Special Edition: 141–207.

Feeser, H.R. and Willard, G.E. (1990) 'Founding Strategy and Performance: A Comparison of High and Low Growth High Tech Firms', *Strategic Management Journal*, 11: 87–98.

Fielder, F.E. (1967) *A Theory of Leadership Effectiveness*, New York: McGraw-Hill.

Findley, M.C. and Williams, E.E. (1981) 'Financial Theory and Political Reality under Fundamental Uncertainty', *Journal of Post Keynesian Economics*, Summer: 528–49.

—— and —— (1985) 'A Post Keynesian View of Modern Financial Economics', *Journal of Business Finance and Accounting*, Spring: 1–18.

Freeman, R.B. (1978) 'Job Satisfaction as an Economic Variable', *American Economic Review*, 68(2): 135–41.

Freeman, R.B. and Medoff, J. (1984) *What Do Unions Do?'*, New York: Basic Books.

Friedman, (1953) *Essays in Positive Economics*, Chicago: Chicago University Press.

Gallagher, C.C. and Doyle, J. (1986) 'A Reply to Storey and Johnson', *International Small Business Journal*, 4(4): 47–54.

Ganguly, P. (1985) *UK Small Business Statistics and International Comparisons*, London: Harper and Row.

Gephart R.P. Jr and Wolfe R.A. (1989) *Qualitative Data Analysis: Three Microcomputer Supported Approaches* Canada: Department of Organisational Analysis, Faculty of Business, University of Alberta.

Goodman, P.S. and Pennings, J.M. (eds) (1977) *New Perspectives on Organisational Effectiveness*, New York: Jossey-Bass.

Greene, C.N. (1975) 'The Reciprocal Nature of Influence between Leader and Subordinates', *Journal of Applied Psychology*, 60: 187–93.

Greiner, L.E. (1972) 'Evolution and Revolution as Organisations Grow', *Harvard Business Review*, 50(4): 37–46.

Grieve Smith, J. and Fleck, V. (1987) 'Business Strategies in Small High Technology Companies', *Long Range Planning*, 20(2): 61–8.

Gudgin, G., Brunskill, I. and Fothergill, S. (1979) *New Manufacturing Firms in Regional Employment Growth*, Centre for Environmental Studies, Research Series No. 39.

Gupta, A.K. and Govindarajan, V. (1984) 'Business Unit Strategy, Managerial Characteristics and Business Unit Effectiveness at Strategy Implementation', *Academy of Management Journal*, 27: 25–41.

Hage, J. and Dewar, R. (1973) 'Elite Values versus Organisational Structure in Predicting Innovations', *Administrative Science Quarterly*, 18: 279–90.

Hambrick, D.C. (1987) 'Top Management Teams: Key to Strategic Success', *California Management Review*, 9: 88–108.

—— (1989) 'Putting Top Managers Back in the Strategy Picture', *Strategic Management Journal*, 10: 5–15.

—— and Finkelstein, S. (1987) *Managerial Discretion*, in L.L. Cummins and B.M. Staw (eds) *Research in Organisational Behaviour*, Greenwich, CT: JAI Press: 369–406.

—— and Mason, P.A. (1984) 'Upper Echelons: The Organisation as a Reflection of its Top Managers', *Academy of Management Review*, 9: 195–206.

Handy, C., Gordon, C., Gow, I. and Randlesome, C. (1988) *Making Managers*, London: Pitman.

Hansen, G.S. and Wernerfelt, B. (1989) 'Determinants of Firm Performance: The Relative Importance of Economic and Organisational Factors', *Strategic Management Journal*, 10: 399–411.

Hitchens, D. and O'Farrell, P. (1991) 'Comparative Performance of Small Manufacturing Firms Located in South Wales and two English Regions', *International Small Business Journal*, 9(2): 64–70.

Honkapohja, S. (1989) *Information and Incentives in Organisations*, Oxford: Basil Blackwell.

House, R.J. (1971) 'A Path–Goal Theory of Leader Effectiveness', *Administrative Science Quarterly*, September: 321–38.

Hunt, H.G. (1986) 'The Separation of Corporate Ownership and Control: Theory, Evidence and Implications', *Journal of Accounting Literature*, 5: 85–124.

Hunt, J. (1979) *Managing People*, London: Pan Publishing.

Hurst, D., Rush, J. and White, R. (1989) 'Top Management Teams and Organisational Renewal', *Strategic Management Journal*, 10, Special Issue: 87–106.

Jensen, M.C. and Meckling, W.H. (1976) 'Theory of the Firm: Managerial Behaviour, Agency Costs and Ownership Structure', *Journal of Financial Economics*, 3: 305–60.

—— and Murphy, K.J. (1990) 'Performance Pay and Top Management Incentives', *Journal of Political Economy*, 98: 225–64.

Kalleberg, A.L. and Leicht, K.T. (1991) 'Gender and Organisational Performance: Determinents of Small Business Survival and Success', *Academy of Management Journal*, 34, 1: 136–61.

Kamerschen, D.R. (1968) 'The Influence of Ownership and Control on Profit Rates', *American Economic Review*, 58: 432–47.

Kamm, J.B., Shuman, J.C., Seeger, J.A. and Nurick, A.J. (1990) 'Entrepreneurial Teams vs New Venture Creation: A Research Agenda', *Entrepreneurship Theory and Practice*, 14: 7–17.

Kast, F.E. and Rosenzweig, J.E. (1985) *Organisation and Management: A Systems and Contingency Approach*, 4th edition, New York: McGraw-Hill.

Keasey, K. and McGuinness, P. (1990) 'Small New Firms and the Return to Alternative Sources of Finance', *Small Business Economics*, 2: 213–22.

Keeble, D.E. (1990) 'Small Firms, New Firms and Uneven Development in the United Kingdom', *Area*, 22: 234–45.

Kimberly, J.R. and Evanisko, M.J. (1981) 'Organisational Innovation: the Influence of Individual, Organisational, and Contextual Factors on Hospital Adoption of Technological and Administrative Innovations', *Academy of Management Journal*, 24: 689–713.

Knight, F.H. (1921) *Risk, Uncertainty and Profit*, New York: Houghton Mifflin.

Kochan, T. (1980) *Collective Bargaining and Industrial Relations*, Homewood, Ill: Irwin.

Kotter, J.P. (1982) *The General Managers*, New York: Free Press.

Lafuente, A. and Salas, V. (1989) 'Types of Entrepreneurs and Firms', *Strategic Management Journal*, 10: 17–30.

Larner, R.J. (1970) *Management Control and the Large Corporation*, Massachusetts: Dunellen Publishing Co, Inc.

Lawler, E.E., Hall, D.T. and Oldham, G.R. (1974) 'Organisational Climate: Relationships to Organisational Structure, Processes and Performance', *Organisational Behaviour and Human Performance*, 11: 139–55.

Lawrence, P.R. and Lorsch, J.W. (1967) *Organisation and Environment*, London: Unwin.

Lawriwsky, M.L. (1984) *Corporate Structure and Performance: The Role of Owners, Managers and Markets*, London: Croom Helm.

Lee, L.F. (1978) 'Unionism and Wage Rates: A Simultaneous Equation Model with Qualitative and Limited Dependent Variables', *International Economic Review*, 19: 415–533.

Levicki, C. (ed.) (1984) *Small Business: Theory and Policy*, The Acton Society, London: Croom Helm.

Levin, S.G. and Levin, S.L. (1982) 'Ownership and Control of Large Industrial Firms: Some New Evidence', *Review of Business and Economic Research*, Spring: 37–49.

Locke, E.A. (1982) 'The Ideas of Frederick W. Taylor: An Evaluation', *Academy of Management Review*, January: 14.

Luthans, F. (1985) *Organisational Behaviour*, 4th edition, Singapore: McGraw-Hill.

Machlup, F. (1967) 'Theories of the Firm: Marginalist, Behavioural, Managerial', *American Economic Review*, 67(1): 1–34.

Macmillan Committee (1931) *Report of the Committee on Finance and Industry*, Cmnd. 3897, London: HMSO.

McNamee, P.B. (1988) *Management Accounting, Strategic Planning and Marketing*, Oxford: Heinemann Professional and Chartered Institute of Management Accountants.

McConnell, J.J. and Servaes, H. (1990) 'Additional Evidence on Equity Ownership and Corporate Value', *Journal of Financial Economics*, 26: 595–612.

McEachern, W.A. (1975) *Managerial Control and Performance*, Massachusetts: Lexington Books.

—— (1976) 'Corporate Control and Risk', *Economic Inquiry*, June: 270–8.

McGuinness, T. (1987) *Markets and Managerial Hierarchies*, in R. Clarke and T. McGuinness (eds) *The Economics of the Firm*, Oxford: Basil Blackwell: 42–61.

Malcomson, J. (1984) *Efficient Labour Organisation: Incentives, Power and the Transactions Cost Approach*, in F.H. Stephen (ed.) *Firms, Organisation and Labour: Approaches to the Economies of Work Organisation*, London: Macmillan: 119–26.

Marlow, S. and Storey, D.J. (1992) 'New Firm Foundation and Unemployment: A Note on Research Method', *International Small Business Journal*, 10(3): 59–67.

Marris, R. (1964) *The Economic Theory of Managerial Capitalism*, London: Macmillan.

Martin R. (1989) 'The Growth and Geographical Anatomy of Venture Capital in the United Kingdom', *Regional Studies*, 23(5): 389–403.

Mason, C.M. (1985) 'The Geography of "Successful" Small Firms in the United Kingdom', *Environment and Planning A*, 17: 1499–513.

—— (1991) 'Spatial Variations in Enterprise: The Geography of New Firm Formation', in R. Burrows, (ed.) *Deciphering the Enterprise Culture*, London: Routledge, 74–106.

—— Harrison, J. and Harrison, R.T. (1988) *Closing the Equity Gap? An Assessment of the Business Expansion Scheme*, London: Small Business Research Trust.

Mason, E.S. (1949) 'The Current State of the Monopoly Problem in the United States', *Harvard Law Review*, 62: 1265–86.

Meng, R. (1990) 'The Relationship between Unions and Job Satisfaction', *Applied Economics*, 21: 1649–60.

Miles, R.E. and Snow, C.C. (1978) *Organisational Strategy, Structure and Process*, New York: McGraw-Hill.

Milgrom, P. and Roberts, J. (1992) *Economics, Organisations and Management*, Englewood Cliffs, NJ: Prentice Hall.

Mintzberg, H. (1973) *The Nature of Managerial Work*, London: Harper and Row.

Monck, C.S.P., Porter, R.B., Quintas, P.R., Storey, D.J. and Wynarczyk, P. (1988) *Science Parks and the Growth of High Technology Firms*, London: Croom Helm.

Monsen, R., Chui, J.S. and Cooley, D.E. (1968) 'The Effect of Separation of Ownership and Control on the Performance of the Large Firm', *Quarterly Journal of Economics*, June: 435–51.

Morck, R., Shleifer, A. and Vishny, R.W. (1988) 'Management Ownership and Market Valuation: An Empirical Analysis', *Journal of Financial Economics*, 20: 292–315.

Mueller, D.C. (1988) *The Corporate Life Cycle*, in S. Thompson and M. Wright (eds) *Internal Organisation, Efficiency and Profit*, London: Phillip Allan: 38–64.

Murali, R. and Welch, J.B. (1989) 'Agents, Owners, Control and Performance', *Journal of Business Finance and Accounting*, Summer 385–98.

Murray, A. (1989) 'Top Management Group Heterogeneity and Firm Performance', *Strategic Management Journal*, 10, Special Issue: 125–42.

Nicholson, N. and West, M. (1988) *Managerial Job change*, Cambridge: Cambridge University Press.

Noreen, E. (1988) 'The Economics of Ethics: A New Perspective on Agency Theory', *Accounting, Organisations and Society*, 13: 359–69.

O'Brien, D.P. (1984) *The Evolution of the Theory of the Firm*, in F.H. Stephen (ed.) *Firms, Organisation and Labour: Approaches to the Economics of Work Organisation*, London: Macmillan: 25–50.

O'Farrell, P. and Hitchens, D. (1988) 'The Relative Competitiveness and Performance of Small Manufacturing Firms in Scotland and the Mid West of Ireland: An Analysis of Matched Pairs', *Regional Studies*, 22(5): 399–416.

—— and —— (1989) 'The Relative Competitiveness of Small Manufacturing Firms in Scotland and the South of England', *Environment and Planning A*, 21: 1241–63.

O'Farrell, P.N. (1986) *Entrepreneurs and Industrial Change*, Dublin: Irish Management Institute.

Oakey, R.P., Rothwell, R. and Cooper, S. (1988) *Management of Innovation in High Technology Small Firms*, London: Pinter Publishers.

Ouchi, W.G. (1980) 'Markets, Bureaucracies and Clans', *Administrative Science Quarterly*, 25: 29–41.

Pennings, J.M. and Goodman, P.S. (1977) *Towards a Workable Framework*, in P.S. Goodman and J.M. Pennings (eds) *New Perspectives on Organisational Effectiveness*, New York: Jossey-Bass: 146–84.

Penrose, E.T. (1959) *The Theory of the Growth of the Firm*, Oxford: Basil Blackwell.

Perrow, C. (1961) 'The Analysis of Goals in Complex Organisations', *American Sociological Review*, 26: 854–66.

Perrow, C. (1967) 'A Framework for the Comparative Analysis of Organisations', *American Sociological Review*, April: 194–208.

Peters, T.H. and Waterman, R.H. (1982) *In Search of Excellence, Lessons from America's Best Run Companies*, New York: Harper and Row.

Pfeffer, J. (1983) *Organisational Demography*, in L. Cummings and B.M. Staw (eds) *Research in Organisational Behaviour*, Greenwich, CT: JAI Press: 72–83.

Phillips, B. and Kirchhoff, B.A. (1988) *Survival and Quality of Jobs Generated by Entrepreneurial Firms*, Washington DC: US Small Business Administration.

Porter, M.E. (1979) 'The Structure Within Industries and Companies Performance', *Review of Economics and Statistics*, 61: 214–27.

—— (1980) *Competitive Strategy*, New York: The Free Press.

Pritchard, R.D. and Karasick, B.W. (1973) 'The Effects of Organisational Climate on Managerial Job Performance and Job Satisfaction', *Organisational Behaviour and Human Performance*, 9: 126–46.

Putterman, L. (1984) 'On Some Recent Explanations of why Capital Hires Labour', *Economic Inquiry*, 22: 171–87.

—— (1989) 'Commodification of Labour Follows Commodification of the Firm on a Theorem of the New Institutional Economics', *Annals of Public and Cooperative Economics*, 60: 161–79.

Radice, H.K. (1971) 'Control Type, Profitability and Growth in Large Firms', *Economic Journal*, Sept: 547–62.

Ramsey, J.B. (1969) 'Tests for Specification Errors in Classical Least-Squares Regression Analysis', *Journal of the Royal Statistical Society*, 31: 350–71.

Reid, G. (1987) *Theories of Industrial Organisation*, Oxford: Basil Blackwell.

Reid, G.C. (1991) 'Staying in Business', *International Journal of Industrial Organisation*, 9: 545–56.

Rothwell, R. (1986) 'The Role of small firms in Technological innovation, 'in J. Curran, J. Stanworth and D. Watkins, *The Survival of the Small Firm*, 2, Farnborough: Gower: 114–42.

Schumpeter, J.A. (1934) *The Theory of Economic Development* Cambridge, MA: Harvard University Press.

Schwochau, S. (1987) 'Union Effects on Job Attitudes', *Industrial and Labor Relations Review*, 40: 209–24.

Scott, M. and Bruce, R. (1987) 'Five Stages of Growth in Small Businesses, *Long Range Planning*, 20(3): 45–52.

Shearman, C. and Burrell, G. (1988) 'New Technology Based Firms and the Emergence of New Industries: Some Employment Implications', *New Technology, Work and Employment*, 3(2): 87–99.

Silver, M. (1984) *Enterprise and the Scope of the Firm*, Martin Robertson: Oxford.

Simon, H.A. (1957) 'The Compensation of Executives', *Sociometry*, 20: 32–5.

—— (1964) 'On the Concept of Organisational Goals', *Administrative Science Quarterly*, 9: 1–22.

Slatter, S., Ransley, R. and Woods, E. (1988) 'USM Chief Executives: Do They Fit the Entrepreneurial Stereotype?', *International Small Business Journal*, 6(3): 10–23.

Solem, O. (1989) 'Factors for Success in Small Manufacturing Firms – with Special Emphasis on Growth Factors', in M. Virtanen (ed.) *Proceedings of the Conference on SMEs and the Challenges of 1992*, Helsinki School of Economics and Business Administration Publications M–47.

Song, J.H. (1982) 'Diversification Strategies and the Experience of Top Executives of Large Firms', *Strategic Management Journal*, 3: 377–80.

Sorenson, R. (1974) 'The Separation of Ownership and Control and Firm Performance: An Empirical Analysis', *Southern Economic Journal*, 41: 145–8.

Spence, A.M. (1974) *Market Signalling: Information Transfer in Hiring and Related Screening Processes*, Cambridge, MA: Harvard University Press.

Spicer, B.H. (1988) 'Towards an Organisational Theory of the Transfer Pricing Process', *Accounting, Organisations and Society*, 13: 303–22.

—— and Ballew, V. (1983) 'Management Accounting Systems and the Economics of Internal Organisation', *Accounting, Organisations and Society*, 8: 73–96.

Stanworth, J. and Curran, J. (1973) *Management Motivation and the Smaller Business*, Epping: Gower Press.

—— and —— (1989) *Employment Relations in the Small Firm*, in P. Burns and J. Dewhurst (eds) *Small Business and Entrepreneurship*, London: Macmillan.

Steer, P. and Cable, J. (1978) 'Internal Organisation and Profit: An Empirical Analysis of Large U.K. Companies', *Journal of Industrial Economics*, 27(1): 13–30.

Stephen, F.H. (ed.) (1984) *Firms, Organisation and Labour: Approaches to the Economics of Work Organisation*, London: Macmillan.

Storey, D.J. (1982) *Entrepreneurship and the New Firm* London: Croom Helm.

—— (1985) 'Manufacturing Employment Change in Northern England 1965–78: The Role of Small Businesses', in D.J. Storey (ed) *Small Firms in Regional Economic Development: Britain, Ireland and the United States*, London: Cambridge University Press.

—— and Johnson, S. (1986) 'Job Generation in Britain: A Review of Recent Studies', *International Small Business Journal*, 4(4): 29–46.

—— and —— (1987) *Job Generation and Labour Market Change*, London: Macmillan.

—— Keasey, K., Watson, R. and Wynarczyk, P. (1987) *The Performance of Small Firms: Profits, Jobs and Failures*, London: Croom Helm.

—— and Strange, A. (1992) *Entrepreneurship in Cleveland 1979–1989: A Study of the Effects of the Enterprise Culture*, Employment Department, Research Series No. 3.

—— Watson, R. and Wynarczyk, P. (1989) *Fast Growth Businesses in Northern England*, Department of Employment, Research Report No. 67.

Stulz, R.M. (1988) 'Managerial Control of Voting Rights: Financing Policies and the Market for Corporate Control', *Journal of Financial Economics*, 20: 25–54.

Thompson, J.D. (1967) *Organisations in Action*, New York: McGraw-Hill.

Thompson, S. (1988) *Agency Theory*, in S. Thompson and M. Wright (eds) *International Organisation, Efficiency and Profit*, London: Phillip Allan: 65–85.

Thompson, S. and Wright, M. (eds) (1988) *Internal Organisation, Efficiency and Profit*, London: Phillip Allan.

Toyoda, T. (1974) 'Use of the Chow Test under Heteroscedasticity', *Econometrica*, (3): 601–8.

Turok, I. and Richardson, P. (1989) 'Supporting the Start up and Growth of Small Firms: A Study in West Lothian', *Strathclyde Papers on Planning*, 14.

Utton, M.A. (1984) 'Concentration, Competition and the Small Firm', in C. Levicki (ed.) *Small Business: Theory and Policy*, London: Croom Helm and The Acton Society.

Variyam, J.N. and Kraybill, D.S. (1992) 'Empirical Evidence on Determinants of Firm Growth', *Economic Letters*, 38: 31–36.

Wachter, M. and Wright, R.D. (1990) 'The Economics of Internal Labour Markets', *Industrial Relations*, 29(2): 240–62.

Walsh, J.P. (1988) 'Selectivity and Selective Perception: An Investigation of Managers' Belief Structures and Information Processing', *Academy of Management Journal*, 31: 873–96.

Waterhouse, J.H. and Tiessen, P. (1983) 'Towards a Descriptive Theory of Management Accounting', *Accounting, Organisations and Society*, 8: 167–93.

Watkins, D.S. (1983) 'Development, Training and Education for the Small Firm: A European Perspective', *European Small Business Journal*, 1(3): 29–44.

Watson, R. (1990) 'Employment Change, Profits and Directors Remuneration in Small and Closely-Held UK Companies', *Scottish Journal of Political Economy*, 37(3): 259–74.

—— (1991) 'Modelling Director's Remuneration Decisions in Small and Closely-Held UK Companies', *Journal of Business Finance and Accounting*, 18(3): 85–98.

Westhead, P. and Moyes, A. (1992) 'Reflections on Thatcher's Britain: Evidence from New Production Firm Registrations', *Entrepreneurship and Regional Development*, 4(1): 21–56.

White, H. (1980) 'A Heteroskedasticity-Consistent Covariance Matrix Estimator and a Direct Test for Heteroskedasticity', *Econometrica*, 48: 817–38.

Williams, A.J. (1990) 'Measurement of Employment Patterns in Growing Small Enterprises', *Proceedings of Fifth Annual Small Business Conference*, University of Newcastle, New South Wales.

Williamson, O.E. (1975) *Markets and Hierarchies: Analysis and Antitrust Implications*, New York: Free Press.

—— (1979) 'Transaction-cost Economics: The Governance of Contractual Relations', *Journal of Law and Economics*, 22: 233–61.

—— (1981) 'The Modern Corporation: Origins, Evolution, Attributes', *Journal of Economic Literature*, 19: 1537–68.

—— (1984) 'Efficient Labour Organisation', in F.H. Stephen (ed.) *Firms, Organisation and Labour: Approaches to the Economics of Work Organisation*, London: Macmillan: 87–118.

Williamson, O.E. (1985) *The Economic Institutions of Capitalism*, New York: Free Press.

Wilson Committee (1979) *The Financing of Small Firms, Interim Report of the Committee to Review the Functioning of the Financial Institutions*, Cmnd,7503, London: HMSO.

Wilson, H. (1980) *Committee to Review the Functioning of the Financial Institutions*, Cmnd 7937, London: HMSO.

Woodward, J. (1965) *Industrial Organisation: Theory and Practice*, Oxford: Oxford University Press.

Yarbrough, B. and Yarbrough, R.M. (1988) 'The Transactional Structure of the Firm: A Comparative Survey', *Journal of Economic Behaviour and Organisation*, 10: 1–28.

Yarrow, G. (1972) 'Executive Compensation and the Objectives of the Firm', in K. Cowling (ed.) *Market Structure and Corporate Behaviour: Theory and Empirical Analysis of the Firm*, London: Gray Mills: 151–73.

Yuki, G.A. (1981) *Leadership in Organisations*, Englewood Cliffs, NJ: Prentice-Hall.

Index